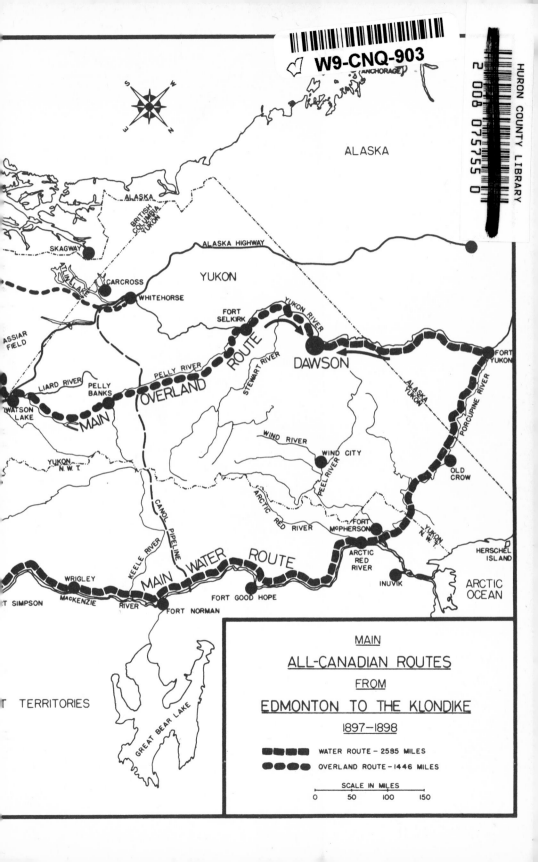

ALASKA

(ANCHORAGE)

ALASKA HIGHWAY

SKAGWAY

ALASKA
BRITISH COLUMBIA
YUKON

ATLIN LAKE

CARCROSS

YUKON

WHITEHORSE

FORT
SELKIRK

YUKON RIVER

CASSIAR
FIELD

DAWSON

OVERLAND ROUTE

PELLY RIVER

STEWART RIVER

FORT
YUKON

PORCUPINE RIVER

LIARD RIVER

PELLY
BANKS

MAIN

WATSON
LAKE

ALASKA
YUKON

WIND RIVER

WIND CITY

OLD
CROW

YUKON
N.W.T.

PEEL RIVER

ARCTIC
RED
RIVER

CANOL PIPELINE

KEELE RIVER

FORT
McPHERSON

YUKON
N.W.T.

HERSCHEL
ISLAND

MAIN WATER ROUTE

ARCTIC
RED
RIVER

WRIGLEY

INUVIK

ARCTIC
OCEAN

T SIMPSON

MACKENZIE RIVER

FORT NORMAN

FORT GOOD HOPE

T TERRITORIES

GREAT BEAR LAKE

MAIN

ALL-CANADIAN ROUTES

FROM

EDMONTON TO THE KLONDIKE

1897-1898

WATER ROUTE - 2585 MILES

OVERLAND ROUTE - 1446 MILES

SCALE IN MILES

0   50   100   150

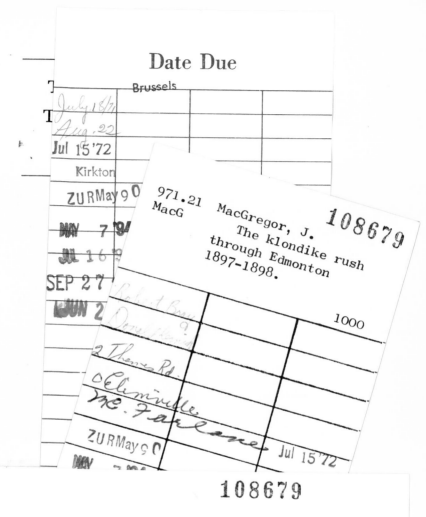

THE KLONDIKE RUSH
THROUGH EDMONTON
1897-1898

J. G. MAC GREGOR

McCLELLAND AND STEWART LIMITED

Toronto/Montreal

The Canadian Publishers
McClelland and Stewart Limited
25 Hollinger Road, Toronto 374

CONTENTS

ILLUSTRATIONS

Facing page 114: Gold washing with a "grizzly" at Edmonton, 1890 — Gold dredges on the river at Edmonton, 1898 – Mrs. Garner of the Fresno party – Some of the Garner (Fresno) party, 1897 – The Fugard party with toboggans, 1897 – The Helpman or O'Brien party, 1897, camped adjacent to Fort Edmonton – The Mason party on Jasper Avenue – The Ferriss party, 1898 – The Hastings-Crozier party – "Barrel" Smith's contrivance – To the Klondike with oxen – Loaded pack horses in John A. McDougall's yard – The Glen Campbell party – Red River carts at Fort Smith, 1898 – Athabasca Landing, 1898, the steamer *Boston* – Athabasca Landing, 1898, Jim Wallwork's paddle-wheeler the *Daisy Bell* – Athabasca Landing, 1898, Klondikers building boats – The Jenner brothers' party.

These photographs are from the E. Brown Collection of the Provincial Museum and Archives of Alberta

MAPS

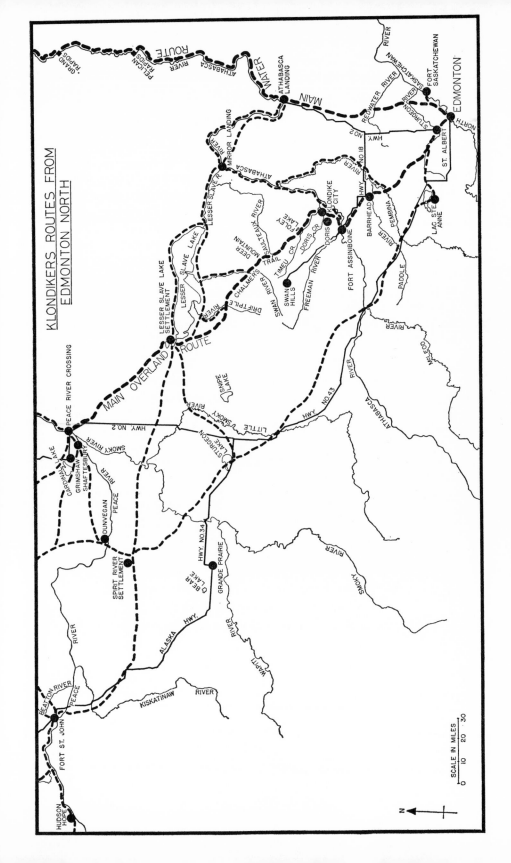

KLONDIKERS ROUTES FROM
EDMONTON NORTH

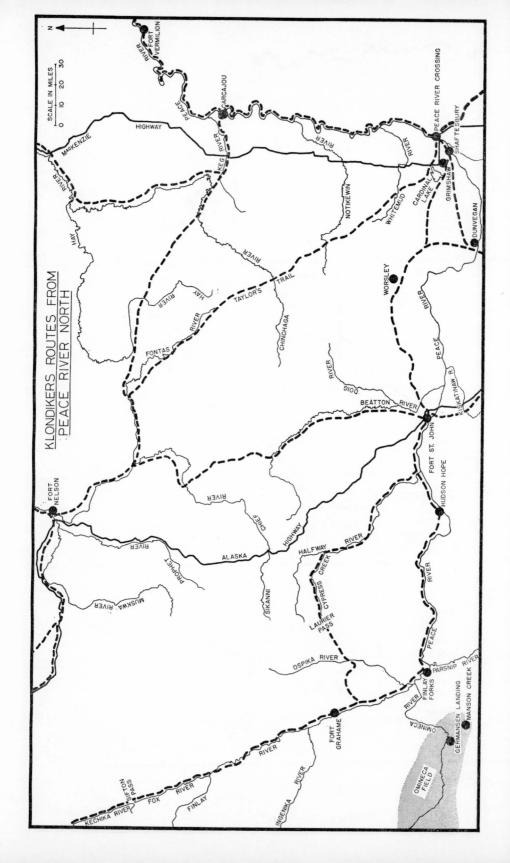

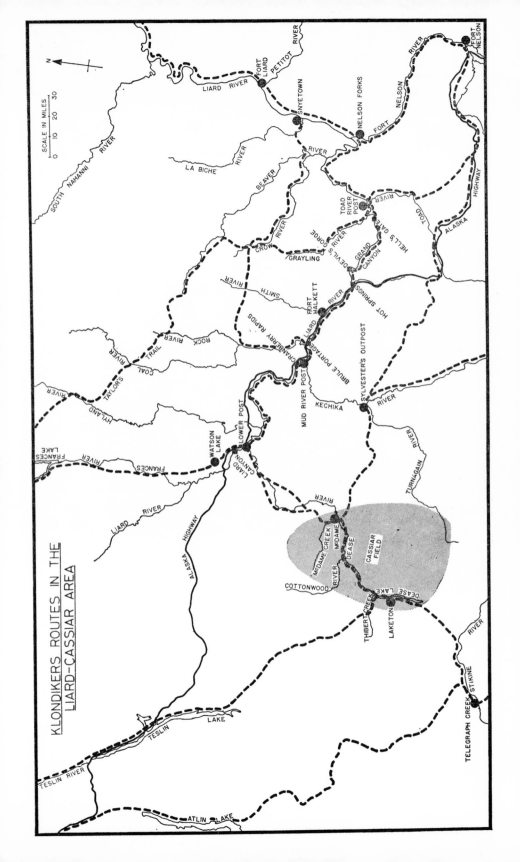

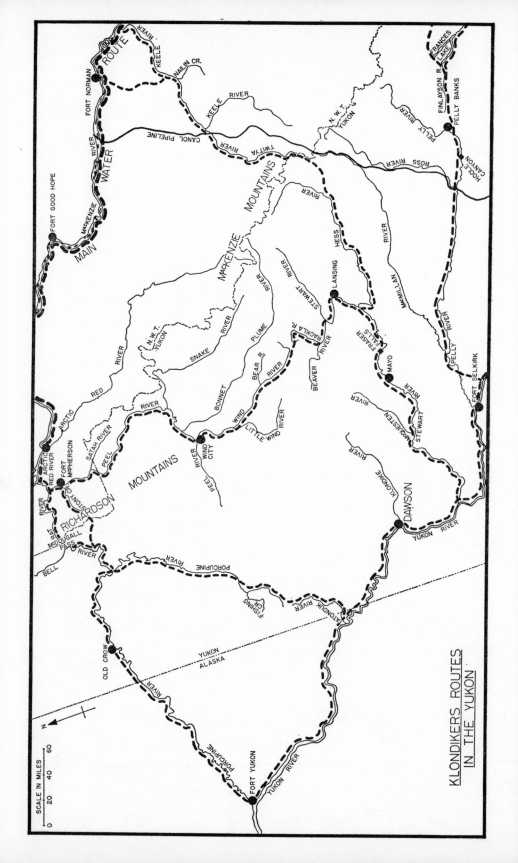

KLONDIKERS ROUTES
IN THE YUKON

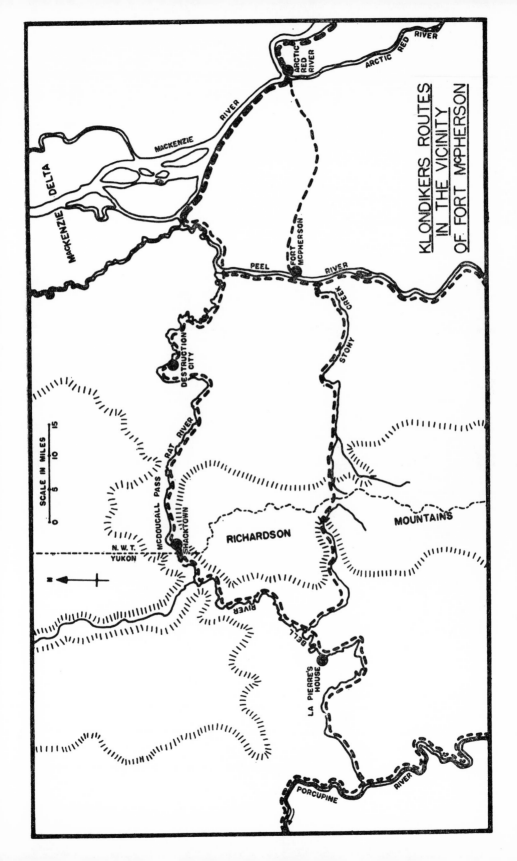

KLONDIKERS ROUTES
IN THE VICINITY
OF FORT McPHERSON

ACKNOWLEDGEMENTS

Several individuals and libraries have been very helpful in supplying information on the Klondikers who passed through Edmonton and in making available their diaries and memoirs. Foremost among these has been W. E. Ireland of the Provincial Archives of British Columbia, who provided me with the diaries of Ernest Corp and Scott Gillespie and copies of correspondence dealing with the relief expedition in the Cassiar. The staff of the Provincial Library and Archives was most helpful in supplying me with the files of the *Victoria Colonist* and other papers.

I obtained much background material from a study of various newspapers and records in the Public Archives of Canada. With its usual efficiency, the staff referred me to a narrative written by Alphonso Waterer from which, with the kind permission of the Archives, I have made some quotations.

Through the kindness of Mrs. J. B. Tebbutt, Librarian of the *Hamilton Spectator*, I was able to study the excitement created in the Hamilton area by the Klondike Rush. The Hamilton Public Library very kindly made available old files of the *Hamilton Herald* which contained copies of letters from former mayor A. D. Stewart besides material on R. H. S. Cresswell.

Miss Dorothy I. Hamilton of the Rare Book Room of the Cameron Library, University of Alberta, kindly allowed me to peruse the diary of Eben McAdam and graciously permitted me to make quotations from it. Bruce Peel, the librarian, supplied me with some material he had gathered on Captain J. S. Segers.

Through placing microfilm and other facilities at my disposal, Eric Holmgren of the Alberta Provincial Library has, as usual, helped considerably. The staff of the excellent new City of Edmonton Public

Library has also been helpful in making a great deal of information available, particularly the files of the *Edmonton Bulletin*.

The Ryerson Press kindly permitted me to quote extracts from Charles Camsell's *Son of the North*.

Mrs. Virginia Reid of the San Joaquin Valley library system at Fresno, California, went to considerable trouble to dig up material on the Fresno overland party and sent me several extracts from the Fresno paper.

Mr. E. H. Milvain of Cheltenham, England, has been particularly kind in sending me photographs and copies of his father's memoirs from which he has allowed me to quote.

So many others have been helpful and have volunteered information. Not the least of these has been T. E. Rodie of Calgary who, upon hearing that I was interested, sent me much material he had collected.

I have been most fortunate once more in being able to call on Les Collins's dedication in drawing the careful maps which illustrate the text.

The Provincial Museum and Archives of Alberta has graciously allowed the use of the photographs used as illustrations, taken from the Ernest Brown Collection.

Most gratitude, however, should and does go to my wife Frances who has edited and typed every one of my manuscripts and who besides that has spent untold hours in various phases of research, much of which is extremely tedious.

CHAPTER ONE

"THE BACK DOOR
TO THE YUKON"

The year-long procession of fifteen hundred Klondikers from Edmonton over the All-Canadian Routes to the Yukon should form at least a page in Canadian history. Unfortunately no one has paid it more than passing and derogatory mention. In a Canada that has been won by courage, endurance and even foolhardiness, its story deserves a better fate.

For magnitude, daring and adventure, this year-long migration of prospectors over routes which varied in length from 1,500 to 2,500 miles is unparalleled in Canadian history. On it youths grew to manhood, hoary heads found their graves, twenty women faced the rigours of travelling through a Canadian winter, two babies died and another was conceived and born. Even though about half of the gold-seekers turned back, even though in the remote fastnesses of Canada's northwest 70 lie buried or unburied, even though all but a score of the 725 who reached the Klondike returned empty handed, this trek of 1,500 outward-bound from Edmonton was not a failure but a rare chapter of courage and endurance.

When compared for magnitude or success with the migration of thousands along the American Oregon Trail (of which to some extent it was an offspring), it was minor. But there is no other parallel. The famous 1874 summertime march of some three hundred North West Mounted Police across the prairies to Fort McLeod, backed by the resources of the Dominion Government, was only three months and one thousand miles long.

The rush of homesteaders to the Canadian West came mainly by train. The prospectors who poured in to open Ontario's and Quebec's northern mines travelled a scant two or three hundred miles. Even the Fraser River and Cariboo gold-rushes swept their participants a mere

1

three or four hundred miles. But the shortest route from Edmonton to the Klondike, through terrain as difficult and a winter as severe as any on earth, was some 1,500 miles and the most roundabout was 2,500 miles. The Oregon Trail from the vicinity of Kansas City, Missouri, to Portland, Oregon, was some 2,100 miles. For comparison, the milage from Toronto to Edmonton by CNR is 2,012.

The nearest comparison was the main Klondike Rush itself, when thousands flocked over the perilous Chilkoot and White passes or stumbled in by other difficult routes. Because the trek starting at Edmonton was only a part of the much larger migration of Klondikers, its story has been neglected. Because the much larger migration included Soapy Smith and streets full of dancing girls, whereas the trek of 1,500 from Edmonton had no girls filling their pokes by supine submission and no Smith, it has been overlooked. To sweep it aside as a mere part of the major push to the Klondike is not good enough. In its own right it forms an episode in Canada's history and an episode colourful and courageous.

And yet its participants wasted no thought on whether or not they were colourful or courageous. They were bound for the Klondike and their maps indicated that Edmonton was the end of steel nearest to it. Thenceforth they were heedless of other considerations. When the first of them arrived at the end of the railway, Edmonton's businessmen, surprised by the influx, rallied round to serve them. Then, never blind to a good thing, these merchants began to advertise the godsend which had fallen into their laps – their All-Canadian Routes to the Yukon.

Hearsay, ever ready to embellish a good tale, has produced two generally held opinions regarding the Edmonton routes to the Yukon. The first is that all the suffering on the way to the Yukon and the disappointment were brought on because Edmonton merchants solicited. The second is that only a handful of prospectors ever reached the Yukon by way of Edmonton. The truth is a far cry from both these opinions.

Actually, in the beginning at least, Edmontonians did not solicit; they were themselves seduced, and before long relaxed and enjoyed the unwonted exercise. Actually, 725 Klondikers reached the Yukon by the Edmonton routes.

The image of all Klondikers is clouded by yet another misconception. Romantic, holier-than-thou writers, seeking alliteration, grasped the phrase "Greedy for Gold" and with it damned those who took part in the great rush. The bulk of the Klondikers were not pathologically greedy for gold. There were men like you and me – generally decent men, entranced by the gamble of the Klondike and embracing adventure. Unlike our generation, pampered by pelf and swaddled in security, they had the chance to go on an odyssey and the courage to harken to its call. When their gamble did not pay off, they shrugged their shoulders and came home. But they had embraced adventure and that satisfaction never deserted them.

Greedy for gold? No more than we. Gold-fever had infected them – a disease eluding drug or doctoring, infectious, contagious and hereditary, but not necessarily greedy.

For years before the rush of 1897, various Edmontonians had set out for the Omineca and the Cassiar gold-fields and for the Yukon. While of interest to Edmontonians, the news that some of their number were doing so was nothing unusual. In May 1897, for instance, before the news of the Klondike broke, James Shand, like others in previous years, announced that that summer he was setting off for the Yukon.

Going to the Yukon, then, was no new venture for Edmontonians. Neither was a general knowledge of the many possible alternative routes to that destination. Of these there were two main ones: the Water Route down the Mackenzie River to its delta and thence west over the mountains to the Yukon, a total of some 2,500 miles; and the Overland Route heading along dimly marked trails through forest and muskeg, touching the Omineca and Cassiar gold-fields and finally descending the Pelly River and the Yukon River – some 1,500 miles. Each of these routes presented a host of alternative ways and at various points far back in the vast forests of the northwest they anastomosed. When Edmontonians travelled them they planned to build a shack, spend the dead of the winter somewhere out there, and then push forward in the spring.

When the Klondikers arrived in Edmonton, many of them were but vaguely aware of what lay in store for them. Generally those from the Great Lakes, the St. Lawrence River, or the eastern seaboard came with the intention of floating down the Water Route. Those from the other two-thirds of the continent, some of them sons or even daughters of parents who had taken the famous Oregon Trail, planned to buy pack horses and travel overland. Some were woefully ignorant of all phases of travelling in the northland and of the rigours of a Canadian winter but most were types who with ordinary luck might have been expected to get through. That they did not have ordinary luck was partly their own fault and partly owing to the intransigence of the North. It allowed no man a second mistake.

What bedevilled them more than any other factor was that each Klondiker had to take along a food supply that would last two years. Travelling to the Yukon would have been a pleasant jaunt if there had been man and horse filling stations along the way but instead, every man had to transport a ton of food to feed him for the year he would be travelling and for the year after he reached the diggings.

That 725 out of 1,500 got through is a measure of the Klondikers' hardihood. Because this was no 2,500-mile steamship voyage where a miner paid his fare and for a week or so sat in a salon smoking away the hours between meals and finally arrived at the diggings fat and soft; this 2,500-mile water route was vastly different. On this trip, with his own muscles, a man whip-sawed lumber for his boat, propelled it for two thousand miles through roaring cascades or quiet reaches to the mouth of the Mackenzie River and there cut it down to a smaller craft. Then, up to his waist in freezing water for all the hours of daylight, he pulled or poled or pushed it up icy rapids or lifted it past drift-piles until finally, halted by winter, he had to stop and build a shanty. Next, in the intervals between hunting through blizzards for meat and making his own meals, he cut up the reduced boat to fashion a sled for the succeeding stage of his "voyage." After that, in the frigid air relaying his loads forward over the deep snow and up steep grades, tugging his sled ten miles to move his goods one mile, spring saw him at the top of the pass whip-sawing lumber for another boat with which to risk his life in seething whirlpools until finally, after twelve months of living in the open, he reached the diggings, frost-scarred and bruised, thin as a pike pole, but fit as a fiddle.

Neither was the overland trip an affair of stagecoaches and hotels with hot and cold water, a menu and a warm, dry bed at the end of the day; this 1,500-mile trek was markedly different. For on this trip, horses and dogs and snowshoes played a part: double sleighs or toboggans till the snow melted, then pack horses, then dogs and then whip-sawn boats dashing down rapids, dragged up cascades, or inched over portages. On this trip a tree provided the night's shelter, and the next day began in the drizzling rain of dawn when, rounded up after a couple of hours' search through the dripping underbrush, seven or eight horses had to be packed and whacked on their way. Driving them into rivers or dragging them out of the sucking mud of muskegs, unpacking, carrying their loads to firm land, wading back to other horses, dragging them to dry land and repacking them all, the prospectors pressed on, only to repeat the performance amid clouds of sandflies and no-see-ums at the next muskeg a mile away. Swatting mosquitoes, struggling along, wet through for days at a time, often starving or scurvy-ridden, these men, versatile and determined, drove their horses, snowshoed after their dogs and at times built and steered their boats along the fifteen hundred miles to the Yukon.

4

After setting the stage for the rush through Edmonton and telling of Edmonton's strenuous efforts of seventy odd years ago to clear roads for the Klondikers and to obtain a railway to the Yukon, we can follow the routes the Klondikers chose by presenting their adventures in their own words, using their diaries, letters and verbal reports. Some of these concern: Nellie Garner of Fresno, who spent a year on the trail before returning to Edmonton; John Rudolph Smith, the young lad who wrote home so cheerfully just before disaster overtook his party; Old Man Lang, who drove his cattle and died on the way; Young Moffatt from Pembroke who, in sight of safety, turned back to save a companion and perished; Meneely, whose last entries in his diary were: "My partner deserted me . . . awful foot . . . crippled on an island alone. The pain . . . is terrible"; Mayor Stewart of Hamilton, Ontario, writing hymns as he lay dying of scurvy; Jim Wallwork, the cowboy who rode his steamboat along the Water Route, over the pass and downstream to Dawson; Milvain, Robertson, Woodward, Cresswell and a few who reached the Klondike and made it pay; the death of Sophia the white mule, and of four thousand pack horses; and many other stories.

Some of these diaries tell of making a hundred miles a day, floating downstream in placid summer weather. Some tell of fighting up icy cascades, taking all day to make a mile, or of dragging hand-sleighs in forty-below weather back and forth, making five trips totalling twelve miles to lug their supplies forward two and a half miles. Some give day-to-day accounts of the intense suffering before death ended scurvy's agony. Some tell of starvation and some of rejoicing when the caribou came.

Using these diaries, letters and verbal accounts, we have tried to resurrect a page of history showing what manner of men (and women) took the Edmonton route to the Klondike – a page we think worthy of attention.

But first we must set the stage, or as detractors might say, bait the trap.

CHAPTER TWO

SETTING THE STAGE

When the Klondike Rush started, Edmonton was ready for it. One hundred years of close contact with the vast northwest and some forty years of catering to crotchety prospectors had gone into preparing the old fur-trading post for its role of Gateway to the Yukon. For nearly a century it had supervised or kept an eye on everything that went on in that vast area. No other point in Canada contained such a reservoir of men familiar with the routes and conditions, and no other centre east of the Rocky Mountains had been so closely and continuously connected with the comings and goings of gold miners.

Since 1859, when such adventurous souls as Perry, Love and Tom Clover of Clover's Bar had started panning the Saskatchewan River's gravels, gold-fever had been as rampant in Edmonton as malaria in the tropics. Dying down at times but ever ready to be inflamed by some new rumour and to flare up into some new rush, it kept everybody on the alert. From time to time parties left Edmonton to prospect and some went as far as the Yukon.

Behind Edmonton's preparedness lay a North American background of decades of prospecting and panning. Gold-fever had swept the continent, and indeed the world, when in 1849 the California Rush broke out. Prospectors flocked there till by 1857 California was so flooded with them that they spilled northward and began to trickle into British Columbia. Next year the trickle swelled to a tide as miners of all sorts surged up the Fraser River valley and by 1860 they struck the rich diggings of the Cariboo.

In the Cariboo gravels the lucky few found fortunes. Hundreds of their mates, however, were spreading out into the mountain fastnesses from Mexico to Edmonton sometimes to hunt in vain. For the prospectors were not confined to the Fraser and the Cariboo, but with pack horses, burros or mules, and singly, in pairs or parties, they

6

worked their way up this river or that and down this creek or that. By 1860 they were trying a pan in Alberta's Bow, Red Deer, North Saskatchewan and McLeod rivers and from time to time were dropping into Fort Edmonton.

On the morning of July 22, 1862, when the inhabitants of Fort Edmonton looked across the river, they got their first glimpse of a body of gold-smitten Easterners trekking past the post. The Overlanders of '62 had camped on what is now Walterdale Flats. This group, consisting of about 175 men, reached Edmonton in Red River carts and set out west by pack horses for the Cariboo. Organized in Ontario in a manner similar to the various cavalcades that crossed the United States to California a decade earlier, the party was played up by the Toronto and Hamilton newspapers. Having fallen for the wiles of organizers of dubious reliability, they tramped across the prairies, eventually casting aside their false leaders and finding good ones among themselves. Then, wading through muskegs west of Edmonton and crawling over mountain passes west of Jasper, suffering hunger, exhaustion and sometimes death, they clawed their way through the wilderness to the Cariboo. There they found all the good claims taken up, the food supply costly and precarious and no work to be had. In disappointment they split up and headed for the British Columbia coast to become pioneers in a new land.

Their courage and tribulation formed a pattern for similar parties who were to set out for the Klondike thirty-five years later. Their failure in the Cariboo was to be duplicated by their Edmonton-based, Yukon-bound successors.

But in the 1860's, totally unconcerned with the disappointments of the Overlanders, other hopefuls persevered, and the northward march of miners through the mountains continued. Even before the arrival of the Overlanders at Cariboo, Ed Carey and Bill Cust, Irishmen both, old Forty-niners and men who in due course were to become well known in Edmonton, pushed on north. In 1861, having reached the point where the Finlay and Parsnip rivers join to start the mighty Peace River on its way east, they panned gold in all three streams. Other adventurers followed them and for a few years worked the bars along the Finlay, the Parsnip and down the Peace as far as the Hudson's Bay Company post that had been established half a century earlier, Fort St. John.

In 1868 a party including Ezra Evans and Twelve-Foot Davis discovered gold on the Omineca and for a few years that field, with its towns of Omineca, Manson and Germansen, held the spotlight.

In the Omineca field the miners had established a bridgehead far

7

into the complicated and fantastically forbidding maze of mountains. It lay 450 miles north and 80 miles west of a Vancouver still waiting to be born; it lay 150 miles north and 430 miles west of the decades-old Fort Edmonton. But it was still 770 miles south and east of Klondike Creek, which was as yet without a white man's name and was barely known to the Russians and the Hudson's Bay Company's traders who for a generation or two had operated fur-trade posts in the Alaska-Yukon area.

Some twelve hundred miners flocked into the Omineca field and, as usual, many were disappointed and struck out for new unspoiled mountain streams and for regions not yet prospected. Some went north up the Finlay, some west, and some went hundreds of miles east down the Peace. Edmond Brosseau, for instance, who had lived in Minnesota, descended the Peace to Peace River Crossing in 1866 and then made his way to Edmonton. None of them discovered a new field. That was left to a prospector named Thibert, also of French descent and also from Minnesota, who, after various wanderings, spent the winter of 1869-70 at Great Slave Lake. From there he went down the Mackenzie to Fort Simpson, whence he ascended the Liard and then, with a fellow hopeful named McCollough, worked upstream through the Cassiar Mountains to Dease Lake, where in 1872 he made a major strike on what we know as Thibert Creek.

As soon as the news leaked out, the Cassiar Rush was on and by 1874, 1,600 miners had poured in. Many came from Omineca, many came from other inland points by following the old Telegraph Creek Trail to Telegraph Creek, where they joined forces with others who had ascended the mighty Stikine from tidewater at Wrangell, Alaska. Soon Dease Lake and River and their tributary, McDame Creek, became well known as the heart of the Cassiar country. The focus of mining activity had thus shifted far to the north and west. For Dease River empties into the Liard at what was then known as Lower Post, near the Yukon boundary and some thirty miles south of what we know as Watson Lake on the Alaska Highway. And Lower Post was 740 miles north of the site of the future Vancouver and 240 miles west; it lay 440 miles north and 500 miles west of Fort Edmonton. Ever receding north and west, the golden guide posts were pointing towards Klondike Creek, which was 440 miles beyond Lower Post.

Also aimed towards the Klondike and streaking off northwest over the hills and through the forests, the trail along the right-of-way beside the ruined wires of the Collins Telegraph formed another access which the miners used in working ever northward. The brainchild of the United States Western Union Telegraph Company, in 1866 the line was projected to connect the old world with the new and to join the telegraph systems of America with those of Russia by a land line from the mouth of the Fraser River near modern Vancouver to the tip of Alaska, where it was to link up with a cable across the Bering Sea. Before the click of the Atlantic cable's instrument dealt its death-blow in August 1866, three million dollars had been spent on the scheme. The line ascended the Fraser River to Quesnel and then set off through the forests to cross the Skeena and the Stikine rivers and to continue to the Yukon. At widely spaced intervals along the right-of-way the company had built cabins and one of these, at the crossing of the Stikine, became known as Telegraph Creek, a place that was to loom large in many a Klondiker's life. Although long before the Klondike was ever suspected of being a gold-field the old telegraph trail had grown over, its right-of-way had been blocked by fallen timber and its cabins had caved in, it, nevertheless, served as a route trending ever north and west.

Moreover, long before the Klondike Rush several eager prospectors, wandering in parties of two or three, were also heading northwest beyond Dease Lake and beyond Telegraph Creek. These were strong, cautious men, resolute and reliable, who could cope with the country as they found it. They were men who enjoyed the empty solitudes and who might wander in them for years, panning gold when they could, trapping when they could, and at the isolated Hudson's Bay Company posts trading their gold and furs for food and supplies which the forests or streams did not provide — flour, beans, sugar and salt, and maybe tobacco or a tot of rum.

Such men were Arthur Harper and his colleagues, who tramped the same ground and panned the same creeks that twenty-five years later the Klondikers were to work. In the winter of 1872-73 they made their way to Fort St. John, up the Halfway River and over to the Fort Nelson River and the Liard. When spring came they floated down it to Fort Simpson on the Mackenzie River and, once again foreshadowing the Klondikers, descended that magnificent stream to the mouth of the Peel River near Fort McPherson. Crossing McDougall Pass, they descended the Porcupine River and began prospecting along the Yukon River.

Such a man too was LeRoy Napoleon McQuesten, who came to be known far and wide as Jack. With one or two cronies he left the Cassiar and Omineca regions and by way of the Mackenzie eventually reached the mouth of the Peel River. From there, instead of taking the route Harper took, McQuesten ascended the Peel and worked his way up to the headwaters of the Wind River and over to those of the

Beaver River and found a pass to the stream that now bears his name. In 1874, descending it to the Stewart River, at a point some eighty miles upstream from the Yukon River he built a cabin.

Harper and his friends and McQuesten and his associates, the earliest prospecting predecessors of the Klondikers, thus became the first known miners from the south to move into that part of the Yukon. But others arriving by a variety of routes trickled in until by 1886 some two hundred prospectors began to feel their way about the vast mountainous Yukon.

Thus in the space of less than twenty years after Twelve-Foot Davis and Ezra Evans had discovered the Omineca diggings, prospectors were wandering about the Yukon. And a straight line of some 1,160 miles from where a few miners were working the Saskatchewan River gravels at Edmonton to where their confreres were busily panning in the Yukon passed through or near all the main gold-bearing regions: Fort St. John, the Finlay River, the Omineca area, the Upper Liard, the Cassiar and Frances Lake. Off to the west of it lay Telegraph Creek with its exit to the coast at Wrangell.

When it became obvious that more and more men were going to head for the Yukon, the Canadian government at Ottawa sent the first of its famous geologists to explore the region: G. M. Dawson, R. G. McConnell and William Ogilvie. In due course they issued their reports and at the height of the Klondike Rush in 1898 Ogilvie wrote a book entitled *The Yukon Official Guide*.

Long before the miners and the telegraph line and the geologists, however, the centuries-old Hudson's Bay Company, using the Mackenzie River trade route, had explored the Yukon and its approaches, built posts in it and maintained a system of communication from one to another. Along the Mackenzie waterway the company established Fort Smith, Fort Resolution, Hay River Post, Fort Providence, Fort Simpson, Wrigley, Fort Norman, Fort Good Hope, and finally, in 1840, Fort McPherson on the Peel River, just off the Mackenzie – nine posts, like nine tiny dew-drops glistening on a long clothesline. Nine posts each occupying a space of but two acres carved out of the thirty million acres of unending spruce, pine and poplar forests, incredibly beautiful but incredibly aloof, encompassing each one of them on every side.

From the Mackenzie River the Hudson's Bay Company began sending feelers into all the mountainous area to the west. Its first went up the Liard, which the Klondikers were to come to know so minutely and to curse so bitterly. Ascending it, Robert Campbell in 1836 built a post at Dease Lake. Moving northwest, in 1848 at the mouth of the

Pelly River he established Fort Selkirk on the Yukon River. Then in 1851 he explored that river down to where he linked up with his confrere W. L. Hardisty, who was in charge of Fort Yukon.

Whereas Campbell had approached the Yukon from the east and south, Hardisty and his colleagues had entered it from the north and east. They had been led by John Bell, who in 1840 built Fort McPherson, and by 1846 had crossed the Richardson Mountains and descended the Porcupine River to its mouth. There in 1848 Alexander Murray built Fort Yukon.

Thus by 1851, by closing in from the Cassiar country southeast of it and from the delta of the Mackenzie River northeast of it, the Hudson's Bay Company took the Yukon under its wing. From then on for decades its men continued to ascend this river and to descend that, to build posts and outposts in this vast region and to connect them by trails or canoe routes.

Because of the distances involved and the volume of freight needed in the Far North, the Hudson's Bay Company established a line of steamboats on the Mackenzie River system. For decades the bulk of the heavy freight had reached the north by ascending the North Saskatchewan River to a point upstream from Prince Albert and thence by way of Lac Ile-à-la-Crosse and the Methy Portage it had descended the Clearwater River to Fort McMurray and finally floated down the Athabasca.

When in 1883 the CPR pushed its way across the prairies to Calgary, this freight was re-oriented by being shipped to the growing foothills town and then teamed over the wagon road to Edmonton. That year the Hudson's Bay Company sent men out over the old pack trail to Athabasca Landing with instructions to widen it to a wagon road and to build bridges or ferries over the Sturgeon and Redwater rivers and the lesser creeks. Other men were to rig up a crude dock at Athabasca Landing to facilitate transferring freight to the scows which were to take it down-river to the tumultuous Grand Rapids and then through the rough water to Fort McMurray.

At the same time the company built the first of the northern steamboats, the *Grahame*, at Fort McMurray — 135 feet long. At Fort Smith at the lower end of the rapids in 1887 the company put into service the *Wrigley*, a propeller-driven boat of deeper draft and ninety feet long, for use on the stormy waters of Great Slave Lake and the deep Mackenzie River. That year too at Athabasca Landing the Hudson's Bay Company built the *Athabasca* to ply the 167-mile section of quiet water down to Grand Rapids and also to ascend the river to what later came to be known as Mirror Landing, where the river flowing from Lesser Slave Lake enters the Athabasca. With these three steam-boats and a fleet of scows, the old fur-trading organization had established a summer line of communication from Athabasca Landing 1,800 miles to the delta of the Mackenzie. The stage was being set for the Klondikers.

Then in 1891 the Calgary and Edmonton Corporation built the railway line from Calgary to the south bank of the North Saskatchewan River across from Edmonton, and in due course a village, which later was named Strathcona, grew up there. Thus some six years before the Klondike Rush, Edmonton found itself a key point on the only practical line of communication to the Far North.

Finally, feeling their way into the north were the North West Mounted Police based at "G" Division Headquarters at Fort Saskatchewan. As early as 1893, in order to keep better track of the people who were going into the North, the police established a detachment at Athabasca Landing, with an outpost downstream at Grand Rapids and another upstream along the route of travel to the Peace River country, at the mouth of the Lesser Slave River. Eventually the Mounties set up another outpost at Lesser Slave Lake (Grouard). Early in January 1897, only months before the Klondike craze, the Police sent out the first of their northern patrols consisting of Inspector A. M. Jarvis and Staff Sergeant Hetherington. They were provided with three teams of four dogs each and two spare dogs. J. Gullion went along as guide and drove one team, while P. Lutit, Jr., another half-breed, also drove a team.

This patrol illustrates how readily, if not comfortably, men used to the North could travel anywhere, even in midwinter. Setting out by way of Lac la Biche, they called at Heart Lake, McCallum's post on the Clearwater River and Fort McMurray. Going on from there, they stopped at the Métis settlements at Little Red River and two others between there and Fort Chipewyan. The tally of white and half-breed people at the fort, who were mainly employees of the missions, the Hudson's Bay Company or the independent traders, gave Chipewyan a population of about 150 souls without counting some thirty lodges of Chipewyan Indians and twelve lodges of Crees, who seemed to be more or less permanently in residence there. As an indication of the Indian population of the whole area, Jarvis was told that during the summer six or seven hundred Indians came in to trade.

Continuing the trip, the patrol found Campbell Young of Edmonton and a George Martin trapping along Slave River and in due course reached Smith's Landing (Fitzgerald), where some twelve Indian and half-breed families lived. This point was at the head of the rapids of

Slave River where its waters begin their furious rush, dropping 110 feet in tumbling, boiling white water nearly a mile wide and sixteen miles long — magnificent scenery but a maddening obstruction to navigation. For some years the Hudson's Bay Company had maintained a passable road along the sixteen-mile portage to Fort Smith at the lower end of the rapids where a Mr. McKinley was in charge.

The Indians living along the Slave River and the south shore of Great Slave Lake in the vicinity of Fort Resolution were Chipewyans, Caribou Eaters and a few Yellow Knives, and here and there, but very rarely, Jarvis met a small cluster of them. Going on from Fort Smith he reached Fort Resolution, the northern extremity of his trip, on February 13, some six weeks after he had set out from Fort Saskatchewan into the most severe of the winter's weather.

Fort Resolution on the shore of Great Slave Lake was an important point where C. F. Gaudet, a member of a highly respected northern family, was in charge of the Hudson's Bay Company's post. His competition consisted of a well-run post owned by the northern traders Hislop and Nagle. Between the traders and their families and a few native families who lived there most of the time, Fort Resolution had a population of 108. In summer, however, some six hundred Indians who lived in the tributary area came in to trade.

Setting out south again Jarvis retraced much of the route he had taken (and one which the Klondikers were soon to take north of Fort Chipewyan) and turned off to the west and ascended the Peace River. At Little Red River, where navigation was interrupted by the Vermilion Chutes, he found a small Hudson's Bay Company post and then went on to the Fort Vermilion area where W. D. Wilson supervised the company's main establishment. Included in the straggling Fort Vermilion settlement were the Anglican and Roman Catholic missions and the prosperous farm owned by the famous Lawrence family, besides trading posts operated by Twelve-Foot Davis and Fred Brick. On the whole, Fort Vermilion was a substantial settlement of 168 people keeping an eye on 159 horses, 297 cattle and 54 swine. Not far out of the settlement Dan Carey ran a trap line and incurred the policeman's wrath for some of his practices.

Working his way up the river from there, Jarvis called at the Carcajou and Battle River settlements and at Moberly Point with its twenty-six people. Continuing upstream, he passed Peace River Crossing, an insignificant point which contained a Hudson's Bay Company shack and a few other sheds, but without stopping went on to the Shaftesbury Settlement where the Hudson's Bay Company had its main post in the charge of F. J. H. Bedson. After looking in on the Roman

Catholic and Anglican missions, Jarvis went over to the busy settlement at the west end of Lesser Slave Lake, and eventually, after going around by Athabasca Landing, he reached Fort Saskatchewan on April 15.

Jarvis and his companions had accomplished a remarkable trip of over two thousand miles mainly by dog-team and in the very heart of the winter. On his return from that first NWMP patrol into the North he made recommendations about what should be done to protect the Indians and the game animals in the area he had traversed. One result was that starting during the summer of 1897 the police opened an outpost at Fort Smith under Corporal Trotter.

Inspector Jarvis's trip shows how sparse the population excluding Indians was north of Edmonton in 1897. The white men between Edmonton and the Mackenzie delta and the few responsible half-breeds who were in charge of trading posts numbered but a hundred or so. Though their number was so small, their influence was great, and these men – the Hudson's Bay Company factors, Roman Catholic or Anglican missionaries, and the few independent traders – became the keystones of the white man's civilization. They were scattered at strategic points from the far recesses of the Yukon and of the Mackenzie delta south two thousand miles to Edmonton.

To them at trading post or mission the native people, already dependent on the white man's goods, looked for much of their sustenance. Thinly scattered over the whole area, averaging perhaps one soul to every thirty square miles, they and their dogs led a precarious existence on the fish of the lakes and the beasts of the forests. While family by family they dispersed into the corners of the forest to hunt, they congregated from time to time at fishing lakes or at the mouths of rivers to carry on their tribal life or to seek what solace the missionaries could give them or what goods their pelts would bring from the traders.

So much for the Far North. Returning now to Alberta, in 1895, excluding the treaty Indians, the whole of the province had a population of perhaps 35,000. According to the police census taken that year, Calgary, the major town on the transcontinental CPR, contained 3,500 people, Edmonton held 1,165, and the little end-of-steel village of Strathcona 500, while all of the area tributary to Edmonton was home to some 7,000.

In strips west and north and east of Edmonton this little knot of settlement radiated out as much as thirty miles. South of the town a thin straggle of farmers adjoined the railway to Calgary. Eight miles northwest of Fort Edmonton the old village of St. Albert was the seat of the Roman Catholic bishop. Except for a handful of businessmen of French descent, the village and the settlement extending for a short distance up and down the Sturgeon River was made up of a group of high calibre half-breeds who lived by mixing a minimum of agriculture with trapping, freighting, packing or working on the northern rivers. Some twenty miles north and east lay Fort Saskatchewan (population 140), established about twenty years earlier. Also considered to be in the area tributary to Edmonton, two other isolated settlements of half-breeds played important roles. One was Lac Ste Anne, from which came many of the outfitters, packers and pack horses needed by parties venturing into the hinterland. The other was Lac la Biche, where each winter a group of venturesome scow and steamboat men, the best rivermen in the West, returned to their homes.

Edmonton, which had been incorporated in 1892, was just emerging from the straggling stage so typical of fur-trading centres and river towns. From Malcolm Groat's isolated home, located about 124 Street, it rambled along to its eastern fringe some five miles away. Approaching it by the twice-a-week train from the south, travellers observed a few small cultivated fields in the vicinity of Wetaskiwin and were then plunged into the heavy timber which, except for the small siding of Leduc, extended to within a few miles of the station of South Edmonton. There the steel ended at a small knot of buildings which included a hotel or two, some stores, offices and a few houses. To reach Edmonton proper it was necessary to take a stage and set out down the curving roads which descended steeply to either of the two ferries across the North Saskatchewan River.

From these roads winding down the hill, most of Edmonton could be seen at a glance. In the foreground, of course, was the busy river with its steamboat dock, its long rows of pilings and stretched-out log booms. On the flats beside Walter's and Fraser's mills extensive piles of lumber showed whence much of the town's wealth came. Here and there, running entries into the precipitous river banks, coal mines indicated more of the town's rich resources, while on the flats some enterprising individuals had started brick plants. In addition to these, two or three gold dredges widely spaced along the river turned over its gravels. Straight ahead stood the Hudson's Bay Company's decades-old Fort Edmonton, which a few years previously had been shorn of its palisades but nevertheless formed an imposing group.

After gaining the level ground at the top of the long climb and then advancing a block north, the trail brought the traveller to Jasper Avenue not far from its dog-leg bend. Along it, stretching some five blocks from the Alberta Hotel at 98 Street on the east to the Hudson's

Bay Company's brick store, lay the heart of the relatively new business section. This main street and three or four side streets, dusty or muddy as the weather dictated, had been graded up, and along their edges staggered rows of electric light poles. Where the grading stopped, rutted wagon trails stretched out into the bush. The town's central area included a number of well-stocked two-storey stores, alternated with uncleared lots where the original trees still sheltered an occasional rabbit or a squirrel. Here and there huge hip-roofed livery stables stood watch over the squattier buildings.

The streets of this town exhibited the usual busyness of a centre on the agricultural frontier with a procession of wagons, ox-teams, hay racks, coal or lumber wagons, saddle horses and pack horses coming and going. Strings of horses starting out or returning from weeks-long excursions were a common sight. They set out or came back from Edmonton's great hinterland which in every direction, but particularly towards the north and west, began some twenty or thirty miles out from the town at whatever point the most recent homesteader had built his shack. Only two wagon roads made their way beyond these shacks, the Landing Trail and the St. Albert Trail – both soon to be overrun by Klondikers. Between them they provided avenues of entry to Edmonton's two routes to the great northwest.

The Landing Trail led to the broad waterway down the Athabasca, Slave and Mackenzie rivers to the Arctic Ocean, 1,800 miles away. Built in 1883 by the Hudson's Bay Company, it followed the good road leading northeast to the police post at Fort Saskatchewan. Then in the farming areas known as Belmont and Horsehills it swung to the left and headed north to cross the Sturgeon River at Battenburg.

The St. Albert Trail had originally been called the Fort Assiniboine Trail because in 1825 it had been cut from Fort Edmonton for pack horses as a portion of the first Trans-Canada highway connecting the Saskatchewan River to the Athabasca and thence to the coast. Until about a decade before the Klondike Rush it had been in use for transferring goods, furs and personnel from Edmonton to the Pacific Coast. In 1842 when Father Thibault cut a trail to his new mission at Lac Ste Anne he branched off the Fort Assiniboine Trail about fifteen miles out of Edmonton. This branch came to be called the Lac Ste Anne Trail and was the one the Overlanders of '62 had taken. When in 1885 the CPR line across Canada was completed, the Fort Assiniboine Trail lost its importance and for some years saw very few travellers.

It saw a few, however, because it headed north and west and because its shorter Lac Ste Anne branch pointed west towards the mountains and both trails gave access to the vast area between the Athabasca and

Peace rivers, as well as to Fort St. John and far beyond. Within this huge area lived Cree, Beaver and some Iroquois Indians and within it in 1896 the Hudson's Bay Company had small posts: Lac Ste Anne, Whitecourt, Sturgeon Lake, Lesser Slave Lake, Grande Prairie, Spirit River, Dunvegan and Fort St. John. Several independent traders had also set up posts in this area. And the traders, Indians and even several white or half-breed trappers used a variety of routes criss-crossing from one post to another. Furthermore, the Indians revered the Roman Catholic shrine at Lac Ste Anne and early in July each year, heading over hills and through valleys, came by a variety of routes and for hundreds of miles to worship there. From practically every local area in this vast region some trace of a pack trail, sometimes merely a blaze on an occasional tree, and sometimes used only twice a year, pointed towards Lac Ste Anne.

By this time too Ottawa was sending out surveyors and geologists to map the area more correctly and to find out what they could about it. These survey parties usually started from Edmonton and hired guides or packers to take them where they wanted to go.

As a result, supplying pack trains became an important industry and various outstanding men in Edmonton, St. Albert or Lac Ste Anne stood ready to provide the help these parties needed. They were men like the Groat brothers, J. R. Brenton and Dan Noyes of Edmonton; A. Prince and Sam Cunningham of St. Albert; and Walter Bisson, the Taylors and the Iroquois J. F. Calihoo of Lac Ste Anne – men who all their lives had wandered through the vast forests and knew most of the obscure routes. When the leader of some expedition approached one of them and explained what his destination was, the packer, calling upon his knowledge of these obscure routes – not trails – would chose the one the party would take. In short, then, there were many vague pack trails winding their way through the northern and western forests. For instance, a party going from Edmonton to Fort St. John could take one of over twenty routes each materially different from the others.

Lastly, in addition to the Hudson's Bay Company and independent traders, trappers, missionaries and Indians wandering through the northwest, various parties of prospectors had been for many a year examining every river and creek within a radius of three hundred miles of Edmonton and they too used these routes. Year after year, in small parties, they set out from Edmonton and after an absence of many months returned with tales of good or poor luck. Sometimes they never returned but went farther north and west until finally they came out at the Pacific Coast.

By strolling along Edmonton's Jasper Avenue one could usually meet a dozen men who, in the regular course of obtaining a livelihood, had on more than one occasion pushed their way along the river valleys and routes of the North. They were men who had been to the Peace River gravels near Fort St. John or farther on to the Omineca diggings, which had been mined for the last twenty-nine years, or even farther to the Cassiar, where miners had been working for twenty-five years, or indeed, men who had been to the Yukon itself.

Outstanding among these widely travelled Edmontonians were those who were or had been associated with the Hudson's Bay Company. F. A. Hardisty was the son of W. L. Hardisty, one of the earliest traders at Fort Yukon, and had been born at Fort Simpson. W. J. McLean had been in charge of Fort Liard from 1863 to 1873. G. W. Gairdner, who was now secretary of the Board of Trade, had spent the year 1871 at Fort McPherson. While he had been there, James McDougall had discovered the pass that bears his name and crossed it to the Yukon. Then after taking charge of Fort Edmonton during 1883-84, McDougall returned to the Yukon and in 1886 had crossed the Chilkoot Pass. John Campbell, son of old Robert Campbell who had explored the Yukon, had spent some time at Fort McPherson. George Sutherland, who was now farming at Stony Plain, had put in several years at Fort Liard and Fort Nelson. So had Murdoch McLeod, who had taken a homestead at Belmont. And there were several others.

But a knowledge of the far northwest was not confined to former Hudson's Bay Company employees. Many of the real old-timers had made the circuit of the gold-rushes all the way from California to the Cariboo, the Omineca and the Peace rivers. Included among these were Donald Ross, Bill Cust, Jim Gibbons, Ed Carey and Dan Noyes, who made his livelihood as an outfitter for parties wishing to go into the northwest.

Other active frontiersmen were continually going to or returning from various expeditions. There was Swede Larson who had been at Hudson Hope about 1873 when Bill Cust had been there, had then gone on to the Cassiar region and had since shown up in Edmonton still planning to go back to the Liard. There was Baptiste Pilon, who two or three years previously had gone down the Mackenzie and over to the Yukon and was even now preparing to duplicate that trip. Jack L'Anglais was expected back at any time. A little over a year earlier he had taken fifteen pack horses and had set out for the Liard and Cassiar regions. J. R. Brenton had been with the famous geologist William Ogilvie when he descended the Liard and returned to Edmonton by way of Fort Nelson and Fort St. John. Jack "Cayuse" Graham was another whose itchy feet kept him pushing pack horses all over the hinterland. During 1896 he had teamed up with a man named Knight to try the gravels of the upper Smoky River. Then Knight had gone on to see what luck might lie in the Cassiar gold-fields. Cayuse had come back but in March 1897 he had set out again with two other men for the upper Peace and Finlay rivers. He had become a sort of legendary figure far out in the valleys of the northwest and was apt to turn up anywhere.

Edmonton was the headquarters of a score or so of such characters, all of them familiar with the area between the outpost town and the Yukon. And all of them itched for an excuse to go back north. When they could not dream up a venture that would take them that far, a few of them had joined parties to pan the gravels along the McLeod River, the Little and the Big Smoky and the Athabasca River. In 1896 Inspector Griesbach of "G" Division of the NWMP stationed at Fort Saskatchewan reported that during the year a number of miners had flocked in to try their luck on the Athabasca. Going out there, they cleared the fallen timber off the disused Fort Assiniboine Trail as far as the remains of that old fort. Then some worked up-river towards modern Whitecourt and others worked downstream. Griesbach stated that in due course all of them rafted down the river to Athabasca Landing and rode back to Edmonton with freighters. He said: "Not more than fifty of them made expenses and not more than a dozen made wages."

Except for the very real pleasure of the trip they had taken and the thrill of prospecting, they would have been as well off to stay in Edmonton and pan the gravel of the river that flowed at their feet. In fact, that was what scores of men planned to do, as the *Bulletin* of April 15, 1897, explained.

GOLD

Already the rush has commenced, and impatient miners and prospectors, local experts, wandering fortune seekers and businessmen not waiting for the ice to leave the river, have staked claims all along the banks from high to low water mark, all seeking to secure a share of the precious metal whose very name is a magnet to attract the millions. From the high river bank directly back of the business portion of the town can be seen far up and down the river innumerable stakes and pins set up there as soon as the frost had left the ground, staking off the newly located claims.

So with prospectors continually coming and going, with gold dredges operating in the river (with its banks staked for thousands of yards) all in view from the *Bulletin* office, Edmontonians were always in a mild state of gold-fever. Situated as it was at the end of steel, with its navigable route down to the Arctic and its old Fort Assiniboine and other dim pack trails radiating out north and west, and afflicted with chronic gold-fever, Edmonton needed but a moment's notice to be ready for any gold-rush.

Its intimate relations with the Mackenzie River system went back nearly a century. For nearly forty years it had watched miners panning its own river's gravels and for that length of time it had seen a small but ceaseless procession of prospectors coming and going to the gold-fields of British Columbia – the Cariboo, Omineca, Finlay River and the Cassiar. The metal mining boom in the Kootenays was at its height; from week to week men set out for that area or came back to report success or failure. Edmonton was mining oriented.

CHAPTER THREE

LOGISTICS

Then in May 1897 the *Edmonton Bulletin* broke the news of the Klondike Rush. It had been triggered by the gravels of Klondike Creek, an insignificant part of the Yukon which had only become known during the previous few months. Four thousand men were said to be flocking in over Chilkoot Pass. The actual discovery had been made the previous summer, when on August 12, George Carmack, better known as Siwash George, had hit the jackpot on Bonanza Creek. The latest reports said that $20,000 was the going price for a five-hundred-foot claim on its banks. The great Klondike Rush was on. Edmonton buzzed with excitement.

Immediately, many an Edmontonian began dreaming of setting out for the new field. On Jasper Avenue, the town's crooked main street, the talk was of little else and everyone advanced his own theory about the best route to the Klondike. Then, when references in the world's newspapers suggested Edmonton as a jumping-off place and when parties in eastern Canada and the United States wrote and even wired for information, the town council, the Board of Trade and the editor of the *Bulletin* began to sit up and take notice. With their background they needed little prodding to awaken them to the possibility of a rush through the town to the Yukon and once fully awake to it they quickly developed a gold-rush complex. Within weeks the Klondike madness had burst upon them.

As early as August 1896, when they reported that nine hundred miners had gone into the Yukon already that year, the world's newspapers pricked up their ears and eagerly continued to watch the development of the rush and report its progress. Reading these papers, adventurous souls in Europe, Britain, the United States and Canada dragged out maps and atlases to see just where the Yukon was. On

21

this continent many a daring soul, fed up with the dreary days of the depression of the 1890's, day-dreamed of escaping from his rut. Conditioned by two or three generations of westward trekking forebears and by fifty years of gold-rushes, fascinated by the prospect of adventure and the possibility of striking it rich, thousands set out for the Yukon. In offices, clubs and pubs, discussion invariably turned to the question of how one might get there.

Most of those living on the western slope of this continent naturally chose the west coast routes. Viewed from Europe, the obvious way to reach the new gold-fields was to cross the Atlantic, take the CPR to Vancouver and then, like the others, take ship north along the coast. A choice of two routes was available. On the first, starting from Seattle or Vancouver and following the easy route, the ship called at Sitka, some eight hundred miles up the coast. From there it headed westward for a 1,200-mile voyage to Unalaska or Dutch Harbor at the western tip of the Aleutian Peninsula and then a further eight hundred miles across the Bering Sea to St. Michael – a total distance at sea of 2,800 miles or about the breadth of the Atlantic. From St. Michael river-boats ran the 1,600 miles upstream to the Klondike, making a grand total of 4,400 miles.

The second route was to sail from Seattle or Vancouver a much shorter distance up the coast to Skagway on Taiya Inlet. From there the prospectors had to cross the Chilkoot Pass and descend to Lake Bennett, which of course was water that flowed to the Yukon River. The main difficulty with this route was the relaying of supplies over the steep grade of Chilkoot Pass. Conditions were so terrible on this climb that thousands of prospectors literally failed to make the grade.

Of the multitudes who poured into the Yukon, nearly all went by one of these routes. Those who did not favour either of them began to wonder if there were any other and, soaring aloft on the magic carpets of their maps, found their attention caught by Edmonton, which could be reached by the CPR from Calgary. On a map spread out flat on a table, it turned out that in a straight line the end of steel at Vancouver was 1,200 miles from Klondike Creek, whereas Edmonton was only 1,160. Moreover, good atlases indicated that a hundred-mile wagon road ran north from Edmonton to the Athabasca River at Athabasca Landing. There one could connect with a system of steamboats, which, with the exception of two portages, took one downstream a matter of 1,828 miles to the Peel River near the mouth of the Mackenzie River. From the Mackenzie the shortest distance to the heart of the Klondike at Dawson City was only 280 miles. Between the river and the gold-fields rose a range of mountains which prevented

22

anyone from going in a straight line and increased the distance to some six hundred miles. This, however, could be crossed by ascending one large river to its summit and descending another that flowed into the mighty Yukon, on which a system of steamboats plied. The trip looked easy enough.

Surely sailing some 1,828 miles down the magnificent Mackenzie River system would in itself be a thrilling experience and would be pleasure enough to justify the trip. Then too, for the do-it-yourself types nothing was to prevent their making boats and floating down this river system on their own without having to pay any fare. Many decided that they would solve their problem in this way.

Still other do-it-yourself types, studying their maps, felt that though the waterway was perhaps the easiest method, it was nevertheless a long, roundabout route of nearly 2,500 miles, whereas in a straight line overland from Edmonton the Klondike field was only 1,160 to the northwest. Moreover, judging by the information recently released by the Geological Survey of Canada in the form of William Ogilvie's and G. M. Dawson's reports of their trips to the Yukon, travelling overland from Edmonton seemed relatively simple. Accordingly, they decided to use pack horses on this Overland Route, which, because it was circuitous, was said to be about 1,500 miles.

In England, thinking about Edmonton as a point of departure for the Klondike made one man, Frank Richards, write to the *Mercury* of Liverpool about the end of April, 1897. He suggested leaving the CPR at Calgary and striking north towards the gold-fields by crossing the North Saskatchewan River at Fort Saskatchewan and heading for the Liard River some six hundred miles farther north by travelling either by way of Fort Vermilion on the lower Peace or by Fort St. John on its upper reaches. Having reached the Liard, he proposed to ascend it and then carry on overland. While he pointed this out, he explained that his reason for writing was to warn young Englishmen that it was a pretty risky venture and one not to be contemplated on an empty stomach. Richards, like many another, came to his conclusions without consulting anyone at Edmonton.

In fact, up to this point, nobody consulted Edmonton and before the *Bulletin*, the mouthpiece of the prideful town, and its purposeful Board of Trade had awakened to the possibility of capitalizing on a route starting at Edmonton, hundreds of far-away gold dreamers like Frank Richards were casting wistful eyes their way.

When early in May the editor of the *Bulletin* came to realize that the Yukon was an incredibly rich field, he began wondering whether or not it was really practical to think of an inland route starting at

Edmonton. Deciding that it was, he wrote an editorial on the Yukon and the possible routes from Edmonton, advocating that the Dominion Government should see to it that a road be opened up heading north and west to the Peace River country and from there to the upper Liard and the Pelly River.

Thenceforth, the editor, the Board of Trade and the town council were hooked. From that point on they could only go forward, and they leaped nobly into this new, exciting – and profitable – cause. Klondike madness tightened its hold on them. It had taken a while to incubate, but day by day its fever heightened until within a week or so Edmontonians could see no evil in this new thrill that had come upon them, would hear no evil, and certainly intended to speak no evil about their route to the Yukon.

Occasionally during the first days of the attack, one or two voices had queried the value of the Edmonton route. About the middle of May, Louis Couture, a miner who had already returned from the Yukon and who planned to go back, spoke unfavourably of it and stated that he planned to take a train to the coast and a boat from there to Skagway. Hardly anyone listened.

Certainly James Shand and his partner M. Velgue did not, for they set out for the Yukon in a rather routine way and by way of the Mackenzie River on June 9. Although their decision to go must have been made before the news of the big strike on the Klondike reached Edmonton, they were the first to go from Edmonton that summer.

Neither did a group of Couture's compatriots heed his advice, because they prepared to float down the Mackenzie. This party, headed by young Baptiste Pilon who had been north a year or so earlier, consisted of Israel and Louis Lamoureux, E. St. Jean and one of the Verraults, all French Canadians and all men well versed in the ways of the wild country ahead of them. Even that early in Edmonton's history, the Lamoureux were old timers; the patriarch of this group of adventurous frontiersmen had not only settled on the river near Fort Saskatchewan as early as 1882 but had come into Alberta across the mountains from the west. Like most of Edmonton's early settlers, all of this party gained part of their livelihood by working as packers or steamboat hands, or by taking scows down the Saskatchewan or Athabasca rivers.

All these men knew the northland and its climate and the conditions that might be met there. Being the breed they were and knowing what lay ahead of them, they planned to proceed unhurriedly. They would test the gravels of various rivers, such as the Nahanni, as they went down north and govern themselves by what they found. They were

24

no amateurs with the Mecca of the Yukon shining in their eyes, dedicated to a policy of Yukon or bust. Their plans were flexible. If they found gold-bearing bars, they would stop and work them. If not, they would keep on to the Yukon. In any event, they planned to winter somewhere in the North and then, if it seemed advisable, to push forward in the spring. So, taking plenty of supplies to last well into the second year and loading up material out of which to build a scow, they hired friends and relatives to freight their goods to Athabasca Landing and on July 22 set out quietly along the Athabasca Trail.

Since the old ninety-mile wagon road was in reasonable shape, they arrived at the Landing four days later. Being experienced, they quickly assembled their scow and on August 2 slipped off downstream.

Louis Couture, who had already been in the Yukon, accompanied by Messrs. Prevost, Hibert, Bordeleau and Boulois — French Canadians all — left Edmonton five days after the Pilon party. But the Couture contingent left by train for Vancouver, planning to take the orthodox if difficult route by way of Skagway. It is worthy of note that they reached Dawson City on September 29, 1897, two months after leaving Edmonton, whereas the Pilon party reached there about July 25, 1898.

The news of the actual departure of the Shand, Couture and Pilon parties, coupled with an item appearing in the July 19 *Bulletin*, fanned the Klondike fever into a flame and in Edmonton no one talked of anything else. That article mentioned J. J. Clements of Los Angeles, who was reported to have "cleaned up" $175,000. He was said to have brought $50,000 of it to Seattle and to have invested the rest in more claims in the Klondike. Similarly, a man named Lippy, of Seattle, "brought out $65,000 and has $150,000 in sight and claims his mine is worth $500,000." He was reported as saying: "At Dawson sacks of dust are thrown under the counters in the stores for safe keeping. Some of the stories are so fabulous that I am afraid to report them, for fear of being suspected of fabrication."

But none of these news items stirred the townsfolk as much as the unexpected arrival of the advance guard of a Winnipeg party about July 29. Quite independent of any ideas Edmontonians entertained of the feasibility of reaching the Klondike by way of Edmonton and before the Board of Trade had taken any steps to advertise the town as the Gateway to the Klondike, these people came piling in and rushed onward to Athabasca Landing to take the long Water Route.

When, on the same day, the *Bulletin* editor received the latest copy of the *Toronto World*, he rejoiced to find it advocating a route to the Yukon starting at Edmonton. But before the day was out he began to sense competition when a telegraphic item indicated that the people of British Columbia were advocating a rival route along the grown-over clearing of the old telegraph line running from the Fraser Valley to Telegraph Creek, a trail which later came to be called the Ashcroft Route. The hint of a rival All-Canadian Route set his pen off in a flurry of excitement.

Three days later a telegram from Hamilton stated that Alderman J. M. Findley and eight others would entrain for Edmonton and planned to go down the Mackenzie River. When it arrived, the editor was in the midst of enjoying a long article in the latest *Hamilton Spectator* which was most enthusiastic about the Edmonton route. Dazzled by the dawning certainty that at last Edmonton was to find its place in the sun, the editor, gloating over the *Spectator*, exploded into rhapsody.

On the same day his news columns mentioned three local groups that were preparing to go north. The Stephen-Howey party planned to go down the Mackenzie and winter somewhere in the Far North. W. J. Graham was selling his coal business and expected to take the same route. The brothers Fred and H. Jenner were likewise getting ready to go. Evidently Edmontonians, long accustomed to the ways of the northwest, were ready to practice what the editor began to preach. Shand and the Pilon group had led the way, and here were other parties hard on their heels.

Meanwhile, the people of the whole Edmonton area rallied to the cause. Public meetings at Edmonton, Fort Saskatchewan and St. Albert sent resolutions to Ottawa calling upon the government to build a good road to Fort Assiniboine and continue it over the Swan Hills to Lesser Slave Lake.

The August 5 columns of the *Bulletin* advised that a party of New Yorkers, bringing a large boat with them, were expected to reach Edmonton on that night's train while the main Winnipeg party, which had arrived by the previous train, had gone on to the Landing, where they had engaged someone to build a boat for them. The paper also mentioned two more local parties that were getting ready to set out by the Mackenzie River. One consisted of A. E. Lee, S. A. McNeill and F. G. Taylor; the other was made up of Captain Segers, F. A. Hardisty and F. M. Robertson. These news items explained that both parties planned to go as far as they could before the onset of winter and then to camp till spring before making the final push into the Yukon.

But occasionally the editor of the *Bulletin* also had to report the existence of unbelievers. He told casually of Frank Marriaggi of the Alberta Hotel and some friends setting out by train for Vancouver and the Skagway route. He was a little more emphatic, however, in his reaction to rumour from Calgary of a misrepresentation he considered vile and treacherous. For by means of stories of unbelievably terrible conditions along the routes from Edmonton, Calgarians had tampered with the party from Hamilton, which had been intending to go north, and diverted it to the coast. One of the base lies was that, on occasion, as near to Edmonton as Athabasca Landing it had been known to snow sixteen feet in twenty-four hours. If that was what the climate was like only a hundred miles north of Edmonton, what might not the adventurers have to endure if they went beyond that point?

By this time Edmonton merchants were stressing the Klondike theme in their advertising. For instance, Scott Robertson, the sheriff and auctioneer, inserted an ad saying:

TO THE YUKON

Via Edmonton & Peace River

To enable goldseekers to get there I will offer at 2 P.M.
on Saturday August 14th a small band of first class horses, etc.

On his part, on August 5 the editor published a map and wrote a long article pointing out the advantages of the routes from Edmonton and presenting all the available information about them. On the one hand he went into the details of the long Water Route down to the mouth of the Mackenzie. On the other, he looked at the Overland Route by way of Fort St. John and the Cassiar, and suggested two ways prospectors could take to reach Fort St. John.

By either of these overland routes the miners would take pack horses which could carry all their supplies and be useful in prospecting when they got to the Yukon. Shortly after leaving Edmonton, the editor pointed out, the adventurers would pass through potential gold-bearing regions, which, with gaps, would extend all the way to the Yukon – the known areas of Fort St. John, Finlay River, Omineca and Cassiar. They would therefore be in a position to stop at any point that interested them; if luck favoured them, they might find rich diggings, remain at them and never need to go to the Yukon at all. As it turned out, many Klondikers followed this practice.

During the next three days two seasoned prospectors, D. W. Wright and A. M. Pelly, arrived from Vernon, British Columbia, and went on to the Landing. Here indeed was confirmation of the virtue of the All-Canadian Route. Furthermore, another man with experience in the north, ex-Constable J. C. F. Dickson, leading another party from Winnipeg, set out for Athabasca Landing. At the same time, Captain Segers's party set out for the same destination. This group of local men was led by a dominating personality who for years had been captain of riverboats on the Missouri, the Red River at Winnipeg and along the Saskatchewan and Athabasca.

Although all these parties bound for the Yukon planned to take the Water Route, nevertheless interest in the Overland Route increased. More public meetings at Edmonton and St. Albert discussed its problems and, besides urging the Dominion government to open a road through the Swan Hills to Lesser Slave Lake, also asked that the old Red River cart trail from that point to Peace River Crossing be put in good shape. Further, they asked that the government consider a road beyond the crossing to the Nelson and the Liard rivers. All of this would be preliminary to establishing the All-Canadian Route that everybody expected to come into being during the next two or three years.

In addition to reporting all this information, the *Bulletin* found space for a detailed list of the supplies and provisions the Stephen-Howey party had taken with them on the Water Route. It was hoped that this list would be of assistance to other adventurers. The paper made a point of the fact that these quantities of goods were designed to last two years — that is, en route and for several months after the party got to the Yukon.

By this time every Edmontonian was swelled with pride in his town, which fate had chosen to be what was variously called the Gateway to the Yukon, the Beginning of the All-Canadian Route, the Back Door to the Yukon, and the Poor Man's Route to the Yukon. The town council and the Board of Trade were not only persuaded of the superiority of the routes they advocated but were ready to put on a campaign to convince the world. Taking the lead, the editor of the *Bulletin*, sincerely convinced of the righteousness of the cause he espoused, set out to spread the new gospel and to battle anyone who in his ignorance was, or in his malice pretended to be, an unbeliever.

When on August 12, 1897, he brought out his special Klondike issue of the *Bulletin* and in due course mailed it far and wide across the continent, in spite of the fact that he made it sound all too easy, there was nothing untrue in what was said and nothing calculated to mislead.

Headed

TO THE GOLDEN YUKON
THE ALL CANADIAN ROUTE

it contained practically all the information which a score or so of Edmonton's prominent men, who knew about the Far North, had compiled. First it referred to the two orthodox ways of reaching the Yukon along the west coast. One was to make the 4,400-mile voyage from Victoria to St. Michael and Dawson. The other – the Chilkoot Pass route – was to steam up the coast one thousand miles from Victoria to Skagway, then walk thirty-five miles over the summit of a mountain range and finally float six hundred miles down the Yukon. Quite correctly, the *Bulletin* pointed to the nearly insuperable difficulty a man encountered carrying a year's supplies over the worst eleven miles of that route. These supplies, it said, would weigh perhaps 1,300 pounds. Since on the terrible climb up the pass a man could only carry fifty or seventy-five pounds at a trip, he would have to make some twenty-six trips of eleven miles going up loaded and twenty-five trips coming back empty handed. The trip each way would certainly consume a day, therefore he would be at least fifty-one days getting his goods over that eleven-mile stretch, to say nothing of the exhausting labour.

Having made that point, the editor, under the caption

A BETTER ALL CANADIAN ROUTE NEEDED

called for government action to build a road from Edmonton to the Yukon. He reasoned as follows: Although the known area of the Yukon is larger than any other gold-bearing area on earth, and although nearly all of it is in Canada, nevertheless access to it at present is by routes passing through the United States. For that reason alone we need an All-Canadian Route. There are two practical all-Canadian routes, one down the Mackenzie, across the portage to the Porcupine River and thence down to the Yukon River – some 2,500 miles – and the other by the Pelly River.

As compared with 1,600 miles by the Chilkoot Pass, said the editor, the route by the Pelly – an all-land route, in fact the Overland Route – is 1,500 miles long, of which four hundred is downstream on the Pelly and Yukon rivers. On the thousand miles to the Pelly horses can find good grazing and of equal importance is the fact that most of the route passes through areas that are known to be gold-bearing. Here the editor repeated his argument that some prospectors would not find it necessary to go all the way to the Yukon. Moreover, at "moderate cost, it could be made a cattle, pack trail and sleigh route." He went on to point out that for the first six hundred miles various stretches of a wagon road of sorts existed. At little expense they could be connected and improved into a good road.

The Pelly route, he pointed out, had one great national advantage – it was never near the Alaska border and a mail route and telegraph line would not be exposed to attack from the Americans. The mail route and telegraph line were, of course, matters for the future; Canada's immediate interest was to find a quick way to get to the Yukon. The matter was urgent, because already some twenty Californians were preparing to set out from Edmonton along it. The special issue of the *Bulletin* then went on to discuss the many pack trails that intertwined on the way along the route to the Pelly River and published a poorly drawn map to illustrate it.

The route the editor favoured went from Peace River Crossing upstream to the Pine River (our Beatton River, near Fort St. John), up that river, over the height of land to the headwaters of the Fort Nelson River and on down to the Liard River. The route then ascended the Liard, turned off to Frances Lake and, by crossing a low summit, reached the Pelly River, which it descended to the junction with the Yukon. From there, prospectors could float down the broad safe Yukon to the Klondike field — total distance from Edmonton about 1,500 miles.

There were, then, these two general routes out of Edmonton, the Water Route down the Mackenzie and the pack horse route overland to the Pelly River. At various points along each of them the track forked into alternative routes, and these in turn forked into others until each general route offered a sometimes bewildering choice of ways to take to the Yukon. The distances along these routes were revised somewhat later and are given in Appendix I.

The distance by the Water Route was said to be 2,585 miles, considerably more than the milage from Edmonton to Toronto, and the distance by the Overland Route was some 1,500 miles. One of the many problems facing the Klondikers, particularly those who decided to go overland, was choosing which of a multitude of branching and anastomosing routes to take — the same problem of selection which a modern motorist has to solve in driving from Edmonton to Toronto.

When thinking of distances it is worth noting another interesting parallel. The famous American Oregon Trail left the Missouri River near Kansas City and from that point to Portland, Oregon, the distance was some 2,100 miles. In its choice of routes that trail was simple as compared with the large number of choices facing a Klondiker outbound from Edmonton. Here and there the Oregon Trail had a few short cuts and once in a while a major alternative but in contrast to the All-Canadian Route to the Klondike it was a well-defined and well-travelled highway. But there was a definite relationship between the Oregon Trail and Edmonton's Overland Route. The American trail had seen its most active era some forty or fifty years before the days of the Yukon rush. When the Klondike fever was at its height, the western United States held thousands of men who had either come west over the Oregon Trail as children or whose parents had travelled it. It was still an active part of their heritage and when some of them thought of going to the Yukon, they were influenced by the background and practices of the Oregon Trail and applied them to the trek to the Yukon.

It should be noted that there was another entrance from the prairies to the Water Route — one on which the editor of the *Bulletin* did not waste much space. It was promoted by the rival town of Prince Albert, which was probably a little larger than Edmonton, lay some five hundred miles down the winding North Saskatchewan River and was the northernmost end of steel in Saskatchewan. The route actually left the railway at the hamlet of Duck Lake, a few miles south of that town. The hundred or so Klondikers who used this route made use of the century-old fur-traders' trail, largely fallen into disuse, that cut across to Green Lake, went on to Lac Ile-à-la-Crosse and the famous old twelve-mile Methy portage, and then by descending the Clearwater River reached the Athabasca River at Fort McMurray. It was thus an alternative approach to the main Water Route to the Yukon.

By either Edmonton route, the most pressing problem was how to transport the two years' supplies necessary for the venture. Although a Klondiker would pass some traders' posts, he could not rely on buying food there because their stocks were geared only to the needs of their trade with the surrounding Indians. Selling it to a flock of travelling prospectors would soon have reduced it to nothing.

Men with experience in the north recommended certain items as indispensable and Edmonton businessmen advertised that the rations should include enough spare flour and bacon with which to trade. McDougall and Secord, the independent outfitters, put out a folder which, along with considerable information on the routes, also included the list of "Supplies for one man for one year" given in Appendix II.

Food alone for one year came to about one thousand pounds without even mentioning hardware and clothing. A two-year supply, added to the weight of clothing, hardware and other supplies, would weigh at least twenty-five hundred pounds. The problem of getting to the Yukon, then, was not so much a matter of travelling there oneself as of taking in a load which at the start of the trip would weigh well over a ton.

Transporting this gear by the Water Route from Edmonton to Fort McPherson was relatively easy. If one timed everything correctly and could get accommodation on the Hudson's Bay Company's steamers, the trip as far as Fort McPherson could be one long holiday. Mainly because of the cost very few availed themselves of steamers. They either bought boats made in Edmonton and had them hauled to the Landing or bought lumber in Edmonton and built their own boats at the Landing. While boats of all sizes, shapes and designs were produced, depending upon the whims of their builders, most of them were of the York boat type that for so long had served the Hudson's Bay Company on the northern rivers. A typical boat of this kind built by John Walter of Edmonton, an expert in that line, sold for $60, had a 22-foot keel and a 6½-foot beam, and was capable of carrying seven tons. Many of the larger parties of Klondikers built scows at the Landing. These were usually about thirty feet long by twelve feet wide, with bow and stern square and sloping like a punt, drew about eighteen inches of water and were equipped with rowing benches. Canoes were of little service on an expedition like this.

Parties setting out from the Landing in boats or scows usually hired one of the half-breed river-men to accompany them as far as Fort McMurray. Outstanding among these river-men was "Shot," who at that time had twenty-seven years' experience on the Athabasca and had been the very first man to take a boat down Grand Rapids. Except for some minor rough spots, the first 167 miles down the placid Athabasca were smooth sailing but the boiling, swirling Grand Rapids needed the attention of an expert and this the half-breed river-men provided. At Grand Rapids the river, divided by an island into two channels, falls some sixty feet in half a mile, the left-hand side being a raging torrent which no boat could navigate successfully and the one on the right a calmer chute down which boats could be taken empty. Experienced boatmen landed at the upper end of the island, unloaded and carried their goods half a mile on their backs or loaded them on the Hudson's Bay Company's tramway. Then, with strong ropes and much effort, they let their boats down the rough right-hand channel and reloaded them. For the next two or three miles the water was very rough but nevertheless navigable.

Several more rapids had to be negotiated, some of them by portaging, before reaching Fort McMurray. Then for 160 miles all was clear sailing down the broad, forest-lined river as it flowed serenely north to its delta at Lake Athabasca. Crossing the five or six-mile neck of the lake to reach Fort Chipewyan was often a risky venture.

The Slave River, which over a course of 230 miles drains Lake Athabasca into Great Slave Lake, consists of two reaches of easily navigable water interrupted by most violent and dangerous rapids which extend from Smith's Landing (Fitzgerald) for sixteen miles down to Fort Smith. Generally speaking, both boats and loads had to be carried around this obstacle over the good wagon road and put back into the water below Fort Smith. For the next 1,287 miles from there to the mouth of the Peel River, except for the often stormy crossing or skirting of the south shore of Great Slave Lake, navigation was easy.

Travelling beyond the mouth of the Peel River near Fort McPherson, however, was a different story. The long, leisurely summer days of loafing as the boat slipped down the sunlit, placid Mackenzie were over and now work had to begin in earnest, as the men fought their way foot by foot up the Peel or the Rat rivers. This stage of the journey occupied weeks, and in some cases months, and its difficulties went far towards counterbalancing the ease with which the Klondikers had travelled from Edmonton to the mouth of the Mackenzie.

Transporting a two-year supply of goods and provisions over the Overland Route fairly bristled with problems. If it had been possible to purchase supplies at points spaced every two hundred miles or so along the route, thus leaving the Klondiker free to ride along without being loaded down with freight, the Overland Route would have been a cinch. But it was not possible.

Instead, the Klondikers had to arrange horse transport for their twenty-five hundred pounds of supplies, and, as many of them were to find, the logistics of horse transport can be complicated and discouraging. Depending upon the kind of accessories with which he is equipped, a horse can transport up to a thousand pounds. A team drawing a double sleigh can move two thousand pounds comfortably. One horse hitched to what the Yukoners called a flat sleigh, that is, a toboggan fitted with shafts, could make good progress with seven hundred pounds, while if he were merely equipped with a pack saddle he could carry only about two hundred pounds successfully. A very few Klondikers started with two-wheeled Red River carts and a few rigged up travois.

A more or less standard string of pack horses for one man setting out for the Klondike was ten: eight to pack, one to ride, and one spare. Several Klondikers left Edmonton equipped with flat sleighs on each of which they loaded four hundred pounds of goods plus three hundred pounds of fodder. For feed for the horses was of paramount importance. To conserve feed and their horses' strength, several parties hired a freighter to take their goods out forty miles to Lac Ste Anne or ninety to Fort Assiniboine, thus in effect letting their pack horses start their journey from these points.

In summer, theoretically, fodder was not such a problem because then the horses could graze during the evenings. But even then finding meadows on which animals could pasture was no easy matter. That difficulty, combined with the sketchy nature of those traces through the forest called pack trails, was more than many a Klondiker could cope with. For the so-called trails were not tracks cut into the sod by wagon wheels or paths beaten in the moss by passing horses.

Prior to the arrival of the Yukon-bound it was very rare for a pack train to use a trail which at least one member of the party did not know fairly well. A stranger, however, found it hard to recognize or follow these primitive traces. Usually such trails picked their way up or down the valley of some watercourse and sometimes they were marked at intervals of several hundred yards where someone had once blazed a tree. Otherwise, except for occasionally coming upon a previous camping ground, a traveller taking the trail for the first time could rarely be sure that he was really on it.

One of the prerequisites of a pack trail was that at intervals of about ten miles it should drop into a meadow where the horses could feed while the party camped. Knowledge of these meadows was one of the things which made an experienced guide or packer so valuable, because with it he could see that the horses got enough to eat. In areas such as the extensive Swan Hills, which for miles were clothed with pine trees, meadows were very scarce and native pack trails simply did not try to go straight through such regions.

For decades the pack trails that wandered about between Edmonton and Fort St. John had served the relatively light traffic they bore adequately. Most of them saw a few Indians pass and repass and a few trappers or traders make an annual return trip with six or eight horses. Where traffic was that light the horses made no appreciable dint in the grass supply of the meadows and all was well. When hundreds of Klondikers and thousands of horses began to straggle through the forest, however, the animals quickly denuded the camping places and literally hundreds of horses starved.

To avoid falling into such a situation, the Klondikers needed good guides who from long experience knew how necessary it was to take good care of the horses. These guides and packers moreover were invaluable in leading and hazing the horses along, in keeping some order in the straggling procession and in meeting the many emergencies that faced such a cavalcade, such as getting through muskegs and fording rapidly flowing streams. Furthermore, in the mornings these guides, wise to the ways of horses, had far less difficulty in finding any that had strayed away in search of better pasture. The hopes of many a party of Klondikers were frustrated by the time taken in catching their horses in the mornings or by the accidents that befell ponies when they were herded by incompetent drivers.

One of the many cruelties ignorant or careless Klondikers inflicted on their horses was sore backs, where poorly packed boxes or ill-adjusted blankets rubbed them raw. An attentive packer watched and cared for his horses' backs and did everything he could night and morning to ward off sores. Not only that, he also exercised care in balancing and packing the load and lashing it into place. An inexperienced Klondiker had the utmost difficulty in tying on packs and frequently was callous enough once someone else had rigged up the pack to leave it on a horse for days at a time, simply because he knew he dare not try to put it on each morning. Men well versed in trail lore often cursed bitterly when finding such a Klondiker's horses dead with their packs still tied on. Many a party of greenhorns began losing horses at the rate of one every day or two. The occasional loss of a horse was not too serious because as the cavalcade progressed the foodstuffs carried became less, and fewer horses were needed to pack them.

A successful party that made reasonable time and did not lose any horses was in a strong position whenever it came to a point in its journey when it could spare some of its animals to sell to the Indians or traders, or to other Klondikers, or when it decided to change its mode of transport to boats, canoes or dogs. In some cases the wandering prospectors, seeing no way to feed their animals over the winter, killed them and dried or smoked the meat to add to their provisions.

Whether the Klondikers set out by the Water or the Overland Route, they all had one thing in common and that was the money they had to expend for the equipment to make the trip. The majority of them, and mainly the wiser ones, outfitted at Edmonton where they could buy clothes and supplies adapted to the trip lying ahead of them. Each man had to pay out about $180 for his two years' food supply, another twenty for cooking utensils and tools, and for bedding and clothes another ninety, making roughly three hundred dollars in all.

Then, to transport his goods, he needed either a boat or horses. As more Klondikers poured into Edmonton, prices naturally went up, but at the start of the rush, by casting his lot in with someone else, a man taking the Water Route could divide the cost of a boat either made at or delivered to Athabasca Landing and spend only seventy-five dollars. There the pair would have to hire a native to pilot them through the rough water to Fort McMurray and pay him about twenty-five dollars each. Adding these expenditures to the three hundred dollars a man spent for food and supplies brought his total cost to about four hundred dollars.

If he were taking the Overland Route, horses cost twenty-five dollars each, pack saddles six dollars, flat sleighs eight dollars, and double sleighs about fifteen, so that his outlay for transport equipment was of the order of three hundred dollars, and, of course, his supplies added an equal amount to that. If he planned to pull out during the winter, a train of four good dogs varied from fifty to one hundred dollars and a toboggan cost eight dollars. With these, however, if he had the stamina to keep up with his dogs, which dragged a total load of about four hundred pounds, he could easily average twenty-five miles a day.

As the whole concept of the Overland and Water routes came into focus and as Edmontonians realized how much money these eager adventurers with the gleam of gold in their eyes and the clink of gold in the pockets were going to spend, every last citizen came suddenly awake. Thereupon one and all began to advocate the Edmonton route to the Yukon. For money, real money, American silver dollars and American gold eagles, spread into every corner of the community and to every member of it. The farmers had increased calls for wheat for flour, for meat, hay and any cayuses they cared to sell. The merchants were busy bringing in goods and selling them over the counter. Harness-makers and shoemakers riveted and stitched, brewery horses pulled more frequent loads of kegs from the vats on the flats to the saloons where the Klondikers discussed their plans. John Walter's boat-building establishment vied with other lumber yards in turning out boats, sleighs and toboggans. Even the demand for half-breeds, past masters in their knowledge of the routes through the wilds, threatened to overtake the supply.

There was money in the Edmonton route to the Yukon – money for all.

CHAPTER FOUR

SPOTLIGHT ON EDMONTON

Up to the middle of August 1897, six parties totalling some thirty men had left Edmonton by the Water Route and three things should be noted about them. With the exception of one or two men from Winnipeg and two from British Columbia, they were all from Edmonton or its environs. All had experience of travelling in the north, and finally, in spite of the *Bulletin*'s ideas of an Overland Route, all went by water. Regardless of that, however, they demonstrated that Edmontonians were prepared to practise what they preached and to set off for the Yukon.

Six parties may not have been a very great showing but the movement had taken some time to set afloat, and these men had launched it. Moreover, ready to follow in their wake were scores of adventurers on their way to Edmonton. In its issue following the special edition and in a column headed "Yukon Bound," the *Bulletin* listed seven parties that were about to start north. The list included two men from Milton, Pennsylvania, two from Duluth, five from Fresno, California, five more from Duluth, and another large party of nineteen from Fresno. If not the world, at least the United States was beating a path to Edmonton's door.

The paper paid particular attention to the second group from Fresno because, by coming from California, it had turned its back upon the coastal route. After making a careful list of its members, the editor advised that they were going overland, expected to start in a few days, and already had purchased eighty horses.

As week succeeded week for the next month and a half until the end of September, the *Bulletin* faithfully recorded the names, places of origin, and the route selected by those chosen by destiny to start from Edmonton:

Seven from Montreal, who brought three Peterborough canoes and will build a boat at the Landing.

Two from New York.

R. H. Milvain and J. Garnett of Pincher Creek, who are having a boat built at John Walter's yard.

Six from Hamilton, Ontario.

Five from the Morinville settlement twenty miles to the north.

Three from Sault Ste Marie.

Two more from Pennsylvania, and one from Prince Albert, Saskatchewan.

A party from Pembroke, Ontario.

A group from Chicago — a close-mouthed bunch: "the secret of their exact destination is carefully guarded. It is in the possession of Henry Card, one of the party."

E. L. Bell and E. O. Reid of Calgary.

A. J. Bell and party of the Klondiker Intercolonial Syndicate plan to go via Athabasca and Lesser Slave Lake to prospect on the Peace and go to the Yukon in the spring.

Five local men from the Beaver Lake settlement.

Others from Maine, Quebec, Revelstoke, Red Deer, Great Falls, Utah, Texas, Chicago, Oakville, Toronto and Montreal, and a large party from England.

The editor had been a busy man trying to keep abreast of everything that had been going on. For one thing, he began receiving letters from all over the continent asking for information. In answering these he had able assistance from G. W. Gairdner, the Secretary of the Board of Trade. As a side line, Gairdner associated himself with a civil engineer, A. G. Harrison, in opening up an information bureau. In due course these two produced a pamphlet and map giving details of the routes to the Yukon. Some questions the editor had difficulty answering. One man wrote from New York asking if he would have any trouble travelling from Edmonton to the Yukon on a bicycle. Another asked if there were regular boarding houses along the way and whether or not a party would have to fight its way through assorted angry Indians.

On another front the editor had to find time to keep up with what his exchange newspapers were saying. He glowed when during August both the *Toronto World* and the *Vancouver World* made benign references to the Edmonton-Yukon route and the former even published a map of the long trail. The *Chicago Record* also published a map of what it called "The Back Door to the Yukon." The *Winnipeg Free*

Press and the *Hamilton Spectator* also threw their weight behind the Edmonton route.

The *Calgary Herald*, however, was an uncertain ally. Since all Edmonton-bound Klondikers had to change trains at Calgary, that town supported the Edmonton route and, as the prospectors passed, hoped to get the first opportunity at their purses. On September 2 the *Herald* printed several inquiring letters it had received from eastern Canada and the United States. But as if to indicate Calgarians' contrariness, it persisted in spelling the new gold-field "Clondike." Then on September 16 it too printed a "Special Clondike Issue." As a matter of fact, the map which it produced was better drawn than the *Bulletin*'s. In any event, putting out this map showed that Calgary's heart was in the right place, even if on it Calgary was shown in large block letters, while Edmonton was indicated by a scarcely legible scribble in much the same manner as the outposts of Peace River Crossing and Fort Nelson.

Nevertheless, these efforts showed that Calgary too was advocating the Edmonton route and that its people, including the Calgary Wine & Spirit Company, were behind it. That company's advertisement put its finger on one imported item that it hoped would be on every prospector's list, for it stated: "You can't go to the Clondike without some kind of spirit to protect you from sickness and disease," and recommended taking sixty-five per cent overproof wine.

At St. Albert, meanwhile, the high calibre half-breeds held a meeting and enlisted all of their number who were skilled packers or boatmen into one company from which strangers could chose guides for the trip to the Yukon. By this means they hoped to establish uniform prices and to maintain and guarantee reliable service. Prominent in this group were A. Prince, J. Cunningham and a score of others. For just as the Métis at Lac la Biche were without equal as river pilots and boatmen on the great northern waterway, the Lac Ste Anne and St. Albert half-breeds were second to none as guides and packers along the forest trails leading north and west.

They organized themselves just in time, for within a span of ten days three road reconnaissance parties started out and, since each needed packers and guides, the St. Albert men soon found plenty of work to do. The Edmonton Board of Trade sent P. D. Campbell and J. R. Brenton north on August 31; the Ottawa government sent Inspector Moodie of the NWMP towards the Yukon on September 4; while the Northwest Territories government sent T. W. Chalmers, the road engineer, into the Swan Hills on September 9. All these trips were the outcome of Edmontonians' pressure for a road to the Yukon.

Not realizing that the senior governments would act so rapidly, and in any event being too energetic to sit back with folded hands, Edmontonians went to work on their own. If a road were to be built, someone had better get busy and find out just where to build it. And this was why the Board of Trade sent Campbell and Brenton into the field. To raise money to pay them, it took up a subscription. The prominent merchant, Mayor John A. McDougall, and some of his confreres, going further than that, solicited funds from their wholesalers in the East. Most of these responded nobly and the first reply came in a wire from G. F. and J. Galt, wholesale grocers in Winnipeg, to J. A. McDougall, saying: "The firm subscribes one hundred dollars stop If this is not enough make it two hundred."

The response was so good that on August 31 Campbell and Brenton set out overland for the Pelly River, expecting to return "this fall or winter." They took two horses to ride and four packed with supplies, and as the *Bulletin* said: "The idea is to get a definite report on the all land route. The men will keep a diary and send back information. The men received $250 each for the trip and their families will be paid $25 a month during their absence, money to be subscribed. Both men had previously worked on surveys."

The Board of Trade's instructions were that they were to go to Fort Assiniboine, cut across the Swan Hills, and keep on to Peace River Crossing. From there they were to seek a route for a road, preferably from Dunvegan or Fort St. John, to Fort Nelson, and then to descend the Fort Nelson River to the Liard, ascend it, and eventually cross over to Pelly Banks. Based upon the collective experience of Edmontonians, this course was thought to be the best route for a road.

There was so much excitement about all these road-making parties that the editor of the *Bulletin* had his hands full keeping their activities straight and had been too busy to pay attention to his political affairs. As he said on September 9: "The *Bulletin* has been so busy during the past few weeks in building wagon roads and starting steamboat routes to the Yukon that it has not had time to correct some little misconceptions which have been studiously circulated as to the position taken by it towards the government. . . ."

And it was not only the doings of these road-building parties that he had to report but also what other advocates of the route were saying. For instance, Sloane & Sons, large merchants of Cincinnati, wrote to Messrs. Gairdner and Harrison as follows: "We believe 300,000 more will start from the United States for the Alaskan gold fields within sixty days after the opening of navigation in the spring. The fever is spreading, and no doubt the next two years will find 2,000,000 men in that section. The people are going wild for it."

If Edmontonians were entranced by their route to the Yukon, people in the East were enthralled by it. Whereas Edmontonians talked in tens or hundreds, these Easterners dreamed of thousands and millions and made it hard for the editor of the *Bulletin* to keep his feet on the ground. One of them, W. Pugsley of Saint John, New Brunswick, came to Edmonton to dangle a railway before the town council. He proposed to build it to the Yukon and wanted the council's support towards obtaining a charter. And, of course, if they could sweeten the pot by way of a little cash or even a guarantee, he would not consider it amiss. By September 16 he had found a name for his venture (the Edmonton District Railway), had spelled out his charter and had talked the town council into signing an agreement to help it along. For his part he was to build from the South Side, through Edmonton and on to Fort Assiniboine, and to complete his line within two years. By September 16, 1898, he was also to build and set in motion a line of steamers to travel from his end of steel down the Athabasca and Mackenzie rivers.

Then, as if to fling a dash of cold water into the fevered face of all this enthusiasm, one of the newspapers at the coast reported: "Two young Englishmen who have travelled in the Yukon are warning would-be Klondikers against the Edmonton route. One said: 'I don't believe a man could reach the Yukon diggings in a year, no, not in eighteen months going via the Edmonton route.'"

Reaching for his pot of brimstone, the editor of the *Bulletin* demolished them, saying amongst other things: "No doubt the young Englishmen are well paid for the advice they are giving, by parties interested in the coast route." As an offset, the same issue of the paper reported that "W. Pugsley gives notice in the Canada Gazette of application for an act to incorporate the Edmonton, Peace River & Yukon Rly Co. – Edmonton to a point on navigable waters of the Yukon or Pelly Rivers" – a new and more grandiose name.

Gathering encouragement from many sources and many quarters, on October 7, 1897, the *Bulletin* produced a second Yukon issue. By a combination of the editor's talents with those of the Board of Trade and of Gairdner and Harrison, this issue, of which thousands were distributed all over Canada and the United States, contained all the favourable information anyone had about the Edmonton route to the Yukon as well as some that was unfavourable.

It reiterated its criticism of the coast routes. It stressed that the nub of the whole matter was the question of taking supplies into the Yukon, which it insisted could be most easily accomplished by starting from Edmonton. Referring to the bad congestion on these other routes that caused adventurers to mark time for weeks just to get a place in line to cross the passes, the article insisted that by the Edmonton route a prospector "cannot be cornered and the trail cannot be blocked. It is merely a question of time, particularly the latter. That the route is long and difficult everyone will admit – as are all the routes that have been used. . . . The man who has not resolution and ambition and energy and good management and capital enough to carry him to the Yukon by the Edmonton route will be a great deal better off some place else."

While these statements were perfectly true and when considered carefully contained a warning, they also carried a challenge. What man, no matter how inexperienced, having a mind to go to the Yukon, would question himself realistically as to his resolution, energy or ability? The very statement of the hazards in store made them more challenging.

Having issued a warning and thus absolved his conscience, the editor went on to list the advantages of his routes. It was now late fall. Several parties had already set out during the past season and, looking to the future, he began to speculate about the year ahead. The *Bulletin* quite truthfully advised that under favourable conditions a man could travel from Edmonton to the Pelly River in two to three months. Indeed, if he wished to get an early start he should plan to set out during February or March and make the trip to the forks of the Fort Nelson River on the snow. By so doing he could cross the two major rivers, the Athabasca and the Peace, on the ice. Furthermore, by travelling with sleighs a party could take heavier loads and still reach the Fort Nelson River in thirty days, averaging sixteen miles per day. By the time it was reached the snow would be disappearing, so that the sleighs could be abandoned.

Since grazing for the horses might be poor beyond the forks of the Fort Nelson, the prospectors should remain there long enough to build boats. When spring came and the rivers were open, these men would find themselves far in the lead of those who had waited in Edmonton for spring and new grass. After loading most of their supplies into boats, they could float down the Fort Nelson to the Liard and begin to ascend it while some of their party drove the lightly loaded horses along the bank. Finally, having negotiated the difficult upstream pull on the Liard, they could abandon their boats, load up their relatively fresh horses and saunter off towards the Pelly River and the gold-fields.

The editor then turned his attention to the Water Route. He pointed out that during the past summer most of the parties had started out late in the season and that at Athabasca Landing they had been forced to fell trees and whip-saw lumber for their boats. During the spring that lay ahead prospects would be much more favourable. For one thing, Alex Fraser had started a sawmill at the Landing and lumber was now readily available. The rest of the mechanism for going north had been improved considerably and organized on a sound basis. Many guides were on hand whose charge for taking a brigade to Fort McMurray was fifty dollars. Or, if the miners felt competent to deal with the numerous but lesser rapids below the Grand Rapids, they need hire a boatman only to take them down its mile or so of white water.

Having provided information about the Overland and the Water routes, the special edition of the paper looked at Edmonton's merits as a point of departure. The town's outfitters were cognizant of the needs of parties setting out and good experienced guides were available. Not only was the route to the Klondike perfectly safe from hostile Indians, along rivers and lakes abounding in fish and forests harbouring a reasonable supply of game animals, it was moreover an All-Canadian route. Both Edmonton and Dawson and the trails between them were all in Canada, so that one need not be bothered by the expensive and wearying levies of customs officials. While as yet there was no official mail service to the north, the various traders, the Hudson's Bay Company, McDougall and Secord and others would forward mail at every opportunity by their own men who were always coming and going.

As indicated in the special issue, Edmontonians were not alone in taking a hand in opening a way to the Yukon. J. H. Wood and S. B. McNeill of Pembroke, Ontario, arrived with plans to start a boat-building establishment at Athabasca Landing. At the same time, G. T. Leitch, a capitalist from St. Louis, Missouri, called for tenders for freighting his prefabricated steamboat to the Landing, where he planned to go into the carrying business. Various other enterprising individuals began to cast speculative looks at the possibilities of making money in the transportation field. The planners of the Edmonton, Peace River & Yukon Railway were already making progress and had induced the Board of Trade and the town of Edmonton to join them in a petition to Ottawa for a subsidy of $3,200 per mile towards building their line at least as far as Fort Assiniboine.

Perceptive local artisans were beginning to make the most of the opportunities in the rush through Edmonton. For instance, John Kelly and Ed Looby, the blacksmith, were advertising an improved travois which the Yukon-bound could substitute for pack saddles. With it one horse could transport from three to five hundred pounds, or double the load of a saddled horse. Tom Cairns, who operated the brewery near the west end of today's Low Level Bridge, not only applied his talents towards reducing loads but after some experiments announced that he was manufacturing evaporated potatoes. McDougall and Secord investigated his new produce and placed an order.

On November 8 Brenton and Campbell, the two men whom the Board of Trade had sent out to explore a route to the Yukon, came back more or less with their tails between their legs. They had set out on August 31 and at Athabasca Landing had hired an Indian as a guide. On September 12 they reached the east end of Lesser Slave Lake and by riding along its north shore made their way to the settlement at the west end where the Hudson's Bay men discussed routes with them. At Peace River Crossing an Indian who had two canoes charged three dollars to ferry them over to the left bank, whence they took the trail to Dunvegan. There, failing to obtain supplies which they had hoped to get from Brick Brothers, they were forced to turn back to Edmonton by way of the grande prairie, Sturgeon Lake and Lac Ste Anne. Their trip was a failure.

On the other hand, the Northwest Territories government had moved rapidly towards opening up the road over the Swan Hills. Hiring Dan Noyes to take care of the packing and the ten horses, T. W. Chalmers, the engineer, left Edmonton on September 9 to pick a route. When he set out, he took two two-wheeled carts in order to relieve the pack horses as much as possible. The following comments from his report indicate his progress and the state of the existing roads.

> I followed the main road through River Qui Barre to Lac La Nonne. This is a good road and requires no work until within about 2 miles of the lake. . . . From the Pembina River to the crossing of the Athabasca there has been a road cut out which has been pretty badly filled up in places by fallen timber, which can be easily cleared.
>
> We carried a piece of oiled cotton which we soon, on arrival at the Athabasca, converted into a boat with which we crossed the river, swimming the horses.
>
> I found it would be impossible to take the carts any farther, and left them here with some other things we thought we could get on without. . . .

In due course Chalmers picked a route for a trail over the Swan Hills to Lesser Slave Lake settlement. Since he was on a reconnaissance mission, he returned by way of Snipe Lake and, by heading a long distance south, struck the pack trail from the mouth of the McLeod River to Sturgeon Lake. Along this route he met some of the Klondikers and returned to Edmonton on November 7.

Next day Chalmers sent out a party with two teams, a foreman, six axmen and a cook, all under Alex Cameron, to improve the old road to Fort Assiniboine and to hack a new one from there to Lesser Slave Lake. About a month later the Northwest Territories commissioner of public works called tenders for the right to operate ferries at the crossings of the Pembina and the Athabasca, farther north at the narrows near Lesser Slave Lake settlement, and finally across Peace River. By the end of the year Cameron and his crew were chopping their way up the south slope of the Swan Hills.

Inspector J. D. Moodie of the Mounted Police, on whom the federal government laid the task of finding another trail, set out from Edmonton five days before Chalmers went out to work his way through the Swan Hills. Moodie had not been instructed to build a road but only to pick out a route for one from Edmonton to the Pelly River. He was to collect exhaustive information, make a map and mark on it portions over which a wagon trail could be made at little expense, note those portions that would need corduroying, grading or ditching, and report where bridges and ferries would have to be installed. Over the sections where the terrain appeared too difficult to permit the building of a cheap wagon road he was to locate a path which would be practical for pack horses and for cattle drives. Finally, the route he was to find had to bypass the dangerous navigation of the long stretch of rough water on the Liard.

Commissioner Herchmer of the NWMP suggested in pretty definite terms that Moodie should head for Fort St. John, ascend the Halfway River valley, cross the mountains and find and follow a reported pack trail to Sylvester's Post in the Cassiar country. Herchmer further hoped that with luck Moodie would be able to get to the Klondike during the coming winter. Since Edmontonians favoured a trail north and west from the Peace River country to the Fort Nelson River and had sent Campbell and Brenton in that direction, they reacted coolly to Moodie and the route he had been told to follow and were severe in censuring him. It is worth noting that some forty-five years after the Klondike Rush when the Alaska Highway came to be built, it did not follow Moodie's route but generally went the way that early Edmontonians had advocated.

At Edmonton Moodie engaged Richard Hardisty, a son of Senator Hardisty, B. Pepin of St. Albert and an Indian as packers and guides and set out for Lac Ste Anne with twenty-five horses. Following the pack trail to the mouth of the McLeod River, they caught up with the Fresno party, which had started several days before them. Passing Moose Lake and fording the Little Smoky River, they entered the tiny trading centre of Sturgeon Lake on September 28. After crossing the narrows of the lake, they headed for Bremner and Gunn's cattle ranch at Spirit River and on October 8 reached Dunvegan.

Although Moodie had hoped to buy some dogs there, he had to send Hardisty back to the post at Lesser Slave Lake with instructions to buy seven or eight trains of them. While he was gone, Moodie met an odd character by the name of Wilson, an American who had entered the Peace River country in 1890 and for some time had been working at the Spirit River cattle ranch. He undertook to guide the party to Fort St. John along the south side of the Peace River.

Leaving Dunvegan about October 14, the party proceeded reasonably well until it got into the thick timber west of Pouce Coupé Prairie, where Wilson lost the trail. Everyone spread out to try to find it again but when they did, they could not find Wilson. After spending two or three days looking for him they found signs of his wanderings and finally, concluding that he had gone crazy, gave up the search. There is no record that anyone ever saw him again. Moodie's party continued its trip, forded the Kiskatinaw River, and on October 31 built a raft and crossed the Peace River to Fort St. John. A few days later, Stout, Wigmore and Ridell, the more persistent members of the Fresno party, reached that old fur-trading post.

There Moodie, perhaps in some uncertainty of purpose, dallied for a month. On November 6 Hardisty rejoined the party, bringing a boat, thirty-three dogs and five dog sleds. During the long interval at Fort St. John Moodie killed several of his horses that appeared to be fairly well worn out and dried their meat for dog feed. Then he dispensed with Hardisty's services and hired some Beaver Indians.

A day or so before he left Fort St. John on December 3, he sent his party ahead with ten sleighs and horses, three spare horses and six dog-teams. In due course he caught up with them at Cache Creek. The party went up the Halfway River, swung over to the west branch which it followed to Cypress Creek, and started up the creek towards Laurier Pass. Moodie's disagreements with his native guides made the tedious trip difficult and one after another several of his horses played out. From time to time he killed another horse or two but in the pass the day after Christmas he shot seven more and dried the meat. Descending the west slope of the mountains, the party, reduced almost entirely to dogs for transportation, reached Fort Grahame on the Finlay River on January 18. Since the Hudson's Bay post there was short of supplies and lacking dog feed, Moodie immediately sent some of his men to some lakes about twenty miles away to fish, but they had little luck. Thus far his venture had fallen far short of being a marked success.

While Moodie was working his way through the forests towards Fort St. John, the Fresno people who had started out from Edmonton with such fanfare on August 24 were also having problems. Since the organization, disappointments and partial failure of this party were typical of the experiences of so many overland parties, it is interesting to follow it in some detail. It included Mrs. G. E. Garner, who, by accompanying her husband, became the first female Klondiker to leave Edmonton. On August 4, 1897, the *Fresno Daily Evening Expositor* reported:

BY RAIL 2070 MILES — BY HORSE 700 MORE —
AND BY ANYWAY TO THE GOLD FIELDS

Fully 250 Fresnans assembled at the Southern Pacific station this morning to see the Mack expedition start for the Klondyke. There were several damp eyes in the crowd, but the gold hunters were merry and eager for the start for the north.

These gold seekers numbered twenty-two . . . under the leadership of J. S. Mack. Mr. Mack is an experienced mining engineer and surveyor. He has been over the ground before and claims that the Rocky mountains do not extend so far north as is given on the maps.

The party will go from here direct by rail to Edmonton in Alberta province. The distance is 2070 miles. At Edmonton, horses and supplies will be found waiting for them. . . . Mr. Mack states that from Edmonton to Klondyke the distance is but 700 miles. The trip will be made over a comparatively level stretch of country.

It is not intended by the party to reach the Klondyke before spring. The place where they will spend the winter is known only to themselves.

Before it even reached Edmonton the party was beset by an experience that was to be all too common amongst Yukon parties – their leader disappeared with the funds entrusted to him. The headline in the *Expositor* of August 23 said:

CONFIRM THE STORY THAT MACK,
THEIR LEADER, VAMOOSED

A letter received from G. Russ Walton at Edmonton, B.C. [*sic*] . . . states that their guide and manager, Mr. Mack of Fresno, disappeared suddenly from a train on the Canadian Pacific Railroad on the night of August 7th, and it is believed that he skipped by the light of the moon, taking with him whatever funds the boys had advanced on their outfits.

Mack had evidently disappeared with about six hundred dollars, of which each member had contributed at least twenty-five. By this time, moreover, some of the problems of getting to the Yukon had come clearly into focus. As the *Expositor* explained on August 21:

... the Mack party enroute to the Yukon will not have as easy a time as they had hoped. Instead of 700 miles marching they will have more than 2700, though most of it may be done by boats. . . .

The people of Edmonton are trying to draw the stream of goldseekers that way and from the descriptions sent out of the Chilcoot route the Edmonton would seem to be much the preferable.

On August 24 the party got away, and the *Bulletin* commented:

The California party bound for the Yukon pulled out Tuesday afternoon. Their outfit comprised about 120 horses and made a most imposing appearance when lined up on Jasper avenue to be photographed just before the start. The names of the several parties are: — J. W. Cate, T. J. Kelly, L. Boot, L. McDonald, C. C. Hoag, W. R. Hoag, A. S. Cagwin, G. R. Walton, Bert Stevens, O. L. Ingles, H. H. Quick, T. R. Dunlap, N. P. Howsley, W. R. King, Mr. and Mrs. G. E. Garner, K. Emerzian and H. Rustigian, of Fresno, California; John Q. Walker of New York City and Benjamin F. Sears, of Bennington, Vermont. Messrs. King, Garner, Emerzian and Rustigian form a party distinct from the rest of their friends, although travelling with them. The two latter are Armenians. . . . Besides the above, Walter Bisson, of Lake St. Ann, has been engaged as packer by Mr. Walker, and J. F. Cellihou, of Lake St. Ann, will guide the party to Fort St. John, on Peace River. The process of packing is a very intricate one, and it did not appear that the members of the party generally were altogether familiar with it. Consequently there was considerable delay in starting. . . . They do not expect to reach the Yukon region this fall, but hope to get to the upper part of the Liard, where they can drift mine or trap as best suits them during the winter, and make across the divide to the upper waters of the Pelly river early next season. . . . The route they are taking is by way of Lake St. Ann, crossing the Athabasca at the mouth of McLeod river, thence on by way of Sturgeon lake and Grande Prairie to Fort St. John, on Peace river. At St. John they will cross Peace river and will probably take the best available route north to the Nelson river, down which they will go to near its junction with the Liard. Thence up the Liard and across the divide to the Pelly.

The September 22 *Expositor* quoted a letter from Mrs. Garner, saying:

It seemed as though everyone in the town was at the hotel to welcome us, and before leaving Edmonton, by the way, a large crowd of well-wishers surrounded and gave us a sort of "Fourth of July reception." The ladies and gentlemen persisted in approaching and introducing themselves. They all wished us good luck and, of course, gave me plenty of advice as to what I must wear, how to wear it, etc.

48

A couple of photographers took my picture in different poses and attire, and a local author is going to write a book about our party. It will be illustrated.

Tea parties were planned, and I received any number of invitations to attend them.

Mrs. Garner's letter was written in instalments over several days and on each occasion she gave in minute detail just what happened to the party and spoke glowingly of the country. "Its scenery," she said, "is grand, but the weather is something frightful."

After the Fresno party had crossed the Pembina River some thirty miles west of Lac Ste Anne, A. McCorrister, a local man, encountered them and reported that they were experiencing so many delays and difficulties that he feared for their safety. About the middle of September, after they had forded the Athabasca River, Dan Noyes, Jr., of Edmonton, making one of his customary trips in from Sturgeon Lake, met them straggled along the way trying to work their horses through miles of wind-fallen timber. Three weeks of heroic efforts on the trail had taken them about a hundred miles and by this time they had fragmented into four separate parties. They were nevertheless still pressing forward and with the vanguard was Mrs. Garner, carrying on the tradition begun a generation earlier when her parents had crossed to California in a covered wagon.

The leading outfit reached Sturgeon Lake on October 2, but after a few days the arrival of others brought the strength of the Fresno party there to seventeen. At that juncture J. W. Cate and W. F. Hoag decided to drop out. Hoag returned to Edmonton for the winter, intending to go back north in the spring, but Cate went home to Fresno, where, in an interview with the *Expositor*, he provided an insight into some of the party's difficulties incident to reaching Sturgeon Lake.

> The distance is quoted as 280 miles, but fully two miles and a half must be travelled for every mile made. This is due to the crookedness of the trail. . . . However, I am a firm believer in Edmonton as a starting point for parties setting out for the northern gold fields. But I would start differently were I again to attempt the trip. I would have my provisions sent through to Fort. St. John by good reliable traders, and purchase my horses at Edmonton. I would then rush my horses through to the fort, unpacked, so as to have them fresh for the remainder of the journey . . . [for] the difficulties of the trail are death to horses. The trail is filled with spots called "muskeags," which are small marshes, covered for a few miles with moss. A horse, stepping on one of these, sinks to his body. It sometimes takes hours to get him out. Then again, the trail was blocked with fallen timber, thrown down by forest fires. It was necessary to jump the

horses over this. Such work wore our horses out fast, and we were obliged to abandon many of them along the trail.

We lost so many horses that it soon became evident that we could not all get through. I accordingly sold my remaining horses and outfit to T. J. Kelly, my partner. This will materially aid him in his journey to the diggings. . . .

There is no question but that there is plenty of gold in that country. For years old trappers have been bringing out nuggets as large as one's fist. There will be a rush there next spring.

A few of the Fresno party wintered at the little half-breed settlement on the banks of the Spirit River, which they reached on November 6. Three members, however, pushed on and got to Fort St. John before the end of the year. They reported that of the one hundred and twenty horses with which they had started, ninety-four had died or strayed away.

All fall other Yukon-bound hopefuls continued to dribble into Edmonton in twos and threes or to arrive in large parties such as the following:

October 14: Sixteen from Los Angeles planning to go overland. (Regrettably, from Edmonton's standpoint, they had purchased one hundred horses in Calgary.)

October 25: The Fugard party from California, which camped about half a mile north of the town on the road leading to Namao, and purchased 110 horses in Edmonton.

November 22: The Brown-Morse party of twelve, mainly from Ottawa, expected to start north within a few days.

November 29: The Clatworthy party from England, consisting of eleven adventurers, plus a cook, camped on Ross Flats.

Most of the parties did not waste time in Edmonton but, acting on the *Bulletin*'s advice, started overland early in the winter. Between the middle of August 1897 and the end of the year, seven or eight parties, consisting of about ninety-five hopefuls, started overland in a more or less conventional manner with about the right number of pack horses. Some hired well-known half-breed or white guides and some trusted to luck and went without them. A few, because they were experienced or had hired good packers, knew what to expect and made fair progress. Unfortunately, most members of any party had only a very elementary idea of the handling, loading and treatment of pack horses and they soon ran into real difficulties. From the first day that the overlanders started to haze their horses north and west they began feeling the strain of the trip. Within a week or so some of them found it unbearable.

One of the earlier parties to follow the Fresno group consisted of Bray, Fraser and Wood, who had formed themselves into the Pelly-Yukon Mining Company and set out overland with their goods loaded on travois. On November 25 the Fugard party, twenty-three strong, set out and on December 9 the Brown-Morse group started north.

The men of the Fugard party put themselves in the hands of Henry Round, who guided them, and, with his helpers, looked after their 120 horses. This party suffered no major inconvenience and indeed made reasonable time by way of the Swan Hills, reaching the Hudson's Bay Company's post at the west end of Lesser Slave Lake about January 15. By that time Fugard had made up his mind to camp at Peace River Crossing for the rest of the winter and then to sell the horses, descend the river in the spring and take the Water Route.

When the Brown-Morse party arrived in Edmonton, it was vague about what form of transport to use. To start with, it acquired fifty-eight dogs and thirty-six ponies and announced that it planned to head for Fort Chipewyan over the snow by way of Lac la Biche and Fort McMurray. A week of reflection changed their leader's mind, however, and he elected to take his men north and west to Peace River Crossing and thence to the Fort Nelson River. In the spring he hoped to descend this river and the Liard to the Mackenzie and thence down to Peel River. A day or so after leaving Edmonton the men found that driving dogs was much more arduous than they had anticipated and traded most of them for horses.

Towards Christmas, 1897, the Helpman party of twelve from Ireland, the most colourful and perhaps the most ineffective group of all, arrived. It included three colonels, three captains, two physicians and Viscount Avonmore. Their first step was to let a contract to John Walter to build flat sleighs. Meanwhile they camped on the flats west of the Hudson's Bay Company's fort.

By Christmas, Klondikers were camped in little groups all about the town: some behind McDougall's store, others well out along the St. Albert Trail, some along the Namao Trail, and others on the river flats. And they had come from all over, some from France, England, Ireland and Australia, several from Chicago and Duluth, from Toronto and Hamilton, and others from Quebec and New Brunswick – in fact from everywhere including Utah, Great Falls, Matoon, Wabigoon and Woonsocket.

In its December 16 issue the *Bulletin* tried to classify them and to show what progress they had made. One of the tabulations was as follows:

Gone by Edmonton routes:
    Mackenzie River   130
    Overland to Peace   40
    By water to Peace   5
    On snow to Peace   53
    Ready to start   61

In tracing the progress of those who had gone north, the editor had relied partly on reports brought in by policemen, surveyors and the employees of the various trading companies who were always coming and going. Part of his information also came from disappointed or disgruntled Klondikers who were already beginning to dribble back. Some of these soon discovered that financially or physically they were poorly equipped for the realities of the arduous trek. Others were psychologically unequal to the burdens imposed on them by travelling day after day with one or two partners, quarrelled and turned back.

It is possible too that some had heeded the advice in a piece of poetry which came into the *Bulletin*'s hands late in December 1897 in the form of a letter from an Edmonton hotel-keeper. It read:

Dear Sir:
    The following was written in a lady's handwriting on the back of a photograph of a very handsome girl found in the bed room of a lately arrived Klondiker.
    "To rush off to Klondike there is surely no need,
    Where thousands may fail while a dozen succeed,
    When nuggets, as precious as specimen shown,
    At home may be found on a claim of your own."

CHAPTER FIVE

THE 1897 KLONDIKERS

On the whole, such news as had come back from the prospectors who started north during 1897 was encouraging. Let us now see how they were faring and follow their adventures.

James Shand had been the first to write back reporting his progress. With relative ease he and his associates, M. Velgue, also an Edmonton man, and N. Atkinson and P. de Wolf, both of Pine Lake, Alberta, had reached Great Slave Lake, where his most recent letter, dated July 19, had been written. They had left Edmonton on June 9 and spent some days at Athabasca Landing felling trees and whip-sawing lumber to build a flat boat. Leaving the Landing during the afternoon of June 22 they found the river "covered with driftwood. Piles of it that had been lodged on bars and banks during previous high water have this year been lifted and floated off. . . . As the current is very strong we are travelling by drifting, seldom rowing unless we get cold or are in danger of running ashore. After leaving the Landing we drifted and rowed about ten miles, then put ashore and baked bannocks and made tea. Then ate supper on the boat while she drifted down stream. About eleven o'clock we passed the Lac La Biche River about 30 miles from the Landing. The boat drifted all night without running into anything."

On June 26 they passed the Dominion government oil drilling outfit at Pelican Rapids "having in 25 hours travelled about 126 miles." In due course they reached Grand Rapids. "About half a mile from the head of this island the Hudson's Bay Company's steamer unloads, and the freight is then taken down to the island by small boats. Here the company have built a wharf and tramway and have hand cars for taking their freight to the lower end of the island, as it is not possible to run a loaded boat down the channels."

After describing the rapids and commenting that "the water dashing over the boulders throws the spray about 15 to 20 feet in the air," Shand told of loading their boat and freight on the tramway and working all through the night getting the gear back on board at the lower end. "Boat towed into position, fastened bow and stern with ropes and two of us in the boat with poles keeping it off the boulders, one loading the boat and the other carrying the goods down the bank and waist deep in water out to the boat. Finally it was loaded and we were off. We just touched a stone and hung up for a minute, then swung round and down the remainder of the rapid stern foremost. Got through all right into an eddy. Got front end to and continued on."

They set out downstream through the Boiler, Stone and Crooked rapids and others until they came to "one of the terrors of the river, the Big Cascade. The current when the Hudson's Bay party went down was running 25 miles an hour and when we got there about eight. Our trouble was want of water. We had to make three portages. One of them, the last, our boat had to be run out into deep water and the goods carried to her. . . ."

They paused at Fort McMurray, a place of "about three H.B. Co. buildings, two or three houses of half breeds, and some teepees and tents." Next they had an easy and rapid trip down to the delta at Lake Athabasca, where they had trouble finding the best channel. "On looking at a map it seems the easiest possible job to follow the right course, but in fact it is rather more difficult than it looks, owing to the great number of channels at the river mouth. We got into one that added about four miles to the length of our trip. . . ."

Fort Chipewyan they found to consist of "a number of H.B. Co. buildings, smaller in size, but like the present Fort Edmonton; the English and Roman Catholic church missions and a saw mill, besides dwelling houses, but none of us expected such a settlement and it was quite like getting in sight of civilization. . . ."

When Shand came to Smith's Landing (Fitzgerald), he found that "it is usual to hire oxen and carts and make a 16 mile portage or hire a pilot and men for the river. Atkinson chose the latter way, and we were just two days from the time of leaving the landing to arriving at the Fort. . . . There are three full portages and one where our boat was partly unloaded. At the Mountain portage the boat had also to be taken over. Just here we saw a number of pelicans. They seem to breed here on some of the islands, and as the river is very rough and full of fish they are safe and get plenty to eat. They are so fat it is said a quart of oil can be rendered from one of them. . . ."

After his party got past the rough water, the rest of its course down to Great Slave Lake was easy but monotonous, for his letter said: "The river is a big one. With the exception of the St. Lawrence the biggest I ever saw, and as it is very full of islands all very green and timbered, it is beautiful. But one gets tired of the sameness when seeing it day after day; the only changes being in its course, some of which is straight and in other cases a 600 yard channel would cut off 16 miles. But the last few miles are straight – and then the lake." The whole trip this far had been an easy one and the party reached Great Slave Lake about a month after leaving Athabasca Landing.

There was to be an interval of several months before Shand's next letter reached Edmonton. When it did, it indicated that he was still pressing on and that after leaving Fort Smith the party had skirted well over one hundred miles of the south shore of the immense lake, past Hay River Post and on to Fort Providence, a few miles down the Mackenzie River from the extreme west end of the lake. By keeping on down the river, it reached Fort Simpson at the mouth of the Liard on August 14. Here the men decided to forsake the broad river and to ascend the Liard. Poling and tracking up the relatively quiet lower Liard, they finally reached Fort Liard at the mouth of the Petitot River. By December 13, nearly six months after leaving Edmonton and four months after leaving Fort Simpson, Shand and Velgue reached the mouth of the Beaver River, some thirty miles up the Liard beyond the point known as Nelson Forks, which was at the mouth of the Fort Nelson River.

The party had split up when Atkinson and de Wolf decided to remain at Nelson Forks to trade and trap. Shand and Monty Velgue dug a shelter into the river bank at the outflow of the Beaver River and relaxed for a period while they made an unsuccessful attempt at trapping. Just at the time when they were ready to push on along the frozen river with toboggans, Velgue's rifle accidentally discharged and put a bullet through the calf of his leg. While he was laid up, some members of the Stephen-Howey party came along and Velgue decided to throw in his lot with them. Towards the last days of 1897, therefore, Shand alone pushed up the river on his way to the Grand Canyon of the Liard and to the hot springs where the modern Alaska Highway crosses that stream. There he had reached a point some 250 air miles west of Fort Simpson and 650 miles west of Edmonton. By the route he had taken, he had travelled 1,600 miles, and the Yukon was still 700 miles away. He was far ahead of most of those who had started down the Athabasca.

At least twenty-six other parties, varying in size from two men to eleven and totalling some 130, set out along the Mackenzie route before the end of October, 1897. All planned to winter somewhere along the 2,500-mile route and then to make a quick rush to the Klondike in the spring. While it would not be practical to follow them in detail, it is nevertheless interesting to take a look at some of their adventures. By the end of 1897 they were scattered all the way from Athabasca Landing to the mouth of the Mackenzie River, their progress depending upon their experience, their luck and how early they had started.

Two of those who left late in the fall denned up for the winter just a few miles below Athabasca Landing. Eight more lived in two shacks at Pelican Rapids, while seven other men in addition to some of the Merriweather party lived in shanties at Grand Rapids.

That winter the Merriweather party made the headlines and started an episode that was to embarrass the more stable members and to make their leader notorious. The party, consisting of T. W. Merriweather, R. H. Witherspoon, J. E. Enright, W. H. Best, T. C. Stevens and Moses Liebman, left Edmonton late in September. On November 17 Merriweather returned to Edmonton along with J. H. Johnson of a party from Butte whom he had hired to conduct him in safety from Grand Rapids to Edmonton. He stated that the rest of the party were living in a shack at the rapids, where they planned to remain for the winter, and alleged that he was going back to Chicago to organize another group which he would take to the Yukon the following spring.

No one in Edmonton gave him more than a passing thought until the *Bulletin* received a copy of the *Chicago Times* of December 8, which reported a tale of hardship and hardihood of which Merriweather had been the hero. According to it, the other five men of the party were "imprisoned in ice and snow hundreds of miles away in the Northwest." Risking his life for eighteen days, the story said, while at night he sheltered from the 48-degree below zero weather in clefts in rocks, he fought his way back to Athabasca Landing and then came on to Edmonton. There, he alleged, he had arranged with Dan Noyes, an intrepid frontiersman, to lay plans and devise a route along which to lead an expedition to the relief of his stranded and suffering party.

Edmontonians had every reason to brand the story a lie. They were willing to admit that, owing to bad luck or foolishness, the men might be in distress but, if that were so, the time for Merriweather to have sought help was while he was in Edmonton about the middle of November. Certainly the tale of struggling along in temperatures 48 degrees below zero was utterly false, since the temperature at Edmonton at the time Merriweather was on his way out had varied from 32 degrees above to zero. Moreover, eighteen days was a fantastically long time for two men to take to travel the 160 miles from Grand Rapids to Athabasca Landing.

The NWMP heard the rumour of distress and when Inspector W. H. Routledge set out on his midwinter patrol to Fort Simpson, he was instructed to look into the welfare of any Klondikers scattered along the Water Route and to pay particular attention to the Merriweather party. His patrol left Athabasca Landing on December 21, travelled down the river stopping here and there to attend to official business, and reached Grand Rapids on January 1. There he found three of the party, J. E. Enright, W. H. Best and Moses Liebman, occupying the temporarily abandoned police shack. R. H. Witherspoon and T. C. Stevens, whose relations with the other three were a bit strained, were living in a tent about a mile farther down the river. Commenting on these men, Routledge reported: "I found the different parties comfortably quartered, well supplied with provisions, and in good health and spirits, the tent occupied by Stevens and Witherspoon was large and roomy, and had a good camp stove in it. The members of the 'Stevens-Merryweather' party at the police shack expressed themselves in strong terms respecting the stories circulated in Chicago by the man Merryweather, as to their condition, and one and all stated to me that this man was lazy and useless. . . ."

In Chicago, however, Merriweather evidently acted promptly and collected money from relatives of the men alleged to be in difficulties and wired Dan Noyes. About January 3 Dan sent his son Bob to Grand Rapids. When about ten days later he reached there, the men were astounded to see him and even more astounded when he produced letters from Best's wife and Liebman's mother, telling how each had contributed a hundred dollars to pay for the relief expedition. When Bob Noyes returned to Edmonton, Witherspoon, a brother-in-law of Merriweather, came back with him. Shortly after that Stevens also went back to Chicago.

Later on Best and Enright decided that they should leave Liebman to keep an eye on their supplies while they went out to Edmonton. They arrived there on February 10 and wired to their relatives in Chicago. At that time they explained that in November Merriweather had decided to turn back and that even though Best, Enright and Liebman had been the only ones who had contributed to the party's coffers, they had divided the supplies so as to permit Merriweather to go out to Edmonton. Having done all they could to correct Merriweather's misrepresentations, the two men went back to join Liebman and to await the open water of spring to carry them north.

While knavery played havoc with that party, a death, the only one to take place at Grand Rapids during the whole of the Klondike Rush, hit the Patterson contingent from Hamilton, Ontario. This party left Edmonton seven men strong on August 21. Going down the Grand Rapids, Patterson's boat struck a rock with such force that he was thrown into the swirling water and drowned. After discussing the matter with R. Hunter and W. Richmond, two members of the party who, instead of returning to Hamilton like the rest of the group, had come back to the vicinity of Athabasca Landing to trap for the winter, Inspector Routledge reported: "This party had no guide with them, and, apparently, were not aware of their close proximity to the rapids until too late to get their boat about. Men who were working on the island at the head of the rapids, who noticed they were taking the wrong channel, the left going down stream, did everything possible to attract the attention of the boat party, by waving blankets, shouting, firing off guns, &c., but no attention was seemingly paid to them, which leads one to the belief that the men were either asleep or paying little care as to their whereabouts."

The prospectors who left Edmonton during September naturally got farther down the Athabasca. The party of four local men from Beaverhill Lake, led by Rod McKenzie, left Athabasca Landing about September 17, sped down the various rapids without difficulty, and before tying up for the winter reached Fort Chipewyan. One other September party got even farther than that and wintered at Fort Resolution. It was made up of remnants of the Warmolts party from Chicago. Like their compatriots of the Merriweather party, this interesting group, which included R. M. Springer, a correspondent for the Chicago *Inter-Ocean*, and A. C. Craig and his wife, met with friction and frustration. Not only was Mrs. Craig the first woman to set out from Edmonton for the Klondike by the Water Route, but also, as it turned out, she was one of those who got there. When it left Edmonton on September 1, this particularly well-organized party of fifteen was inclined to be unnecessarily evasive about its exact destination.

While most of the group made their way to Athabasca Landing, Henry Card, one of the leaders, who was said to have had some experience in the north as a member of one of the geological parties under Ogilvie, stayed behind to have boats built in John Walter's yard. Friction soon developed. When Card got to the Landing with his craft, he found that some of the party, having grown impatient, had purchased a sturgeon-head boat and departed. He and the others set off downstream and without undue physical difficulties arrived at Fort Resolution.

Months later when on January 25 Inspector Routledge reached the fort, he visited ten of this group, including Mr. and Mrs. Craig. In his report he said that the party had been formed as a result of an advertisement the man called Warmolts had placed in the Chicago papers.

> The party arrived at Resolution on the 12th October and they stated to me that the leader, Warmolts, and his half-brother, Edward Buck had left them in the early morning of the 18th October without having given the members of the expedition any warning of his intention to do so. In consequence of this action on the part of their leader, they were much dissatisfied and discontented at the time of my visit and incensed at the (to them) cowardly conduct of the man Warmolts. . . .
>
> On my return from Simpson I found that the "Warmolts Expedition" had broken up into small parties. Graham and Hore having procured dog trains had transported their effects across Great Slave Lake, and I heard of them from some Indians near Big Island at the [entrance to] the Mackenzie River. Craig was employed in taking his effects by dog train to Hay River en route to Providence. The other members of the party will, doubtless, wait for open water before moving out.

Before Routledge's arrival, R. M. Springer, the newspaper correspondent, had acquired a dog-team and made the 330-mile trip to Fort Simpson.

The inspector evidently did not meet Mr. and Mrs. Horsfall, nor did he report hearing that they were downstream from Fort Simpson. Nevertheless, a couple by this name was said to have crossed to the Yukon by the Rat River Route, accompanied by W. J. Dobbin of the Panet party, during the summer of 1898.

Ten major parties made up of forty-three men left Edmonton during the last two weeks of August and wintered at various points extending from Fort Resolution to Fort Simpson. In general, their members stuck together fairly well: Milvain and Garnett of Pincher Creek; the Langworthy crew, mainly from Fort Saskatchewan and composed of W. F. Langworthy, Frank Braine, A. Marks and two time-expired Mounties, George Woolley and A. M. Watts; the Pembroke party of four, including ill-fated young Roy Moffatt; the Panet party of seven from Montreal; the Rouse group of five from Fresno, California; five from Duluth, including the unfortunate P. Belleveau and led by W. A. Foote; the Esk group of five, also from Duluth; Horsfall and Bain from Winnipeg; W. J. Graham of Edmonton with three other men; and the Griffin brothers with two partners — forty-three men in all. Here and there a few remained by the wayside while their companions or partners pushed on.

W. A. Foote, for instance, soon found that either he or the route did not measure up to expectations and turned back at Fort Chipewyan. Perhaps the last straw of his disillusionment was the fact that when his party emerged from the delta of the Athabasca into the large lake, it went astray. It was a clear day and the men could see some buildings across the narrows of the lake, but after some argument concluded that these were too close to be Fort Chipewyan and so swung off to the right. They worked a considerable distance eastward along the sandy south shore of the lake before they realized their error and that the buildings which had only been a couple of hours' rowing away must have been Fort Chipewyan. As a result of this mistake, they wasted ten days. The other Duluth party also made the same mistake, but it cost them fourteen days. After Foote turned back, his party pressed forward for some weeks and finally built shacks and wintered sixty miles below Fort Providence.

R. H. Milvain and J. H. Garnett, who left the Landing on August 28, took along four small wheels which were of great help in crossing the portages at Grand Rapids and at Fort Smith. Milvain broke through the ice of Great Slave Lake and froze his feet, with the result that he spent some weeks as a guest of Sam Scott, the Hudson's Bay Company manager at Fort Providence, where E. Irving of the Pembroke party, a medical student, attended him. Meanwhile, his partner Garnett hurried forward and wintered with a Duluth party sixty miles below that post.

The two Griffin brothers from Edmonton decided to go into camp at Hay River, but, like several others, their colleagues Ernest Crabbe and Forbes Groat purchased some dogs and pushed along over the ice. Most of the Panet party spent the winter in a building placed at their disposal by Chief Factor Camsell of the Hudson's Bay post at Fort Simpson. With them were a few of the more aggressive members of other parties: A. H. Thompson of Calgary, D. A. McPhee of Pembroke, R. M. Springer, the Chicago newspaper man, and Joseph Lamoureux of Fort Saskatchewan. They had ample provisions and spent a healthy winter.

During the first half of August five parties totalling twenty-six men headed north to Athabasca Landing: Segers-Hardisty (eleven men), Stephen-Howey (six men), Jenner Brothers (four), Wright and Pelly (two) and the Brabant group (three). Starting even earlier than these, of course, were Shand's associates with whom we have dealt and the Pilon party which left Edmonton in July. The five parties that left early in August and these other two, having a good start, got well down the waterway before freeze-up came.

Disappointed at their progress but not discouraged, all these Klon-dikers spent the winter in relative comfort. Some were content to trap and trade and wait to resume floating down north when spring opened the streams. Others, particularly those who found themselves camped along the shore of Great Slave Lake, took time by the forelock, bought dogs from Indians and moved their supplies past the west end of the lake. They knew that the ice would clear out of the Mackenzie long before the lake was navigable, and by moving their goods ahead by relays they could get a much earlier start than if they remained along the shore of the lake.

All these Klondikers who were along the route between Athabasca Landing and Fort Simpson were glad to see Inspector Routledge and nearly all were surprised at the speed with which he had travelled. For he had left Fort Saskatchewan on December 16 and, in spite of having to attend to police matters here and there, he had snowshoed his way to Fort Simpson by February 7. He and everyone else realized, of course, that because he could replenish his supplies at Hudson's Bay posts along the way he had travelled lightly laden. Nevertheless, he had made a remarkable trip.

On his part he was pleased to find the scattered Klondikers faring well, leading normal lives and feeling optimistic. Since he had carried mail to them, he brought a bright spot into their sometimes dull winter days and set them to writing letters which he promised to take out for them. Then, leaving Fort Simpson on February 10, he set out south and reached Fort Saskatchewan on March 26 after accomplishing a most praiseworthy trip. As he said, ". . . the party [was] all in good health and without the loss of any dogs, completing the round trip of 2,172 miles in 80 days of actual travel. The hours of travel each day averaged from 5 a.m. until 5.30 p.m. with 4 'spells' for meals, &c."

On his return to Fort Saskatchewan he made this report on the Klondikers:

I found the greater number of the miners whom I visited satisfied with the Mackenzie River Yukon route as far as they had gone. Of course, many of them realized they had started from the Athabasca Landing too late in the season to complete the proposed journey. Persons who desire to get beyond Great Slave Lake with barges or boats should not leave the landing (Athabasca) later than the first week in August. The lake generally closes about the latter part of October, and the Mackenzie River during the last half of November.

Many of the men whom I met in the north complained of the excessive charges made by the half-breeds and Indians, especially at the Grand Rapids, who act as guides and steersmen down the rapids. These men evidently look upon the Grand and Smith Rapids as their "Klondyke," and it seems to me that some action should be taken to regulate such charges, as is done in the case of pilots in other parts of the country.

For those Klondikers who took the Water Route, Fort Simpson, some 1,100 miles from Edmonton, was nearly the half-way point in their 2,500-mile trip. It was also the place where the first alternative route presented itself. That route lay up the Liard River and several parties of Klondikers decided to follow it.

Looked at on any of the maps of the day, the Liard River must have seemed a most sensible way to get from the Mackenzie River to the Yukon. In a straight line, Fort Simpson lay some 320 miles directly east of Pelly Banks, the point at which boats put into the Pelly would float down the current into the Yukon River. The Liard, however, did not follow a straight line but swept along in a great wiggly semicircle south, then east, and then back to the north again, so that its headwaters in the mountains of the Yukon were seven hundred river miles from Fort Simpson. And all of its seven hundred miles were not only upstream but for most of them its waters came roaring and whirling and gushing down a series of rapids, cascades and canyons. Deep and broad and almost sluggish as it approached Fort Simpson, however, it presented a beguiling appearance. Moreover, the Klondikers knew that some two hundred miles upstream at the mouth of the Petitot River stood the Hudson's Bay Company's Fort Liard and other posts were said to be strung out beyond that.

Unfortunately most of the Klondikers never heard what the Hudson's Bay Company's staffs knew about that river, or, if they did, ignored it. For as early as 1836 the Company had also looked hopefully towards it as the waterway to the Yukon area but, after experiencing some of its harshness and losing some voyageurs, had written it off as too dangerous. With its islands and bars, its crookedness, canyons and general cussedness, it resembled the Fraser River, which the company had been forced to abandon as a route from the Rocky Mountains to the sea.

Since the Klondikers were to come to know every foot of the Liard from Fort Simpson up to the mouth of the Frances River, it might be well to follow its course down from there. For the first twenty-five miles the river ambles along through relatively flat terrain until in the vicinity of Watson Lake it sweeps under the present-day Alaska Highway bridge. From there on for about fifteen miles, however, it gathers its forces and makes the racing leap through the Liard canyon. Then, swinging towards the south for about the same distance and accompanied by the Alaska Highway, its waters flow on to pick up those of the Dease River at Lower Post. Thereafter, with many a minor bend and island and still paralleled by the Alaska Highway, it goes looping across the land for eighty miles, roaring and sizzling and tearing through two or three canyons to Cranberry Portage. Four miles below the last of these rapids it picks up the waters of the Kechika River at Mud River Post and then tumbles on past the Mountain Portage and past the Brulé Portage around Whirlpool Canyon.

As the waters come seething out of the vortices of this canyon they enter a relatively straight section of the stream which carries them past old Fort Halkett some eighteen miles below and on another twenty miles to the Alaska Highway bridge at the Hot Springs. From there for sixty miles onward to the old Toad River Post in stretches each miles long, canyons of seething water or sucking whirlpools bar the way. Of these the Grand Canyon of the Liard, forty miles long, constituted such an effective barrier to communication up and down the river that it even separated tribes of Indians from one another. Below it the Indians looked to the east and traded at Fort Liard. Above it they looked west and went upstream to deal at Lower Post or at Dease Lake.

Looking down on such a stream from a high bank is a fascinating pleasure; trying to navigate down it is an extremely dangerous practice; but for Klondikers trying to make the ascent, it was almost impossible. West of Toad River it fought the voyagers with no holds barred and confronted them with two hundred miles of wild water. Some stretches indeed were navigable, but for most of the way one set of roaring rapids followed another in close succession.

Below Toad River Post the mighty river, narrow and still swift, swings northeast through a deep valley for some forty miles to the mouth of the Beaver River. Then, swinging around to the southeast for about thirty miles, the stream, excessively crooked now, is broad and braided and strewn with shoals and chains of islands for its thirty-mile descent to Nelson Forks. There the large Fort Nelson River joins it and nearly doubles its volume.

At Nelson Forks, where the stream executes a corkscrew bend, it changes direction and sets off for Fort Liard, a river distance of about sixty miles. It pours north and crosses British Columbia's northern boundary some twenty-five miles before reaching Fort Liard. Fifty miles due north of that old Hudson's Bay Company post the South Nahanni enters the larger stream, but because the Liard doubles back and forth upon itself in great loops five to ten miles across, the distance the Klondikers had to drag their boats between these points was about one hundred miles. Throughout that distance there are many strings of islands and bars, as well as an occasional rapid. From the South Nahanni to Fort Simpson, a distance of 120 miles, the course of the river is northeast. It runs in long straight stretches of relatively quiet water with an island or two here and there. There are some minor rapids, but in the lower reaches as the mighty stream approaches Fort Simpson it has finished its fierce course and joins the Mackenzie as an apparently docile partner.

This wild river, some seven hundred miles long, was the stream that scores of Klondikers tried to ascend. Its apparent docility at Fort Simpson deceived them and many started up it. James Shand and his associates were the first to try it. A little later in the 1897 season, several others chose to ascend it. Among these were W. J. Graham, George Purches, George Filadeau, the Jenner and the Stephen-Howey parties, Wright, Pelly, Dan Carey and the Camsell brothers. Altogether that year, for the most part unaware of the three hundred miles of hell ahead of them, twenty-five adventurers set out west up the Liard.

On September 15, 1897, Fort Simpson became infested with Klondikers, for within hours of each other the Segers-Hardisty group and four other parties tied up along the shore. For three days congestion reigned in the hitherto quiet backwater post while the Segers-Hardisty party made plans to continue down the Mackenzie and the other parties revised and overhauled their outfits in order to make the transition from floating down one stream to fighting up another.

At Fort Simpson there was also some rearrangement of crews as the tensions of travelling began to tighten and gall. Probably because they intended to do so before they left Athabasca Landing, Dan Carey and his son Willie left the Segers-Hardisty party and went west up the Liard. Definite friction, however, came to a head in the Graham party which contained a young lad who could not get along with the leader. For a while it appeared that Graham was simply going to abandon him at Fort Simpson but when the boy appealed to the other Klondikers his case was taken before Chief Factor J. S. Camsell, who as a senior Hudson's Bay officer along the Mackenzie had magisterial authority. Camsell directed that, while Graham might leave the boy at Fort Simpson, nevertheless he had to divide his goods and give the lad his share.

While all the men who went up the Liard were well versed in northern travel, the two who had come from Vernon, British Columbia, A. M. Pelly and D. W. Wright, were particularly self-reliant. So, of course, were the old Forty-niner Dan Carey and his son. At Fort Simpson these four recruited two other men of the same calibre in the sons of Chief Factor Camsell, Fred and his younger brother Charles, who within twenty years was to become Deputy Minister of Mines in the Canadian civil service. These young men had been born at Fort Liard and both were well experienced in the ways of the North. Because of their knowledge, they took two steps that gave them an advantage over the other parties: they hired a crew of Indians to take their scow up the river, and Pelly purchased three dogs while the Camsells bought another three. As well equipped as they could possibly be, the Pelly-Wright party set off up the river and soon pulled far ahead of the other three groups.

These others, which also left Fort Simpson on September 18, were the Stephen-Howey party made up of T. H. Stephen, W. R. Howey, H. Woodward, A. Gibney, A. E. Lee, George Purches and George Filadeau; W. J. Graham's group, including S. Schrieves, Meneely and Balaam (or Boland); and the brothers Hal and Fred Jenner and their associates A. S. Weeks and A. E. Schaefer. And for all of them, except perhaps the Camsells, travelling up even the quiet water of the lower Liard came as a rude awakening. Gone was the somnolence of days spent slipping past the silent forested banks of the Athabasca, Slave and Mackenzie rivers when all the party had to do was to keep alert and steer a bit, stopping now and then to stretch and cook meals. In their place had come hour after hour of rowing, poling, pulling and tracking up the tedious miles as, wet to the armpits and cold, they lugged their outfits forward yard by yard.

The Yukon-bound adventurers were weeks getting up the 220 miles to Fort Liard. When they got there, George Purches and George Filadeau had endured enough for the time being and decided to winter there.

When the two Camsells, the two Careys and Wright and Pelly were twenty miles below the mouth of Toad River, their Indians refused to go farther up a stream with such a fearful reputation. Towards the end of October 1897 the prospectors accordingly built a temporary shelter and camped for about three weeks until the ice in the river was firm enough to walk on. During the interval, to keep themselves profitably employed, they trapped fur-bearing animals and shot the only moose they were lucky enough to get all winter. By November 20, when the temperature was twenty below, the ice in the river became firm enough to bear their weight so they pushed on upstream. The dogs they had purchased at Fort Simpson were invaluable here, for the party was heavily laden. Charles Camsell says in *Son of the North*:

Besides our camp outfit we had about 5,000 pounds of provisions, enough to last us all winter but too much to carry in one load. Our plan, therefore, was to load our toboggans to capacity and carry this load up river ten miles or so, cache it there, and then return to camp the same day, making a round trip of about twenty miles. At first it took us over a week to move our whole outfit ten miles. On the last day we broke camp and moved up twenty miles for our next camp, and from that point as a base we brought our supplies up and then carried them forward another ten miles. This, at least, was what we tried to do, but it was not always possible. . . .

It was slow going at first, but as we consumed our provisions the intervals between moving camp shortened until towards spring we were able to carry everything in one trip. By the first of May when we reached Frances Lake, we must have tramped altogether some 3,000 miles on snowshoes.

After a month of this kind of travelling they made another interim camp at the lower end of Hell's Gate. They had advanced a distance of some forty miles at an average of little more than a mile a day. At this camp Dan Carey, who was getting past his prime, decided to stay and trap for the rest of the winter and the party divided its provisions and left the old trapper and his son.

From this camp Charles Camsell and Pelly decided to make a reconnaissance on snowshoes with loads only heavy enough to meet their requirements for a month. They entered the Grand Canyon on the ice and on Christmas Day were through its gap as far as the Devil's Gorge.

We had tried on that day to make our way through the Devil's Gorge, but found this impossible because the force of the stream had kept the water open from wall to wall of the gorge. The only alternative was the portage of four miles over a mountain spur 1,000 feet high by a trail which had never been used in winter and only once in the summer in the last thirty years. This was the notorious Devil's portage, the evil reputation of which was responsible for the abandonment of the Liard River as a trade route from the Mackenzie to the Yukon. . . .

The climb of 1,000 feet was pretty heavy going on account of the deep snow and we had to take turns in breaking the trail ahead of the dogs. We were on the summit by the time the sun began to set and we were ready to make camp. It was the strangest Christmas I ever spent. . . .

From there on they found travelling conditions good, and a few days later reached Mud River Post at the mouth of the Kechika River, 180 miles above Nelson Forks. Its sole occupant, Scott Simpson, who had not seen anyone for four months, was amazed to have visitors in the middle of winter, and particularly visitors who had come up the river from the east. They rested there a few days before starting back to their camp at Hell's Gate. Travelling lightly loaded and with dogs, they made the round trip of two hundred miles in about fifteen days.

At the end of 1897, then, this group and James Shand were the farthest advanced of the Yukoners who had started up the Liard. The others were scattered along the river behind them. Earlier in the fall, Shand and Velgue had stopped at the mouth of Beaver River, and as we have seen Shand himself pushed on. When the Stephen-Howey party reached that vicinity, it too had to wait for ice to form before going on, and accordingly camped. As it turned out, both Stephen and Howey decided to stay there until the following spring. The rest of their party, that is, Woodward, Gibney and Lee, as well as the Shand and Graham groups, merely waited a few weeks before going on westward. When they started again, they split up into new partnerships and groupings and headed upstream singly or by twos or threes. The Jenners camped at the point where running ice stopped them and some weeks later made two unsuccessful attempts at finding a route around the rapids over which to sled their goods. They then settled down and remained where they were for the winter.

With some of the Yukoners camped for the winter and some of them creeping slowly forward, the drive up the Liard had almost ground to a halt.

Up to this time, of all the parties that had started down the Mackenzie River system, only two, the Pilons and the Segers-Hardisty contingent, continued downstream past Fort Simpson. The five men of the Pilon group reached Fort Simpson about September 5 and advised that they planned to go down the river another seventy miles and then to turn up the North Nahanni River. Most of them appear to have wintered along it.

The party led by the capable Captain Segers consisted of F. A. Hardisty, S. A. McNeill, F. G. Taylor, F. M Robertson, W. D. Matheson and his son Mel, M. Sutherland, A. Adamson and Dr. G. Macdonald of Calgary. All of them were well acquainted with life in northwestern Canada, and it would have been hard to put together another large party of men so capable of looking after themselves under all the conditions they were to face. F. A. Hardisty, for instance, was the son of Chief Factor William Hardisty and had been born at Fort Simpson.

The outstanding man of the party, however, was Captain Segers, a man of forceful character whose adventurous life had been bound up with steamboats. He learned his trade on the Mississippi and became

captain on steamers on the Missouri, the Red River and the Saskatchewan. As an experienced pilot he had joined the Canadian Nile Expedition which in 1884 went to relieve General Gordon at Khartoum.
Shortly after his return from there he had been captain of the *North-
cote* when in 1885 it took part in the Battle of Batoche.

Then transferring his attention to the Mackenzie watershed, he
had been in command of Hudson's Bay Company steamers between
Athabasca Landing and Fort Smith during the late 1880's and most of
the next decade. Accustomed to command, he led the Segers-Hardisty
expedition to the Klondike. After a successful if strenuous crossing from
Fort McPherson to the Yukon, he reverted to his old love and within
days of reaching the Yukon River became captain of a steamer navi-
gating that stream. Later he passed on to other adventures, including
being buried in a snowslide in the mining area of Idaho. Segers was
exceptionally well fitted to lead a Yukon expedition.

With very little effort and in forty-one days his party made the
1,890-mile trip from Athabasca Landing to the mission at the mouth
of Arctic Red River. F. M. Robertson kept a log of the trip that throws
considerable light on the method of travel along the Water Route
and mentions briefly some other parties and some of the regular
traders along the river. On Wednesday, August 18, 1897, he reported,
the party left Athabasca Landing and by travelling "day and night"
reached Grand Rapids on Friday, where they "Ran one boat at a time
to head of island. First boat struck several rocks. Going to unload at
head of island. Lower one boat down rapids. Get truck wheels and take
goods to foot of Island. Saw Colin Fraser's and Stephens' outfits leaving." On Sunday, as well as helping the Jenners' and Graham's boats
across, they loaded up at the foot of the island. Going on the next
day they ran "Brule, Boiler, Long and Stony rapids, and pull in at
the Little Cascade. Unload part of cargo, lower boats and load up
again. Unload all at Big Cascade. Load again and pull across the river
to shore and camp for night."

The next day they reached Fort McMurray and on August 28 arrived
at Fort Chipewyan. There they exchanged "our two boats with C.
Fraser for one large one. Fix boat and transship our goods. Get away
about noon. Stick in mud in end of lake. Got off and tied up at mouth
of Stony River, and go back and help Stephen and Connor* off bar.
Get away again and travel till wind held us up."

By September 5 they were across the Smith Portage where the
steamer *Wrigley* was to "pick us up and tow us to Fort Simpson," which
they reached on September 15.

* *Colin Fraser and Connor were two northern traders.*

Three days later they set out down the Mackenzie taking "on H. B. Co. letter packet and some freight. Hoist sail at 2:45 p.m. Baptiste and Jerome came with us as pilots." They reached Fort Wrigley on the morning of September 20 and Fort Norman on the 22nd. When they arrived at Fort Good Hope at 2 p.m. on September 24 it was "snowing and freezing hard." At Arctic Red River, which they reached just as ice made further navigation impossible, the party came to the end of its long, lazy trip down the Mackenzie. During the next two or three days they unloaded their boat and on October 2 Frank Hardisty set out for Fort McPherson, where he hoped to get enough dogs to haul their goods across to that post.

Arctic Red River, the northernmost settlement on the mighty waterway, was about twenty miles above the Mackenzie delta and the delta of the Mackenzie was the hinge of the long Water Route – the point where the work of crossing the mountains began. Like Fort Simpson, it was a transition point where the long simple cruise downstream ended and the short, severe crawl upstream began. At Fort Simpson the prospectors could ascend the Liard or they still had the alternative of continuing to float down the Mackenzie. But the delta of the Mackenzie was the end of the line; the hard work could be postponed no longer.

In the vicinity of the delta lay three strategic points which were to loom large in the lives of all Water Route Klondikers: Arctic Red River on the Mackenzie River, the mouth of the Peel River, and Fort McPherson, the Hudson's Bay Company's main post, also on the Peel River some thirty miles above its mouth. These three points, each about thirty miles apart, were situated so as to form an equilateral triangle. Most of the Klondikers who went by the Water Route had the lower thirty miles of the Peel River as their objective, because that stretch of river provided at least two jumping-off places for their assault on the Richardson Mountains to the west. An ascent of about forty miles by either of two routes took the Klondikers to passes through the summit of these mountains where streams flowing west would carry them down to the Yukon River.

One route which led to McDougall Pass started west from the Peel River at a point some fifteen miles below Fort McPherson and went up the Rat River. From Summit Lake in McDougall Pass a creek flowed to the west and in five miles emptied into the Bell River, which in its turn and about ninety miles downstream poured its waters into the large Porcupine River. Half-way along the Bell River, that is, some fifty miles by canoe, stood LaPierre's House, a Hudson's Bay Company outpost and a point of major significance to the Klondikers.

An alternative route over the mountain range left the Peel River about four miles above Fort McPherson and ascended Stony Creek to an unnamed pass, whence by following another creek down the west side the traveller also came to the Bell River near LaPierre's House.

The men of the Segers-Hardisty expedition chose the Rat River route and during the winter of 1897-98 it occupied their attention for many a weary month. It took Frank Hardisty six days to go to Fort McPherson, purchase dog teams and return to Arctic Red River. In the meantime, Captain Segers kept his men busy taking their boat to pieces and rebuilding it as a much smaller craft which they could take over the snow to Fort McPherson.

On October 8, assisted by five Indians whom they had hired, F. M. Robertson, Frank Hardisty and W. D. Matheson started their dog teams freighting everything across to Fort McPherson. After camping out for one night, they reached the fort the next afternoon and there Mr. Firth, the Hudson's Bay Company man, supplied them with a house and warehouse space. Then, obtaining extra dog teams, they set out for Arctic Red River and fell into a regular routine of travelling back and forth with twelve trains of dogs. By November 6 when they had moved everything across to Fort McPherson they had used up thirty-one days in almost continuous relaying back and forth.

On November 9, the party split up when the two Mathesons, F. M. Robertson and Murdoch Sutherland decided to press on by taking their supplies on to LaPierre's House by dog team. Segers and the others were still committed to going forward with their boat in the spring. According to Robertson's diary, his group remained at Fort McPherson until November 20, a day of which he said: "Thirty-two below. Strong wind. Started with 9 dog trains for LaPierre's House. Camped about six miles from Fort McPherson."

Four days later they got all their supplies over to LaPierre's House and "camped with Indian missionary." On December 2 Robertson concluded his journal by saying: "There is no use giving you the rest as we are not doing anything but killing time, and it is pretty hard work too. However, we have all our lumber cut and everything ready to sail down stream as soon as the ice goes out."

This group now camped at LaPierre's House still had fifteen sacks of flour at Fort McPherson and as the *Bulletin* paraphrased a letter from Robertson which it published several months later:

> . . . just before Christmas Mel. Matheson and Sutherland started to Peel river to bring it. They were caught in the mountains and were lost for six days. For three days they had nothing to eat but tobacco. They left

dogs and sleighs in the mountains and finally got back to LaPierre's house. All the dogs except one found their way home. In a few days Sutherland started back with an Indian guide, got through all right and brought the flour back. . . . They expected to have six weeks start of their friends left at Peel river, in the spring; as they could not start until the ice was out of the Mackenzie. After seeing how successful Robertson and his friends were in getting across they wished to cross in the winter also, but could not get enough dog feed to enable them to make the trip.

Meanwhile, Captain Segers and his five men, including Frank Hardisty and Dr. Macdonald, settled down at Fort McPherson. Although on the whole the time passed agreeably, the inaction of sitting around bore heavily. What actual friction there may have been as differing personalities reacted on each other is difficult to assess, but at times Captain Segers seems to have had to exert his authority. One incident of which he told his daughter and which she revealed in 1955 concerns Frank Hardisty, whom he said he had to place in irons before he exacted obedience. It may or may not have been because of this but during the winter, to relieve the tension of living at Fort McPherson, both Frank Hardisty and Dr. Macdonald of Calgary made separate trips to Herschel Island in the Arctic Ocean.

On his trip Dr. Macdonald heard that "seven whaling ships and 16 men had been lost in the Arctic in the same storm that froze their party in on the Mackenzie." He also spoke of a man named Walker having been sent out to San Francisco by way of Edmonton in order to have relief sent to the crews with the first open water. The crew, 300 men in all, were on half rations when Walker left them. "It was not thought probable that Walker would make the trip."

Frank Hardisty, in a letter written on January 18, 1898, expressed satisfaction with the route his party had taken and the progress it had made. He indicated that by that time they had whip-sawed all the lumber they would need for the next boat, the *Gold Pan*, which they were making and proposed to float and wrestle up to the summit of the Richardson Mountains. He continued:

On Dec. 31st, I left Macpherson on a visit to Herschell Island in company with three Esquimaux who had come from the coast. A jollier lot of fellows than these three huskies I never travelled with. They surprised me very much by their intelligence, modesty and truthfulness. Though we nearly starved before we reached the coast they did not mind and did their best for me, giving me the lion's share, but I would not take it. They are most kind to their dogs and never whip or abuse them. One of them "Oolak" could speak very fair English. In fact English is spoken by a great many of them. The Huskies are the most independent native people from

Labrador to the Pacific. They are all well off and are never in want. They always have plenty of provisions. They are well armed with Winchester rifles purchased from the whalers.

Hardisty also mentioned the whaling ships that were frozen in and gave detailed information about them. He then went on to state that he proposed to leave in a day or so to visit Banks Land, about four hundred miles to the east, and estimated that the trip there and back to Fort McPherson would take three months. Even at that he would be able to rejoin his companions long before they could resume their trip to the Yukon.

It was in such letters that news trickled into Edmonton concerning the scores who had taken the Water Route and wintered at various points along that great river system. Generally speaking, the last days of 1897 found them all optimistic and in good health. Of some 130 who set out down the Athabasca, only one death had occurred and only a handful had returned to Edmonton.

The reports that came in concerning the few overlanders, however, were less optimistic. They had faced a far different prospect from those who had taken the Water Route, merely floating downstream, and were to be weeks before they experienced the full impact of travelling to the Yukon.

In spite of that, the Garners evidently spent an uneventful winter at Spirit River, some 250 airline miles north and west of Edmonton. By the trail they had travelled, it took them seventy-three days; a modern motorist swishing over the paved highway which follows their route closely could breakfast in Edmonton, eat his lunch in Spirit River and have plenty of time to stop for a coffee along the way.

As the year 1897 ended and the snows of a mild winter blanketed the forests from Edmonton to the Yukon, they fell upon some scores of adventurers bedded down fairly comfortably for their long wait for spring. Some overlanders had reached Fort St. John and others were strung out between there and Edmonton. Some of the Water Route wanderers had reached the mouth of the Mackenzie, some were pausing along the Liard River, wondering how to ascend its long, rough Grand Canyon, and others in little groups were spaced along the rivers from Athabasca Landing to Fort Simpson. All of them had known that they would have to spend the winter en route to the Yukon, all of them had hoped to have made more progress than they had accomplished, but all but a few of them looked forward hopefully to completing their trip shortly after the spring break-up.

CHAPTER SIX

EDMONTON'S
EXUBERANT WINTER

At the beginning of 1898, Edmontonians, proud of the town's new-found place in the sun as the Gateway to the Yukon, fondled their pocket-books, pleased that for once pride had been accompanied by a little pelf. They had not however sat idly by, waiting to gobble up any wealth which wandered in. Not only had they put up some of their own money, but, aided by the Boards of Trade and newspapers in eastern Canada and the United States, they had even moved Ottawa to put up some towards cutting a road through to the Yukon.

Meanwhile, the town was knee-deep in Klondikers. Some were eager to set out right away and some intended to start early in the spring. Partly because winter smote the northwest lightly that year, those bound overland left as the mood took them and all planned to reach Peace River Crossing before spring had spoiled the sleighing. When that happened, they planned to change to pack horses. Many who intended following the Water Route did not delay in Edmonton but advanced to Athabasca Landing, where they spent a few busy weeks making boats and scows to be ready for the great day when the ice would go out of the river.

Of those who set out from Edmonton, over half came from the United States, mainly from the eastern half, with especially heavy contingents from Chicago, where some of that city's businessmen put on an extensive advertising campaign. Perhaps fifteen per cent of the total number of Klondikers were from the western states. Eastern Canada supplied about one-third of the total, and these were mainly from Ontario, with a heavy representation from Hamilton. Several parties came from Winnipeg and the prairies. As might have been expected, the Klondike fever was especially virulent amongst Albertans and, of course, particularly so amongst Edmontonians themselves – amongst those who had long been oriented and conditioned to the northwest. The editor of the *Bulletin*, in trying to keep a rough count of the adventurers passing through, often encountered men from all parts of the British Isles and an occasional individual or small party from France, South Africa, or even Australia.

Of most interest during the long winter months were the parties going overland or those who began by planning to go overland but were destined to change their minds at Peace River Crossing and go down the Peace River. Because they spent time and money buying horses and equipment, some of them became well known locally. The big event of 1897 had been the Fresno party, which had taken the trail by way of modern Whitecourt. The winter months saw several parties of the same size prepare to take the Chalmers Trail, which was still in the process of being cut out.

The Fugard party, for instance, caught up to Chalmers's work party shortly after crossing the Athabasca River at Fort Assiniboine and had to strike out ahead making their own trail. Within a day or so its men were wisely spaced out in a column of 120 horses which extended some 15 miles. By January 15 they had reached Lesser Slave Lake post and went on to reach Peace River Crossing on February 2. Writing back to Edmonton, Fugard made light of the difficulties they had overcome in cutting their own trail and described his experiences that far as a "pleasure trip."

The Brown-Morse party, on second thought, decided to follow the lead of the Fugard party and head for Peace River Crossing. By the end of December the party was at Fort Assiniboine and in due course reached the Peace River.

The next large party to set out was the Helpman group, and compared with the first two parties, it made a poor showing. This was the most newsworthy assembly of adventurers ever to titillate Edmontonians' fancy. It consisted of Colonels O'Brien, Helpman and Le Quesne, Captains Hall, Powell and Alleyne, and Viscount Avonmore from Ireland, all with British army experience; Doctors Hoops and Hollwright; and Messrs. C. C. Bannister, E. A. Jeffreys, R. H. Simpson and others. Undoubtedly because they had connections among the British ranchers in the Calgary area, they bought one hundred horses there. Then they descended on Edmonton with supplies of the oddest description, well provided with liquor, and filled with marvellous misconceptions of what lay ahead of them.

Because they were gentlemen of the military caste, Major A. H. Griesbach and his officers of the Mounties welcomed them, while they made a resounding splash in Edmonton's society circles. Less social-minded Edmontonians, particularly the overwhelming majority who hated the English, or the genuine frontiersmen, regarded them with varying degrees of scorn and hostility. Money, however, makes short shrift of hostility. Those individuals who, either honestly or by dubious methods, extracted money from the Helpman party quickly smothered their animosity but left their scorn to simmer. The adventurers' inadequacy on the frontier whetted the eager intolerance of the parochial community and even now, decades after other Yukon parties have been forgotten, stories of the eccentricities of the Helpman party, magnified with each telling, continue to circulate.

One of these which probably has a germ of truth in it concerns their champagne. Amid their copious and varied liquors, that would not deign to freeze, they were said to have "cases and cases" of champagne. Unloading it from the train, they left it covered with a canvas in the middle of the huge pile of their other supplies. When the party began to get the mode of travel which they would have to adopt into focus and when Edmonton's December weather had frozen the fizz out of the champagne, the party held an auction sale of superfluous stores. It is said that the champagne in its damaged condition brought twenty-five cents a case and was consumed on the spot. And the story may well be true, for no tale of the Helpman party's ludicrous misadventures is more plausible.

The fate of Captain Alleyne, who was carried off the train unconscious with pneumonia and died on December 27, got the party off to an unfortunate start. His funeral, carried out with full military and Masonic honours, in which Strathcona's Acacia Lodge took part, provided Edmontonians with a rare spectacle. As laid out in the *Bulletin*, the procession was as follows:

Major Griesbach

and

Detachment of Mounted Police

Rev. A. Grey

Dr. Mostyn Hoops,	Dr. Harrison
Medical Officer of Expedition	

COFFIN

Viscount Avonmore,	Major Helpman,
Director	*Director*
Dr. Hollwright	C. C. Bannister

Capt. Alleyne's Horse
led by groom

Capt. O'Brien,
Leader of the Expedition

Lieut. Col. Le Quesne	Capt. Hall
E. A. Jeffreys	R. H. Simpson
C. Powell, Jr.	Capt. Powell

Employees of Expedition

Members of Mr. Clatworthy's Expedition

Members of Capt. Bernard's Expedition

Members of Mr. Mulholland's Expedition

The Mayor and Mayor-elect of Edmonton

The Masonic Brethren

Mr. Taylor	Mr. Livock	Mr. Kinnaird

representing Hudson's Bay Co.

The Helpman party camped on the flats south and west of Fort Edmonton and soon fell prey to the frictions common to most Klondike expeditions and to other misadventures. A few days after Alleyne's funeral, Colonel Le Quesne fell from a sleigh and broke his arm. In spite of that, the aggregation formed up with their horses and transport behind the fort while Mather, one of Edmonton's early photographers, took its picture. Then on January 3 its advance guard pulled out to begin to discover the rigours of the Chalmers Trail. Most of the remainder of the party followed shortly after them.

At St. Albert, eight miles out, a kicking horse broke E. A. Jeffreys's shoulder blade and he had to return to Edmonton. Curiously, on the same day and in the same place Alex Groat, an Edmonton boy with the Feltham-Mulholland party, was similarly disabled and had to be brought back to town. The Helpman group kept on and about a week after it left Edmonton was reported to be at Fort Assiniboine. In the meantime, Colonel O'Brien and C. C. Bannister, the secretary of the party, both of whom had remained in Edmonton, had a difference of opinion and the colonel appeared before Magistrate Gairdner charged with assaulting his associate. About the same time, Captain Powell, who had gone to Vancouver on the expedition's business, died there.

Despite a discouraging start, the party made reasonable progress as far as the Athabasca River. From there on to Lesser Slave Lake, however, when along with a few members of other parties it had to fight its way over the Swan Hills ahead of Chalmers's road builders, the group fared dismally. When it finally reached Lesser Slave Lake, the Helpman party was thoroughly disorganized and bickering. Up to that time it had fired seven employees but with new guides hoped to make the ninety-mile trip to Peace River Crossing in a reasonable time. Much of the group's delay had been due to ineptness but, since it was among the vanguard pioneering a way through the Swan Hills, at least some of the dawdling was probably beyond its control.

Of a different sort was a well-organized group of thirty-three which had originated in Chicago and was led by a Captain Willis. It called itself the Yukon Valley Prospecting and Mining Company. Amongst other activities, it had a hand in publishing the Chicago *Mining Advocate*. Before reaching Edmonton early in February it had already engaged W. J. McLean, who had been in charge of the Hudson's Bay Company's Fort Liard from 1863 to 1873. Organized along formal lines, with each man paying five hundred dollars into the common cause, it wasted little time. By the middle of the month, with its 101 horses, seventy-eight toboggans or flat sleighs and plenty of feed for its beasts, it set forth for Fort Assiniboine and the Peace River country.

One other group, which seems to have created little stir, was the fourteen-man Philadelphia party under Captain J. H. Mason. It slipped away quietly and was soon pushing through the forests and the maze of hills south of Lesser Slave Lake. In many ways it was similar to scores of smaller parties embracing from three to ten men. Amongst many others, there were the following parties: Detroit (five men), Springfield, Illinois (five), Lexington, Kentucky (fifteen), Billings, Montana (five), the Good Hope Mining Company, the Westmount, Quebec, party, and the Big Four, made up of ex-employees of the Big Four Railway in the United States. Another interesting group was the four or five men associated with F. M. Ferriss from Manitoba.

A number of men mainly from Edmonton or its small adjacent farming area made up several small parties. Many of these men wrote back to friends or eventually returned from the north, or indeed from the Klondike, and told their stories. From them we can form a fair idea of the difficulties everyone faced. They belonged to the parties which pulled out late in the winter or early in the spring of 1898, parties headed by Dr. H. L. McInnis, A. D. Osborne, a local employee of the Dominion government, and W. A. Oliver, an engineer at the Edmonton fire hall. Of interest too was the party from Fort Saskatchewan led by Frank Walker, which included his brother Albert, J. Carscadden, T. Cinnamon, J. H. Reid and W. Hepburn and left Edmonton on March 8.

Another local party under C. P. Braithwaite, which included Allen Omand whose farm was the land that is now Edmonton's Windsor Park, engaged the famous frontiersman Joe McDonald to guide and pack for them. McDonald's report of the trip and the trails throws considerable light on conditions.

But it was not only men with horses and dogs that took the trails to the Yukon. There were also three parties that set out northwest driving cattle. The previous September, G. W. Lang of San Antonio, Texas, arrived, bringing cattle he had purchased in southern Alberta, and took them out to Egg Lake (modern Whitford Lake) to winter. Early in February, accompanied by J. P. Mansfield, W. S. Craig and August Kraft, he started to drive sixty-five steers and forty horses north. He planned to go by way of Athabasca Landing and the trail running up the Athabasca River and along Lesser Slave Lake. He took ploughs and haymaking machinery and intended to stop in August to prepare for the winter, with the expectation of reaching the Klondike in the fall of 1899.

A month later the Geddis-Harris party of six Americans left to herd fifty more cattle along the same route. Still later, H. Y. Jones of Swift Current, Saskatchewan, accompanied by J. Butler and three other assistants, started for the Yukon driving seventy-five cattle he had brought with him.

Just as during the previous fall Mrs. Garner of the Fresno overland party had accompanied her husband and Mrs. A. C. Craig had gone down the Athabasca, so during the winter several other hardy wives bound for the Yukon passed through Edmonton. At least twenty women, and possibly one or two more, set out, and even though in most cases we know little of their experiences, the presence of a woman in a party always heightened everyone's interest in it. Undoubtedly there may have been some women who went through without leaving any record. Nine of those we know about started overland: Mesdames Allen, G. E. Garner, C. B. Heizer, G. W. Larrabee, Nansen, H. S. Neisler, A. P. Toneilli, H. M. Woods and Miss Semple. Eleven others went by the Water Route: Mesdames A. Booth, S. Brown, A. C. Craig, Horsfall, Hoffman, L. L. Lampman, Le Francois, O. Sommer, C. Westhead, Miss Jones and Rosie the German girl. All of those who set out were vigorous types who carried on for months under strenuous conditions. At least six made it through to Dawson, of which one was delivered of a baby which reached the Klondike.

Late in January a party of seven arrived from Montana, planning to go overland with twenty-five horses. It was made up of J. Johnes, P. Ferguson, Mr. and Mrs. H. S. Neisler and Mr. and Mrs. G. W. Larrabee and their three-month-old baby. These were hardy pioneering women from the western states, and undoubtedly this baby must have been the youngest Klondiker to set out from Edmonton.

About the same time, eight Cincinnati adventurers came in and camped near McDougall and Secord's store. They were J. B. Heizer, J. H. Myers, Dr. Domhoff, Mr. and Mrs. C. B. Heizer, H. M. Woods and his wife and her sister, Miss Semple. On February 19 the Heizer party set out for the north but a few days' experience of the harsh realities of such a trip during the winter induced the Woods family and Miss Semple to head back to Cincinnati.

Then in February the Harry Sommer party of five, including his brother Otto and Otto's bride, arrived from Chicago. Several months earlier Otto had planned to go to the Klondike but held back because of his girl friend's reluctance to allow him to expose himself alone to the sins and sufferings of a gold-rush camp. With the Klondike calling on the one hand and the girl clinging on the other, he solved the problem by marrying her and bringing her along.

While many parties were merely loosely organized groups of friends, several started out with a complex corporate structure. Of these some were genuine organizations banded together for mutual support but others were merely a front behind which unscrupulous promoters fleeced the unwary and vanished with the funds.

Typical of the various corporate setups was the Klondike Co-op Grubstake Company, designed so that each participant contributed some cash for the expedition. When the men got to the gold-fields, half of whatever gold they found was to go to the company and the rest was to be divided amongst them. This organization published a short-lived paper called the *Klondike Reporter*. The company planned to recruit a hundred men, of which half were to go to the Klondike by the coastal route and the other half by way of Edmonton. It hired J. R. Brenton, the local guide, to conduct the overland expedition.

The Mackenzie River — Klondike Expedition of Hamilton, Ontario, was a company in which Arthur H. H. Heming of that city was a leading spirit. Being the work of an author of some note in the field of outdoor books, his writings created quite a following and were instrumental in inducing so many Hamilton men to head for the gold-fields. Originally the company was planned to include fifty men and on the way one of the officials, W. J. Skynner, was to teach the members the elements of prospecting and mining. While Heming did not go and the company fell through, Skynner threw in his lot with former mayor A. D. Stewart of Hamilton and took the Water Route.

Fraud and trickery were not uncommon. In April 1898 the *Bulletin* noted the presence of seventeen Montreal men who were awaiting the arrival of J. C. Hogmard who, they claimed, had collected $250 from each of them and was supposed to be in Edmonton making preparations for their departure. When they arrived they could not locate him and discovered that he had neither purchased the outfit nor made any arrangements but instead was rumoured to have gone to New York. A month later he had still not shown up, and finally about the middle of June the men, muttering imprecations, returned to Montreal in the hope of catching up with him.

The Klondike Rush presented a first-rate opportunity to inventive persons who put their minds to devising means, generally unsuccessful, to make their long trek less arduous. About the middle of January 1898, nine members of the Chicago Steam Sleigh Company reached Edmonton with an idea that they thought would revolutionize travelling to the Klondike. This was a steam traction engine where the driving wheels were replaced by a steel drum which weighed 373 pounds. Projecting from the drum were spikes which were supposed to provide traction. This contraption was said to be capable of making 15 m.p.h. on the level and to be similar to other machines used in the Michigan lumber camps. It was intended to pull three cabooses to carry supplies and serve as sleeping quarters.

On a vacant lot near the corner of 102 Street and Jasper Avenue, the machine was assembled with care. When it was completed, the party had a little ceremony, christening their steam sleigh the *I Will*, amid the applause of the crowd. The furnace was lit, black smoke belched from the funnel, steam hissed and, to the farewells and cheers of the onlookers, it started to roll. The trip was the shortest on record. The machine scrabbled along for a few feet with the great cylinder clawing its way ever deeper into the ice at each revolution. Finally with a snort the *I Will* gave up. Two or three weeks later K. A. McLeod, a local contractor, purchased the machinery and cabooses, with the intention of renting the latter as residences.

Another party of nine, led by J. T. Montgomery of Toronto, brought along his invention, a combined sleigh, boat and cart. It was a sort of canoe hinged in the middle. One section was fitted with four wheels while the other had runners. When water was reached, it was proposed to take off the runners and wheels. But the craft never reached water because it wore out half-way to the Peace River country and the party had to get more horses and pack its gear that far. Some of the rest of the party continued towards the Klondike but about the end of June Montgomery returned to Toronto.

C. L. Smith from Houston, Texas, arrived in May to rig up his conveyance, which he stated was a duplicate of one he had frequently used with success in Mexico. In Edmonton it succeeded only far enough to earn him the name of "Barrel Smith." Keeping in mind the swollen streams he would have to cross, the muskegs, the high land, the snow and the mud, he and his partner assembled a vehicle which had three axles instead of two. Instead of terminating in a pair of wheels, each axle was run through a whisky keg so that the machine rolled on three wooden barrels. Into the three barrels were loaded 1,000 pounds of supplies, while two horses drew this go-devil. It looked feasible, this contraption, so Texas Smith started off towards St. Albert. In the first mile one hoop came off and in the next mile several more came adrift. In the third mile all the barrels collapsed at once, like the famous "one-hoss shay," and another attempt to conquer the fifteen hundred miles to the Klondike came to naught.

Ideas for these unusual creations were not confined to incoming Klondikers. An Edmontonian named Bruno Fabian took steps to patent an amphibious contrivance weighing five hundred pounds and alleged to combine the useful qualities of a boat, a sleigh and a cart. It, like Montgomery's vehicle, had a long body sheeted with galvanized iron and hinged in the middle. Like many inventions of the era, it passed down the stream of time without making any permanent impression.

This early in Edmonton's history both strangers and local people were seeking a solution to the problems of travelling over the muskegs and the difficult terrain of Canada's northwest. One ingenious method was never actually tried. In May two Parisians arrived to start down the Mackenzie. They advised that they had spent some time arranging to go to the Klondike by balloon but had given up the idea.

All these efforts were ahead of their time, and for a few decades more the onslaught on the north had to be spearheaded by pack horses, draft animals and sleighs. During the winter of 1897-98, John Walter continued his boat-building activities and also did a thriving business in land vehicles. Both he and his rival, the Edmonton Carriage Works, turned out over three hundred Klondikers' sleds each. Since even these were not enough, the Carriage Works sent east for a quantity of two-wheeled Red River carts.

To pull all these vehicles hundreds of horses were required and Edmonton became a busy market which received these animals by the carload. In less than a year the price of a very ordinary horse jumped from fifteen dollars to between thirty-five and fifty dollars. Even in March 1898, when most of the demand had been met, the *Bulletin* reported that there were six hundred imported horses for sale, while five hundred more were available at Calgary, another five hundred were for sale on the prairies, and another 150 could come from Battleford. As late as the middle of April, three carloads of horses reached the city in the same train with two carloads of "burros."

Edmonton's unexpected prosperity was not confined to horse traders stalking the unwary. Everyone had some article or service to sell. Edmontonians had really no need for the advice given them by W. H. Woolums, editor of the Yukon Valley Prospecting and Mining Company's Chicago *Mining Advocate*. He came to town and inserted an ad in the *Bulletin* reading:

W A K E   U P
Edmonton has a Klondike at home,
outfitting prospectors for the goldfields.

But Edmontonians were already fully awake. Their offerings varied from those of E. A. Potter, who opened a school of placer mining, to the work of an unknown author who produced and sold a song entitled "The Spirit of the Klondike." The clergy felt called upon to assist in its own way. On Sunday, January 30, the Rev. Mr. Dyke of the Methodist Church preached to an overflow crowd of homesick adventurers, enjoining them to "Stand fast in the faith. Quit you like men. Be Strong. Let all your things be done in charity" — advice they were soon to need to apply.

While in one way or another every Edmontonian was enjoying the greatly increased excitement or the influx of cash, or both, nevertheless the leading citizens were genuinely concerned with making their route to the Klondike a practical road. They were not even deflected from their purpose by an unfavourable article in a March issue of *Le Temps* of Paris which told of the terrible hardships of the Overland Route. That newspaper had some good things to say about the Water Route down the Mackenzie but viewed the other with horror. It was, so the paper said, the route on which "the Temperature often fell to fifty below," so that a man had to "stuff his nose and ears with cotton to keep from freezing to death while in summer the mosquitoes were unendurable."

Disregarding comments of that kind (comments uncomfortably close

82

to the truth) Edmontonians persisted in trying to realize their dream of a road to the northwest — persisted, and put up cash. They had three irons in the fire: Pugsley's Edmonton, Peace River and Yukon Railway, the Dominion government's Inspector Moodie, and the Northwest Territories' engineer Chalmers, with his road gang. Of them all only Chalmers was really heating up.

In January 1898, Pugsley extracted four thousand dollars from the town. It was the last the citizens saw of that money. Moodie, who had chosen a route they decried, was temporarily out of fuel at Fort Grahame. As a matter of fact, Edmontonians had criticized Moodie's choice of route and bothered Ottawa again until the federal government promised to advance a thousand dollars to finance a study of another proposed trail running northwest from Peace River Crossing to Fort Nelson. With the assurance that this grant would be forthcoming sometime during the summer, the Edmonton town council decided to take time by the forelock and late in February hired W. P. Taylor, with instructions to set out immediately. He was to receive $950 for the trip, of which $500 was to be a down payment, and he was to blaze a trail from Peace River Crossing to Pelly Banks.

By the spring of 1898 Chalmers, the engineer, had actually cut a road most of the way through to Lesser Slave Lake, finishing it at the end of July. From Fort Assiniboine his men had chopped out a new trail which at first ran easterly for a few miles and then struck off north into the relatively open, sandy jackpine country until it crossed Timeu Creek, near modern Timeu. From there the crew headed northwest along the creek; by the end of February they had passed over Deer Mountain and the height of land in the Swan Hills and were starting to follow down a creek which ran into Swan River. Deer Mountain is some eighteen miles north and east of the modern town of Swan Hills, and while the southern portion of the Chalmers Trail ran parallel to modern Highway No. 18, it was always at least twelve miles away from it.

After crossing the Swan River the road cutters continued in a northwesterly direction across the almost mountainous portion of the Swan Hills and kept well up the northeast flank of House Mountain until they struck the headwaters of Driftpile River, some twelve miles south of Lesser Slave Lake. Not only was the terrain rough here, but this twenty-five-mile section of the trail had to be cut through a heavy pine forest in which little grass grew. For the remaining twenty-five miles from the headwaters of Driftpile River the men pressed on to the northwest until they struck the lake shore between modern Enilda and Joussard. From there on around the west end of the lake to Lesser

Slave Lake post the land was fairly open prairie. The actual post was on the north shore of the lake, and to reach it travellers had to cross a narrow neck of water.

Early in August 1898 Chalmers returned to Edmonton and stated that by July 28 the trail had been completely cut through to Lesser Slave Lake. By that time, of course, the bottom had dropped out of the Overland Route and the editor of the *Bulletin* was referring to the "now historic Klondike rush." Chalmers reported:

> The trail is cut from 10 to 16 feet wide from the Athabasca river to the Lake [Lesser Slave Lake]. . . . Of course a great deal more, chiefly in the way of grading up in low places, will have to be done, and it will have to be smoothened by travel before it will be really good. But it is now passable for wheeled vehicles moderately loaded, clear through [the 257 miles to Lesser Slave Lake settlement.]. . . Goose Lake [Foley Lake], which is about three quarters of a mile off the trail about half way between the ford and leaving of Deep creek, offers splendid feed and a good chance to put up hay; but is difficult to find from the trail.
>
> From Vermillion creek to Swan river over the Swan hills . . . there is very little feed, except about a mile south of Salteaux river. Some feed and water may be had at the foot of the hills, a little off the trail.
>
> At Swan river there is plenty of feed, but it is scanty from there to the lake shore. . . . A trail follows Swan river down to the lake shore and then follows the shore of the lake. There is plenty of feed along this route but it is considerably longer than the direct trail, and the creeks, which have to be crossed at their entrance to the lake, are more difficult than where the new trail crosses them. . . .

Of the Swan Hills, Chalmers said:

> Great fear of their horses being poisoned in these hills is felt by many travellers, and they sometimes drive from Salteaux river to Swan river without stopping. The distance is 34 miles and as the road is bad it is most trying on horses. . . . This is a mistake, both because of the overstrain on the horses and because being famished when turned out at Swan river they are more apt to eat the poisonous weed, if any is found. The weed is a species of larkspur and has the qualities of aconite. It grows in wet places. The top is harmless and is not particularly relished by horses. The danger is that if the ground is soft from rains and the horses greedy from hunger they will pull the plant up and eat the root, in which the poison is. If symptoms of poisoning are noticed the horse should be bled. In the mouth (not too far back) is the best place to start the blood, and once the blood is started there is very little danger. If the horses are not famished there is no danger of their eating the weed.

Supplementing Chalmers's efforts, the Northwest Territories government let the rights to construct and operate ferries over the Pembina

84

and Athabasca rivers and over the narrows of the lake at Lesser Slave Lake post. W. H. Humberstone of Edmonton had his ferry at Fort Assiniboine ready to run by May 6, 1898. Another was installed at the Pembina at what came to be called McDonald's Crossing, where during the spring of 1898 Gordon McDonald built a store and stopping place and a barn capable of holding forty horses. The trader Picard put the ferry across Lesser Slave Lake.

Another instance of civilization along the Chalmers Trail was that J. Livingstone (son of one of Alberta's earliest gold-panners, Sam Livingstone) worked out an unofficial mail service from Fort St. John to Edmonton. He undertook to carry letters once a month for all prospectors at a rate of one dollar per month. On one such trip he left Edmonton with 150 pounds of mail matter. On the return trip he left Fort St. John on July 30, rafted down to Peace River Crossing in four days and then rode into Edmonton in another nine. About the same time, in association with a man named Greer, he built a hotel and stables at the Fort Assiniboine ferry landing and also let a contract to some half-breeds to cut and cure 150 tons of hay.

At about this time a group of entrepreneurs in Montreal set up the Commonwealth Development, Mining and Transportation Company to start a stage service from Edmonton to the Yukon. They proposed to put steamboats on all the navigable stretches of the streams encountered on the way to the Yukon and to organize a series of stages and wagons to transport passengers and freight from one river to another. Although for some weeks their plans created considerable excitement, they fell through.

Other enterprising individuals also looked into some of the problems and day-dreamed of the profits to be derived from providing transportation in the northwest. The names of a school of such transportation companies spawned during the rush were as pompous as their routes and destinations were nebulous. The Edmonton-Alaska Mining and Transportation Company of Rutland, Vermont (which should not be confused with the Alaska Mining and Trading Company of Chicago), was one of these. Because Dan Noyes, who had originally come from Vermont, became associated with the Rutland company when in the spring of 1898 he went to his home state for a holiday, it was a little more credible than most of these companies.

On March 10, 1898, J. C. Jones, an employee of the company, arrived in Edmonton. He announced that with Dan Noyes as manager it proposed to start a system of transportation to the Yukon by way of Peace River Crossing. As far as that point the organization would put a stage line into operation, but beyond there it would use pack horses.

Here and there at strategic points along W. P. Taylor's trail it would build stopping places, and in due course hoped to have steamboats operating on the Fort Nelson, Liard and Pelly rivers. Along this route the company would be prepared to carry hundreds of Klondikers. When, at the end of March, Dan Noyes returned to Edmonton, he confirmed this story and at the same time inserted a large advertisement in the *Bulletin* outlining the plans. Unfortunately this scheme fell through, for on June 13, A. L. Taylor, secretary of the company, returned to Boston, leaving word that the project had failed.

With all this activity centred on the Chalmers trail, with all the strings of pack horses frisking around, and with all the Klondikers, greenhorns or otherwise, coming and going, Edmonton's days were one round of excitement. All through January the trains from the south disgorged new hopefuls, and during February the influx increased. The *Bulletin* of February 17 listed sixty prospectors who had arrived individually or in parties of anywhere from three to seven during the previous week and who "are purchasing their outfits here preparatory to starting overland."

Most of the overlanders planned to buy horses and sleighs and, therefore, were anxious to get started while the snow was on the ground and the sleighing was good. Some well-organized parties arrived which spent little time in acquiring what they had to buy locally and set out promptly. Many of those who came in individually spent some weeks looking around before banding together with other footloose men or small groups.

On March 3 the *Bulletin* editor recorded these impressions:

> The rush over the snow to the Yukon by the Edmonton route is at its height. Parties are arriving by twenties and thirties on every train and hurrying forward to take advantage of the last snow, which is gradually, but steadily disappearing. The main street is now in a state of semi-slush and the strings of loaded flat sleighs travel along the side in preference to the centre where the travelling is heavier. In the open the snow is soft and commencing to settle.
>
> So numerous are the pilgrims who are pouring in that it is practically impossible to keep track of the many different parties. Some immediately upon arrival go to the hotels, some remain for a few days at the south side, all available rooms and shanties are occupied by "batchers," and the great majority leave the train and go immediately into camp. A walk through the bluffs in the vicinity of the Hudson's Bay Company and McDougall & Secord's stores reveals the fact that literally the woods are full of them. Around the bluffs are clustered tents and teepees while bare patches on the

ground, from which the snow is thawed, show where some passing pilgrim had made his transient home. In the open all is activity and life. Loaded flat sleds are everywhere and the work of packing and collecting their outfits is being pushed by every party with all possible speed. The open space offered by the race track is utilized for breaking horses, both to ride and drive, and the scene it offers is not only lively, but amusing to the spectator.

The warm weather of the past week has greatly facilitated the work of packing and a great number of parties were enabled to complete their final arrangements, and as a result, a large exodus took place on Tuesday. All day long the streets were filled with loaded flat sleighs and bobs pulling out on their journey. . . . At least fifty left on Tuesday alone.

For the months during which its population of 1,200 was augmented by an influx of nearly that number of Klondikers, Edmonton was a bustling and a bewildering place. During the ten-day period ending March 28 the *Bulletin* counted ninety-four hopefuls who arrived. Of them the editor said: "The following parties have arrived, en route to the Klondike, since the 17th. A large number are on the train coming in this week, and the list would have been much larger only for the blockade in trains which prevented any movement for the past week." As late as April 7 they were still flocking in, for the *Bulletin* recorded that during the current week over 190 had arrived by the two trains from the south. Since most of those who came that late in the season planned to take the Water Route, hoping to go down the Athabasca as soon as the ice went out, the number of arrivals dwindled rapidly after the early part of April.

It is not possible now to arrive at any accurate tally of the number of Klondikers who set out from Edmonton during 1898. From data available in the *Bulletin*, it appears that some 650 souls started out for Athabasca Landing to follow the Water Route, while possibly 675 planned to push on overland.

CHAPTER SEVEN

HEROES, ENTREPRENEURS
AND WATER-ROUTE
KLONDIKERS, 1898

On April 14, 1898, from the Saddle Lake Indian Reserve one hundred miles to the northeast Edmonton's startled telegraph operator received a message reporting a stranded whaler. Saddle Lake, some six hundred straight-line miles from the Pacific Ocean and nine hundred from the Arctic Ocean, was an unusual place from which an officer of an ice-bound whaling vessel might be expected to report. But there Charles A. Walker, mate of the wrecked S.S. *Orca*, had calmly walked in desiring to wire his principals, the Pacific Steam Whaling Company of San Francisco.

Two days later he nonchalantly drove his dog train into Edmonton. In contrast to his exploit, his story was simple. He had come to get relief for his stranded sailors. Through the dark days of the depths of winter, after having walked some five hundred miles from Point Barrow he had driven his dogs from Herschel Island, another distance of well over two thousand miles. At Fort Saskatchewan he fell in with Forbes Groat, who accompanied him to town and promised to sell his dogs for him. Now he was ready to take the train to San Francisco.

The *Orca* with three companion ships, the *Freeman*, *Jeanie* and *Newport*, had left San Francisco in April 1897. That fall the ice off Point Barrow nipped all four ships. For a few days they had worked through the floes until they were off Point Tangent, and there on September 31 their crews had been forced to abandon them. On November 1, Walker had set out on foot for Herschel Island. There he had purchased a team of dogs, arranged for two Indians to guide him into the mouth of the Mackenzie River and set out for the nearest telegraph line at Edmonton. From there on, except that he called at all the fur-trade posts along the way, he was on his own. He reported meeting various members of the Segers-Hardisty party at Fort Mc-

Pherson. As he came south, he had picked up mail from all posts and prospectors and turned it in at the Edmonton post office.

His feat was the talk of the town. The hardihood of a man who could complete such a long, lonesome trip was unexcelled, for he had walked the best part of 2,500 miles with no companions save his dogs. Edmontonians could admire a man like that, who had travelled in the wilderness for 167 days in all.

And yet his trip was perhaps no more remarkable than many another made with dogs or on foot. Three weeks before Walker arrived, Inspector Routledge had returned from his round trip of 2,172 miles, made in eighty days. That too had taken stamina, even though there had been three or four men travelling together to keep each other company. Edmontonians, thinking back, could call to mind some other strenuous trips. Among them was the one made by Chief Factor W. J. Christie, who until 1871 had been in charge of Fort Edmonton and then had moved north to Fort Simpson. In 1873, finding it necessary to go to Fort Garry, some two thousand miles away, he set out alone, and in fifty-five days reached his destination. Travelling through the same terrain but on a much longer trip, Chief Factor Robert Campbell set out from Fort Selkirk on the Yukon River on September 6, 1852, and reached the Company's head office in London, England, by the middle of the following April. His actual walk was perhaps one of the longest on record. For some distance on the Pelly and Liard rivers he had been able to use a canoe but after leaving Fort Simpson he took to snowshoes and tramped to Fort Garry. After relaxing there a day or so, he continued on foot to Crow Wing on the Mississippi River, whence he bought passage on a boat. When reminiscing about his trip, he estimated that he had covered three thousand miles on foot in what was a remarkably short time.

It was exploits like these that native Edmontonians were nurtured on and men like Christie and Campbell, Routledge and Walker, that they had grown up to respect – men who could meet the North on its own terms. It was because every young man in the town and in the surrounding area felt that, if called upon, he too could make his way unaided into the North, that so many Edmontonians set out for the Klondike. To them it was not a bit surprising that hundreds of men from afar had come flocking to head out into the North.

While, on their separate ways from Fort Simpson, Inspector Routledge and Mate Walker had been tramping south, other enterprising individuals had been casting their eyes north. We have already seen how the men from Vermont who had been willing to identify themselves with Edmonton's Overland Route to the Klondike had associated themselves with Dan Noyes and risked their capital in the Edmonton-Alaska Mining and Transportation Company. Other easterners were casting a speculative eye over the Water Route. Late in 1897, J. H. Wood and S. B. McNeill of Pembroke, Ontario, had started a boat-building yard at the Landing. Their plans went only as far as building boats, not to operating a transportation system.

G. T. Leitch of St. Louis, Missouri, however, who was the leading figure in the Mackenzie River Steam Navigation Company, had larger plans. In February 1898, he arrived in Edmonton to complete arrangements for freighting the pieces of his prefabricated steamer, the *Sparrow*, over the ninety-mile trail. By the middle of April she was ready to float, and Leitch advertised that she would leave the Landing on May 1 with any passengers who were prepared to pay for the trip.

A company from Chicago as well, incorporated as the Alaska Mining and Trading Company, made ambitious plans. (Some sources refer to this company as the Alaska Mining and Transportation Company.) It distributed three thousand copies of Gairdner and Harrison's pamphlet and map. Late in December 1897, J. A. Brewer of the company announced plans for a line of steamers which it hoped to launch on the Athabasca and Mackenzie rivers. By the end of January the Alaska Mining and Trading Company had printed a booklet of its own. It advertised that it was prepared to transport passengers with five hundred pounds of baggage from Chicago to the Stewart River in the Yukon for three hundred dollars each. The company was also arranging to establish supply houses at Athabasca Landing and at Fort McPherson on the Peel River. It claimed that at present its fleet consisted of the *Edmonton*, the *Chicago* and the *J. B. Griswold*. The last was 150 feet long with 26-foot beam and was to run on Great Slave Lake and the Mackenzie River.

This booklet came out a little prematurely, because a week or so after its appearance the company's plans had changed and it announced that it was going to build ten boats about forty-five feet long at Athabasca Landing and would use them instead of a lesser number of larger steamers.

While these entrepreneurs were only looking into the possibilities of making money out of supplying transportation, scores of Klondikers began trickling into Edmonton to get ready to float down the Athabasca's waters. As a rule, these parties going by the Water Route were small, varying from a pair of partners to six or seven persons. Like the overland parties, they were made up of individuals from as far afield as Australia and South Africa. Perhaps because physicians are an adventurous breed, many of these small groups counted a doctor amongst their members.

The memoirs left by Ernest J. Corp, who was a member of the Phillips party from Hamilton, give a good idea of the way many of the Klondikers commenced their adventure and what they did at Edmonton. He wrote:

> We bought most of our outfit from the local [Hamilton] wholesale houses, excepting flour and rolled oats, which we bought later in Edmonton (as it had probably come from around there). At that time aluminum utensils were but little used, and, wanting to avoid unnecessary weight when packing on the portages, two of us went to Buffalo, N.Y., and bought a complete outfit of cooking utensils, all aluminum.
>
> Our heavy winter clothing, sleeping bags and oil skin clothes were all made in Phillips' tailor shop, and when we were ready to start we had as complete an oufit as could be secured for such a trip. . . .
>
> For a while each Monday morning in March and April, various parties for the Klondyke or the Prairies left the Railway Station on Hunter Street, and quite a crowd would gather to watch the departing travellers. For many of these it would be a final farewell. . . .
>
> Arriving at Edmonton, we found it a small prairie town, with one main street (Jasper Avenue) North of the Saskatchewan River. South of the River, apart from the sheds of the railroad terminus, there were but few houses. . . .
>
> We got our outfit freighted across the river, and pitched our tents in a cottonwood grove in what is now near the heart of the city. . . .
>
> Just to show what greenhorns we were about cooking, I mention this incident. One day while camped at Edmonton, we had a piece of bacon cooking, when someone of our party suggested that, as bacon and beans would soon be our main diet, we try some now. So I put a large cup of beans into the boiling pot, thinking they would be soft and ready to eat by suppertime, but after many hours cooking they were still like bullets from being put into boiling water instead of cold. Another man made a plum duff and put it in cold water on the stove, so you can imagine the result. . . .

Some of these groups which arrived in January and February 1898 immediately began to place orders for boats to be built for them or bought lumber and had it hauled to the Landing and hurried there to build their own. Others paused only briefly in Edmonton and then went on to the Landing to buy lumber there from Fraser's mill. Many Klondikers, of course, arrived in Edmonton without having decided whether to take the Overland or the Water Route. As a rule, however, those who came from the Atlantic Coast or the Great Lakes region were marine minded and had made up their minds to go north by water. In any event, March saw the heavy inrush of those bound for Athabasca Landing.

All of this vastly increased activity involving steamboats, Klondikers and an incredible assortment of their gear kept every available freighter busy all winter and spring hauling to Athabasca Landing. The volume of traffic was so heavy that, although many parties rode out with the freighters, there was enough demand by the middle of March for a regular stage to start operating. It made the round trip over the old trail in a week, and so great was the rush that by May 1 the operators were running two stages a week.

The trail itself was a fascinating entity. It left the Fort Saskatchewan Trail at Belmont (which is well within Edmonton's city limits) and turned north to cross the Sturgeon at Battenburg. Then it continued some seventy miles, winding along hillsides and around sloughs and wherever possible keeping to the high land. All along its course, great spruce and pine trees hemmed in the wheel tracks, shutting out the sunlight. After crossing the height of land it followed Tawatinaw Creek until it swung around its last bend, and there, three hundred yards away, the muddy waters of the Athabasca lay below. Between that point of vantage and the river was the town of Athabasca Landing.

Along this trail during March, April and May several hundred hopefuls directed their steps. Everyone whose business brought him to Edmonton from the Landing passed scores of Klondikers heading north. Even as late as May 26, on his way back from Athabasca Landing, W. S. Edmiston, the mayor of Edmonton, reported meeting fifty north-bound prospectors and seeing seventeen boats and one steam yacht being freighted north. Yet by that time the peak of the traffic was over.

Along the Athabasca Trail passed the fit and the unfit, the seasoned veteran of other rushes, and the office clerk at a dead end who should have stuck to his stool. Along it passed the quiet, competent man trying to dodge the know-it-alls who, by assuming a mantle of knowledge they did not possess, revealed their inward uncertainty. Along it passed many a man whose untried resolution was doomed to dribble out before the grim reality of the trek or whose untested courage was destined to soar above that of his fellows. But as they finally turned their faces north out of Edmonton, whether they were experienced or ignorant, seasoned or soft, all of the adventurers, old men or young, or even women, found their life lifted to a new plane and their spirits and strength soaring to a new level. When at last the trail carried them over the hills and into the scented pine woods, each one shucked off the restraints and trammels of the city in the fierce excitement of his life's greatest gamble. In that moment many a man lived for the first time and entered a world of adventure denied to all but a chosen few in any generation.

The pocket of pay dirt at the end of this trek was merely the sop that put the conscience and the more logical parts of their brains to sleep so that they could embark on this venture. Many of a grasping disposition really believed that in the Yukon they would get rich but many others had no such determined hope. Man has been disappointed so often; nevertheless, while his head tells him that there is no pot of gold at the end of the rainbow, his heart insists that he must go and look.

Taking part in the trek to Athabasca Landing therefore, were all sorts of men. Taking his place in the procession was the one-time Edmonton agent of one of the New York life insurance companies whose principals finally awakened to the fact that he had looted the office, locked its door and vamoosed with the funds.

Taking their places were Jim Wallwork and his partner Charlie Roberts, who rode with the freighters hauling their steamboat to Athabasca Landing. A young man on his father's ranch (on which part of Lethbridge is now built), Jim had talked to Klondike-bound Montana people who, while trekking to Edmonton, stopped over for the night. Before long he could resist the pull of adventure no longer and set off for Edmonton. There he met John Gainer, who was later to start a packing plant, and from him bought the little sternwheeler *Daisy Bell*, which had seen service on the North Saskatchewan River. By doing so, he immortalized the *Daisy Bell* as the only boat that had plied the Saskatchewan and had then made the trip down the Mackenzie and finally crossed the mountains to dip its paddles into the Yukon River.

Travelling the trail too was George Mitchell, whose experiences were incorporated in a book published some decades later. So was Alphonso Waterer from Pincher Creek, who wrote a graphic account of his contact with scurvy along the Rat River.

Also rolling north was a party of prospectors loaded into a freighter's wagon including a boastful individual decorated with pistols and armed to the teeth, who wore everyone down with the tales of his prowess as a northerner. About the third day, when his companions' patience was wearing thin, what was obviously a sleigh dog was sighted trotting along the trail towards them. "Look," he cried, "a wolf! a wolf!" With silent malice, no one tried to stop the man with the artillery, who, determined to be able to recount to his grandchildren a harrowing tale of killing a wolf in the far reaches of the North, shot this fine beast. Jumping off the wagon and hurrying over to pick up his victim, he was surprised when W. H. Connors, a northern trader, and his team approached over the hill, enraged by this senseless slaughter. Abjectly, amid the quiet smiles of his companions, the boastful one paid fifteen dollars for the dog, and rode on to the Landing in silence.

A. D. Stewart, one-time mayor of Hamilton, Ontario, also headed for Athabasca Landing. Stewart, a forceful, restless man of many parts and of considerable education, was well known in Ontario. He had risen to national prominence when at the close of the Northwest Rebellion of 1885 he was the man who, on behalf of the people of Canada, laid the formal information and complaint against Louis Riel that led to his trial and hanging at Regina. About the same time Stewart was promoted to Chief of Police in the City of Hamilton but resigned in 1886 because of a difference of opinion with a newly elected mayor. At the next opportunity Stewart ran for alderman and was elected. During 1894-95 he was mayor of the city, but lost the ensuing election and went into private business.

When the Klondike excitement swept Hamilton, he gathered up the remnants of the party which Heming, the writer, had started. Stewart's group consisted of R. H. S. Cresswell, W. J. Skynner (a mining expert), and Messrs. W. Tallman, Brock, Duncan and Irvine. The men left Hamilton on April 14, 1898, and about a week later arrived in Edmonton. At Athabasca Landing on May 24 they launched their "GOLDEN HOPE trusting we should be taken to the land of gold by her." Fortunately Cresswell kept an interesting diary and A. D. Stewart wrote long and descriptive letters which from time to time were published in the *Hamilton Herald*.

Of similar stature was John Wilson, a former mayor of Kalgoorlie, Australia, who had wandered far over the wide world. Heading for the Landing also was the pair from Chicago whose combined assets amounted to fifty dollars in cash and a cheerful capacity for making their way. When they reached the river they mysteriously, but without arousing any animosity or spending any money, acquired lumber, obtained nails and built a boat. So well were they regarded that when their boat was ready, many in the camp gave them flour and provisions and collected money to enable them to set out down the river – two men who were completely competent to look after themselves. About the same time, Frank J. Nash of Haverhill, Massachusetts, took the trail. He had reached Edmonton with a grin, a willingness to work, and $4.50. By pursuing his calling of carpenter through the winter, he built up a stake sufficient to set out north.

Taking the trail too, all unaware of the tragedy, hardships or eventual success which lay in store for its different members, was the Hoffman party of Sandon, British Columbia, which included Mrs. Hoffman and Rosie, a German girl whose last name is not recorded. At Athabasca Landing, A. D. Stewart got to know the members of this party. Both Hoffman and Hoffmeir were recent immigrants from Germany where as soldiers they had taken part in the battles of Sedan and Metz and hence felt competent to overcome all lesser risks they might encounter on the way to the Yukon. Stewart noted that Mrs. Hoffman was obviously pregnant.

Along the trail also went a man named Jones from England and his sister, as well as Mr. and Mrs. Westhead, recent immigrants from England to Buffalo Lake, Alberta. They too were to experience mixed success and failure. Otto Sommer and his new bride, filled with the joy of their joint adventure, also made their way to the Landing. So did the Woonsocket party from Rhode Island, of which Mrs. Le Francois was a sturdy member.

Ernest Corp, too, who had made a mess of cooking beans at Edmonton, took the Athabasca Trail, and said in his memoirs:

> We camped here about a week, then arranged to have our whole outfit freighted to Athabasca Landing over the old H.B.C. road, being about seventy-five miles. The freighter made two trips to take our six tons of freight. Arrived here, we made our camp, and started to get our boat ready. It had been made for us in Hamilton by an old boat builder, and had a rock elm keel and ribs, and Georgia pine planking, each piece marked and knocked down, which made it easy to reassemble. This, I think, was the strongest boat built here; the scores of other boats built here were constructed of fresh sawn local lumber, and were just flat bottom scows. . . .

For an idea of the stimulating reception awaiting the travellers at the Landing we have the evidence of an unnamed Athabasca Landing correspondent, who wrote in April 1898:

> Less than three months ago the "Klondiker" upon descending the winding slope leading to the river bottom which constitutes the location of the village, saw only the Hudson Bay fort warehouses and out-buildings, the Athabasca, saw mill and English church, the police barracks, two houses, a few shacks, and train dogs galore; high hills, snow two feet deep and all is told. To-day the scene is changed. The scores of white tents that dot the hill side and the river bottom almost succeed in sustaining the snow impression of two months back. The Hudson's Bay Company have surveyed a town site from a portion of their property and shops of different kinds are being erected so the north bound traveller will be able to replenish his stock. . . . All kinds and shades of people are here, old and young, big and little. A Hollander, six feet seven inches tall, is the longest man in

95

camp, and a French Canadian, four feet six inches, holds the hot cross bun, made at the local bakery, and presented on Good Friday to the smallest on record. . . .

East and West Chicago are places or camping grounds east and west of the village proper and so-called because of the Chicago men there who outnumber their fellow campers four to one. The north town is on the north side of the river where Woods & McNeil have their boat building yard, and several other parties — mostly from Ontario — are camped. There is only one street and that revels in the name of "Fifth Avenue," and the visitor upon walking up the trail leading from the river will notice a sign upon a spruce tree, painted in red paint, which tells him that he is on the bonton street of the town. Sturgeon's landing is further up the river and is named after its first settler, Jim Sturgeon. This location is familiarly known as "The warmest baby in the bunch," and it is certainly entitled to its name as it catches the first sun in the morning and has among its campers a colored man who sings exceedingly well the popular song from which it takes its name. A row of shacks southeast of the H.B. fort enjoys the distinction of being the first thing in the village to resemble a street and it bears the title of Bohemian Row.

Every shade of opinion, on topics ranging from gold mining down to the qualities of pain killer cordial, is here nightly discussed. Ten different languages are spoken among the tenants of this row, and they boast among their number, an artist, two miners, three carpenters, two ex-tramps, one actor, an ex-policeman from Boston, one reformed temperance lecturer, an Englishman who plays the banjo very well, one boat builder, one butcher, two old men occupation unknown, destination Peel River, and seventeen dogs of every species known to science. To reside in Bohemian Row is considered an honor and room is at a premium. All things considered the Landing is about as orderly a place as a man would care to live in. Bishop Young, of the English church, is a very familiar figure and can be seen daily walking from camp to camp, where his council, both spiritual and practical, is well given and received. The church is well filled every service night by men of all denominations.

The different steamboat companies are busy on their boats. The "Sparrow" is very nearly complete and will be without a doubt a splendid boat, built on graceful lines. She is 65 feet over all, twelve foot beam, six feet depth of hold and 60 horse power screw engines, with Scotch marine boilers. The Alaska Mining & Trading Co.'s yard is a very busy place and work on their boats is being pushed ahead rapidly. Their machinery comes from Chicago. Mr. John Fraser has a staff of men working on the Wilson & Macdonald boats and work is being pushed along with all speed. Their machinery is from the C. H. Willard Co., of Chicago, and the Polson Iron Works of Toronto. Hundreds of other boats, after the York, the scow, and sturgeon head models are being built by the smaller parties. There are also seven or eight steam launches here, and a busier scene it is hard to find.

The appearance of the ice indicates a break shortly, and the 600 or 700 men sojourning here are eagerly waiting its move, when some of their pent up excitement can be got rid of.

Writing somewhat later, the correspondent continued in the same vein.

The town boasts two hotels, one restaurant, one butcher shop, half a dozen boat yards, four general stores, a barber shop, two bakeries, a Solomon Moses, a number of dances every week and excitement to burn. A most enjoyable concert was held last week, over which Bishop Young presided most acceptably. The talent displayed was surprising, yet when one stops to consider the wide field from which this cosmopolitan town is drawn it it not so surprising after all. Every number received a determined encore – no getting away from the audience. They thought of long years to come with possibly no other opportunity of this kind in store for them and it made them slow to let the performer rest. The rear of Mr. Simmons' butcher shop made a capital stage as an annex was being built which left one side open. Mr. Wood, the genial H. B. Co.'s agent here, lent an organ for the occasion which was placed at the left opening of the stage. The back and right sides were arranged with chairs, real store chairs, and was reserved for the chairman, the ladies and the artists. The seating arrangement of the pit consisted of two pair of bob-sleighs, discarded for the present, and temporary lumber benches while a lumber pile made a capital gallery and the body of the field was "standing room only." Your correspondent enjoyed the concert hugly [sic] from the second row on the first "bob." The proceeds of the concert went for a good cause, the benefit of Mr. Struthers, an old trader, trapper and scout who had just come in from Cold Lake. He was to have been sent to the Edmonton hospital to be treated for a throat disease, but died within forty-eight hours after the benefit, called to a world where the trails and trials of life are unknown.

The number of boats is legion and their names varied and peculiar. I notice one bearing the pretty name of "May." It is far from appropriate as she is built like a cart horse and will carry ten tons. The "Shamrock," "Thistle" and "Rose" are the names of three boats built exactly alike, only one is painted green. They belong to one party. The "Anna" is a launch and as pretty as her name. She is certainly a beautiful little craft and it seems too bad that her destination is where it is. As a pleasure launch she is ideal. The "Montana" is the name of a boat owned by the Buck Co., of Great Falls. A rather staunch looking boat built after the scow pattern. The "Enterprise" is a stern wheeler belonging to a Detroit party and is very strongly built and manned by some practical sailors from the great lakes. She sports a big staff and pennant. Peterborough canoes are strongly in evidence here, also all kinds of punts and every conceivable kind of row boat darting here and there across the river, up and down and nowhere in particular, just trying the current and testing their boats; some out on shooting trips. Game is scarce, but poor shots very numerous. After looking over the different kinds of boats that are here and going down the river, I must confess that I think no port in the world, Liverpool included, can boast so many different models. It looks as though every man who ever had an idea that he was a boat engineer was here and had tried his hand and the result is boats, – beautiful, practical, pathetic, ludicrous boats, all the owners, however, with one end in view, and one man's chances are about as good as another's. . . .

The ice went out on the 22nd of April and shortly after, within a few hours, the Milne party left and took with them the distinction of being the first to get away. The following parties have since gone: Clarke, Barnes, Bolton (a colored man who is much missed as he was an entertaining chap and sang negro melodies very well), Brown, Daroack, Walker, Cole & Calwell Nugent, Clatter, Jim Sturgeon, Paradis, Cooper, Hilber, Buck, Pritchard, Knee, Smith, Groath, Spaffen, Matchet, Hugal, Flavin, Farney and an old forty-niner, D. Hutry. . . .

Mr. Myers, a gentleman from Pittsburg, Pa., met with a rather painful accident. He was handling a revolver supposed to be empty, but which (the old story) had one cartridge left. The cartridge was discharged and the bullet passed through his hand, entering at the palm and coming out between the third and fourth bones in the back. Dr. Barr is attending him and he is doing well and will continue his journey north.

Somewhat later, about May 26, W. S. Edmiston returned to Edmonton and reported to the editor of the *Bulletin*: "All along the river front for a distance of two miles the tents have clustered – many are yet there and more have gone but left the signs of their owners' tenancy behind, in half deserted, new cut streets which the sign boards on the trees show to have revelled in the names of 'The Strand,' 'Piccadilly' and the 'Bowery'. . . ."

Even as late as that there were 250 prospectors who had still not started down the river. The Landing had also been congested by the arrival of 120 of the Hudson's Bay Company's boatmen who had gathered to take its flotilla of some twenty York boats downstream. The company's old steamer, the *Athabasca*, had been condemned and these boats, each manned by a crew of eight, had been substituted for her services.

At about the same time, another correspondent wrote to the *Mail and Empire* of Toronto, giving his version of the excitement at Athabasca Landing. Speaking of the Klondikers' boats, he said:

The remaining thirty are scows, York boats, and large canoes, of all forms and sizes, but the majority are scows with good run fore and aft. One wise precaution taken by nearly all the miners is that they load only five tons in an eight or ten ton boat. . . . Yesterday two miners came down

98

the Athabasca on a raft from Lesser Slave Lake. They report that several parties who left Edmonton with cayuses have got through as far as the Peace River.

There are three steamers here which will start as soon as completed. Of these the Alaska Trading Company is building the largest. The boat is only put together temporarily, to be built permanently below the rapids. . . . Mr. George Leitch, a capitalist, of Minneapolis, Minn. [*sic*], has a steamer about ready to be launched, of thirty tons, twin screw, staterooms for fifty passengers. The other boat is a private party's boat. I learn that Dr. Lister, of Detroit, is now at Edmonton. His party has a steel sectional steamer.

This correspondent noted some prospectors coming down from Lesser Slave Lake and other traffic on the river above the Landing was not all going one way. A number who had taken the trail to Athabasca Landing ascended the river, intending to go to Peace River Crossing. Jim Wallwork with his *Daisy Bell* was one of these because he thought he saw an opportunity to start a passenger and freighting business. As it turned out, his one attempt to ascend Lesser Slave River failed. Jim Cornwall, who was to rise to prominence in the history of the Peace River country, had decided to start trading and had formed a partnership with Fletcher Bredin. Jim Wallwork undertook to carry the pair and their goods to the west end of Lesser Slave Lake. All went well till he tried to force the *Daisy Bell* up the rapids of Lesser Slave River and found that the rough water was too much for the little steamer. When Bredin and Cornwall had to take canoes to complete their trip, Jim's partner, Charlie Roberts, joined them. The traders in due course started a post at Peace River Crossing. Wallwork was forced to run back to Athabasca Landing where he teamed up with some Klondikers and set off down north.

The miners coming down from Lesser Slave Lake were just a few of those overlanders who became fed up with prodding pack horses through the woods and decided to switch over to the Water Route. Many others made this decision when they reached the Pembina River, sixty miles out from Edmonton. At the beginning of May, twelve camps of prospectors were reported as waiting for the ice to clear out of the Pembina so that they could float down to Athabasca Landing. Others continued overland to Fort Assiniboine before they decided to take to boats. Still others, such as the Gifford brothers of Cobourg, carried a canoe to the Pembina and then set off down it to its mouth, with the intention of descending the Athabasca for a few miles and then turning up the Lesser Slave River, bound for Peace River Crossing, whence they proposed to ascend the Peace to Hudson Hope. If one looks at a good map of Alberta, it is almost impossible to find any combination of trails or waterways leading northwest that some party of Klondikers did not use.

The article in the *Mail and Empire* gave some information about a few of the steamers that were to go down the river and mentioned the Alaska Mining and Trading Company. By May 16 that company had finished its first 40-foot steamboat and had another well along. By June 9 the *Chesrown* was finished – a propeller job which was to be used on Great Slave Lake and the Mackenzie. It left the Landing that day with J. Kelly as chief engineer, a crew of three, twenty-two labourers, three teams of horses and a few paying passengers. The men and teams were to be used to get the boat over the Smith Portage and then to continue down-river and be put to work again portaging in the Fort McPherson area. Accompanying the *Chesrown* was the *Alpha*, towing two barges laden with machinery for the larger craft. It was hoped that once the *Chesrown* crossed the Fort Smith portage she would complete her trip to Peel River in time to make another trip back to Fort Smith and home to Peel River again.

The *Mail and Empire* also mentioned George Leitch's steamer, the *Sparrow*, which was to have a troubled career. In addition it noted a number of boat builders – Woods and McNeill, Cinnamon brothers, Colin Johnstone, Fraser and Company, Jackson and Company and George Gullion – who among them still had over fifty ordinary boats for sale.

The *Edmonton Bulletin* eventually compiled the incomplete register given in the Appendix III of the boats and parties that went down from the Landing. This tabulation listed 113 craft, including twenty-five belonging to the three traders, Loutit, the Hudson's Bay Company and Ed Nagle. It also indicated that some five hundred souls set off aboard them, of whom 115 were employees of the traders. Undoubtedly the list was not complete but it was a fascinating tally of the gaily named craft which amid cheers went bobbing off downstream for their joust with destiny.

CHAPTER EIGHT

THE RIVER ROUTE
TO FORT SMITH, 1898

While the trip from Athabasca Landing to Fort Smith was relatively easy (there was only one death on this leg of the voyage in 1898), nevertheless its labour and perils served to toughen any of the prospectors to whom life in the open was a novelty. The diaries, memoirs and letters of some participants present a vivid tableau of the trip. Ernest J. Corp's memoirs, for instance, start the Argonauts off on the great adventure of floating down from Athabasca Landing.

When we were all ready to start down the river, our party, in conjunction with another party of nine men, also from Hamilton, engaged a river guide [Billy Clark] to go with us until we were past the rapids on the Athabaska River. He, of course, went on the larger boat. We started down the river about noon the day after the ice went out, early in May of 1898, and after a while we got separated from the other boat with the guide aboard in one of the several channels occurring in any river. Thinking it was the intention to run all night, when it got dark we hoisted a hurricane lantern to the mast top, and all turned in and went to sleep, leaving the boat to drift on its own, which none of us would have thought of doing after some experience of what rivers are like. My own idea of a river was somewhat like a canal with nice banks, instead of what many are – real death traps, especially under a cut bank with overhanging sweepers which could easily overturn a boat. This was certainly a case of "ignorance is bliss."

However, when daylight came, our boat was grounded on a bar at the tip of an island, but easily pushed off. Then a few miles below, we were carried sideways on to a succession of bars just off the main stream from which with all our efforts we failed to get our heavily loaded boat off. Now we began to worry lest our guide on the other boat was so far ahead of us that we might not be able to overtake him, when suddenly we heard a voice from the other boat passing by in the main channel. "What are you fellows doing over there?" We said, "We are hung up on a bar, and can't get off!" He said, "You will have to lighten the boat by taking some of your freight over to the bank in the dinghy, and we will wait for you a short distance down river — it may take hours of hard work, but that is your only chance of getting off."

Reluctantly deciding to take the guide's advice, we were in the act of starting, when suddenly a stiff breeze sprang up and I had a happy idea. We had several hundred feet of ¾ manilla rope on board, and it occurred to me that, if we could get a line across the main channel to the bank, and make it fast, if the boat went ahead the rope would haul it round in an arc to the channel. To this all agreed, in that while it might not succeed it was the only alternative to a lot of hard work. This was done, and, when the rope was made fast to the bank, the big square sail was hoisted, and the boat went across the bars like a scared cat and into the channel, and we were ready to go on our way. When we pulled in to where the guide was waiting, about half an hour behind him, he said "How in H— did you get here so soon?" When we explained what we had done, he said, "Nobody but a bunch of greenhorns would have tried it."

Continuing our journey, we next came to what is called the cascade.* This is caused by a rim of rock stretching across the river, over which the water flows as over a dam, the drop being from six to nine feet according to the stage of water. Empty boats can safely be jumped over, whereas a heavily laden boat may quite likely dive in headfirst and swamp. The accepted procedure is to lower the loaded boats along the bank to the very brink of the falls, tie them to rings fastened in the rock by the H. B. Company for this purpose, after which the empty boats are hauled back upstream a short distance, rowed out, and jumped over, and brought back to the bank about fifty feet from where they were unloaded and again reloaded. Here again we came very near to losing the big scow of our party, and all its contents. A loaded boat going down the river is brought to the bank, a strong stern line attached and held on to by several men, and lowered slowly toward the cascade, while a light line is attached to the bow of the boat, with just one or two men to hold it. The guide, getting on board, called out, "All right, let her come!" This went all right until the men holding the stern line, instead of climbing up over the point of the rocks, mistakenly followed the river bank until they arrived where the rock jutting out into the deep water cut off further advance.

Now the guide began shouting, "Let her come, let her come!" We answered, "We can't!", but the roar of the falls nearly drowned our voices. Then the guide shouted, "Why in H— don't you let her come?" Now, one after another, the men holding back on the stern line dropped off as they came to the rock, which jutting out into the water, cut off any view between the boat and the men on the line. Finally, with the guide's frenzied

---

* *This was actually the Big Cascade, which was well downstream from the Grand Rapids.*

shouts of "Let her come!" we let go of the stern line. The boat immediately swung out, and we heard the guide say, "My God, they have let us go — make fast the bow line!" The boat swung around in an arc, and was hanging half over the falls, with nothing but the light tracking line holding it from certain destruction. Luckily, there were lots of men waiting here, and they jumped into the boat at the risk of their lives and unloaded about eight tons in as many minutes. The empty boat was then dropped over the falls, hauled out, and, with the help of a Spanish windlass, pulled back into shape, and was ready to proceed after a little patching and caulking. The other boat was lowered without incident.

At Grand Rapids the Corp party paid Billy Clark his one hundred dollar fee and he went back up-river to fetch other parties down. Ernest Corp considered the money well spent and well earned, because piloting was "an uncertain and risky occupation, especially with a bunch of greenhorns like us."

In due course Billy Clark made a trip in to Edmonton. Leaving Grand Rapids on June 21, he and Otto Sommer tracked a skiff to the Landing in five days, and on June 29 arrived in Edmonton. He gave the editor of the *Bulletin* the following list of the thirteen new steamboats that either had left the Landing or were about to do so.

ATHABASCA TRANSPORT

"Enterprise," stern wheel, 50 × 10 feet, drawing 18 inches.

A canvas propeller, 36 feet long, drawing 32 inches.

Sectional iron propeller, built in Detroit, 48 feet long. These three reached McMurray safely on June 3rd.

"Garden City," stern wheel, 50 × 10 feet, drawing 16 inches.

"Minnehaha," stern wheel, 50 × 8 feet, drawing 22 inches. This boat struck a rock in the Long rapid and was delayed two hours.

Ferneke's Chicago party, propeller, 45 feet, built by J. Walter. Over Grand Rapids safely.

"Alpha," Alaska Mining & Transportation Co., propeller, 40 feet.

Also hull of steamer 60 feet long 12 feet beam, owned by the same company. The machinery was being taken on a flat boat and would be fitted in after passing the Fort Smith rapids. These two boats were through Grand Rapids.

"Sparrow," propeller, 60 feet long. Best built steamer on the river, all machinery in place, owned by Geo. T. Leitch. Hung up in Grand Rapids uninjured, waiting for a rise of water. She had fifteen passengers.

"Anna," propeller, 36 feet long.

"Daisy Bell," stern wheel, belonging to the Holt party,* with two flat boats, Pelican rapids, 120 miles from the Landing.

* *The* Daisy Bell *was actually owned by Jim Wallwork.*

"Upas," propeller, at Landing.

Fringe's party with steamer 36 feet long, just launched at the Landing. Would try Lesser Slave river with a view of reaching Peace river. If they found that impossible they would go down the Athabasca.

The Grand Rapids had washed out Otto Sommer's hopes of carrying out his great adventure. For some months, as we have seen, he had been held back until he had solved the immediate problem by marrying his girl friend and bringing her along. In June 1898, as the couple faced up to the exigencies of the Grand Rapids, fate or his new bride took a hand and turned them back. Now he was on his way home again.

While the Klondikers had no particular difficulty until they got to Grand Rapids, 167 miles downstream from the Landing, its white water made them stop and think. As a *Bulletin* correspondent writing on May 15, 1898, expressed it:

> Nine men out of ten pick out a convenient rock and seat themselves gazing long and thoughtful at a scene that is hard to surpass. . . . The right hand side is the one the pilots use in lowering their boats down. It has more rocks in it than the left side, but the fall is less and the volume of water not so great. In low water of course the boats are lowered with a line, but in high water they shoot the rapids and the sight is one worth seeing. With one man in the bow with a long pole and another at the stern with a sweep, the lines are cast off and away they go like mad, dashing down the turbulent stream, darting first this way then that till they at last make the shoot at the foot, and the rubber-necks on the bank once more breathe easier and the cool headed pilots with their stoic faces and powerful bodies walk back again along the winding path that leads to the anchorage at the head of the rapids, and prepare to repeat the performance.
>
> I, for one, advocate taking a pilot and when he comes aboard your boat don't "know it all." Do as he tells you and only what he tells you, and remember the old sea precept: "Don't talk to the man at the wheel." In every case where a pilot has been engaged not a single accident has occurred. Some who have not engaged pilots have also gone through in safety, but others have met with very serious accidents. . . .

Just as Edmontonians had taken steps to get a trail cut through the Swan Hills, so they also tried vainly to improve the Water Route. It appeared that the channel of Grand Rapids would be improved vastly if two or three dangerous boulders could be blasted out. To accomplish this the citizens raised a fund of six hundred dollars to have them dynamited. Of this amount they collected ninety dollars from Klondikers who were going that way and arranged with Ed Nagle, the trader, to have some of his employees, including D. McCallum and

W. Clarke, do the work. They went in and blew pieces off two or three rocks, but their efforts did little to make navigation any safer.

Fortunately during 1898 no lives were lost at Grand Rapids, but there were some close calls, which the correspondent described.

On the afternoon of the 10th the De Belleue party, six in number, while lowering their boat down the channel lost control of her and she upset, letting eleven sacks of clothes out into the river. Five were recovered shortly afterwards and a member of the party went down the river after the remainder, but up to the time of writing had not returned. The boat is jammed between two large rocks over which heavy waves are breaking and she will be a total loss.

On the afternoon of the 13th, a man by the name of Loundy was upset half a mile below the Little Grand. He was attempting to run the rapids in a small skiff; to "learn the rapids" he told us when we inquired after his health. He said it was his intention to run his larger boat in the event of his being successful. He barely escaped with his life and I since learned that he has changed his mind and will take a pilot.

A rather serious accident occurred here yesterday, 14th, when Joseph Cardinal, a guide from Pelican rapids, while steering an outfit over to the island and making the shoot, was struck by the sweep and thrown clear of the boat and on a rock. He received four broken ribs and fractured his leg. Drs. Buck and Dillabough attended, gratis, and Sergt. Anderson circulated a subscription, getting a neat sum for him. He is getting along splendidly and is being well looked after by the police detachment.

A large number of parties take the tramway over the island in portaging their boats, but they all — with a few exceptions — pack their goods. It is here the first hard work of the trip is experienced. The stout, able-bodied man shines from now on, and the "Chappies" are objects of charity. Speaking personally, your correspondent made 23 trips over the island and packed 100 lbs. each trip; next morning he felt like a man 150 years old. He has since slightly limbered up, but it would take forty-eight hours sleep and a half a dozen Turkish baths to get him back where he belongs. I overheard a man remark the other night after he had got his last load safely deposited at the foot of the island: "It is all here now, but this morning it was all at the other end." I asked him if he was glad and he replied, "Yes, but young man I'm ten years older."

Writing again towards the end of May, the correspondent added more descriptive touches to the picture of the rapids:

On or about the 18th of May, boats to the number of sixty-four left the rapids here, practically one fleet, bound north. Some guides had a round dozen of boats to chaperone, while others had but two, some four and others six. The system was a good one and speaks highly for the good judgment of the pilots. A pilot would steer the lead boat and two or three more would follow him as close as was considered prudent. If one of the consort was a large boat or a small boat with a large draught of water, a steersman was placed aboard to steer her. At the rapids the pilots would run one boat at a time and in this way every boat that left here in the fleet I speak of, reached McMurray safely.

A few accidents happened, but none of a serious nature. Thos. Bowen, a pilot, met with the only accident that befell any member of this large flotilla. A boat was being snubbed to a tree on the bank by an inexperienced man, a member of one of the parties, and Bowen, seeing the way it was being done and the danger that would accrue, rushed up to the tree. He was a little too late, for just as he reached the tree the line drew taut and the current at this point (it being 300 yards above the Big Cascade rapids) is very swift and when the boat tightened upon the line something had to give. In this case it was the tree, which was torn out by the roots and just as Bowen reached it the trunk swung around and landed on his neck and shoulders, putting him out of the pilot business for a few hours. Drs. Buck and Dillabough attended him and he is now on deck again little the worse for wear. Drs. Buck and Dillabough have done enough free doctoring to entitle them to a large immediate, as well as a future award, if any men deserve gold these men certainly do. It's the whole-souled, gratis business you read about and seldom see.

Their practice here has also an amusing side. About every half day some old pilot or riverman will get a very bad cramp and one of the doctors will be brought to see him and, through an interpreter, the sick man will tell that he is subject to those attacks and that there is a remedy, but as he cannot speak English he has forgotten the name. The doctor, on being asked to name over the different medicines likely to be beneficial will eventually get around to "hot drops and ginger" and it's worth the trip here to see the old rascal's eyes blink and he nods an eager assent.

Eventually the rush down the rapids slowed to a dribble, and another correspondent writing from Grand Rapids on June 24, 1898, said:

The rush is over and the different steamboat outfits are having their day.

The Halifax City and Minne-ha-ha, stern wheelers, have got through to McMurray perfectly safe, as also the Enterprise, and the Uncle Sam, a steel sectional steamer with an outfit headed by Dr. Lester, of Detroit.

The Lillian B., a steamer owned by a Chicago outfit, headed by a Mr. Butterfield, left Big Eddy this morning for McMurray.

Mr. Leitch is here with the Sparrow yet, waiting for pilot McDonald to come up from McMurray. He is expected any day.

The Alaska Mining and Trading Co. with Mr. Brewer in charge, are here and are making good time. . . . Mr. J. B. Griswold, the superintendent of construction, is here and under his direction the largest of their steamers was skided out of the water, cut in two, bulk heads put in, caulked and launched in eight hours. Quick time, and the workmanship was of the highest order. . . .

The Capt. Hall party is here, all hands safe and sound. Pilot Atkinson will take them to McMurray.

The "Daisy Bell" in all the glory of a new coat of paint, arrived this morning. I think that Edmonton people have seen the last of her, as she is bound for an uncertain goal.

Mr. and Mrs. Westhead and party, from Buffalo Lake, passed through here on Monday; Pilot Shot will be in charge to McMurray. They were travelling in consort with Mr. and Miss Jones, of England. The ladies enjoyed themselves pleasantly while here, and departed north with a more determined air than plenty of men who viewed for the first time the wild and turbulent waters of the Grand rapids. . . .

At last on June 3 the first steamboat reached Fort McMurray. Fortunately someone there with a gift for writing described the natives' surprise at the influx of Klondikers.

When McMurray was reached, a happier lot of men it would be hard to find, laughing, shaking hands and congratulating each other on their safe arrival. And to see the natives stare when the fleet of boats arrived and the rush of men trooped up to the Hudson's Bay Company's store to post letters and make a few purchases. Its hard to tell what they thought, but they were certainly too dumbfounded to speak, merely standing at a safe distance to view the advancing crowd. It was enough to make others besides the natives stare. Fancy a little hum-drum hamlet three hundred miles from civilization, so to speak, dead to the world for half the year and in the other half they perhaps see or hear of a single boat passing down the river. Then of a sudden to have their solitude disturbed and the even tenor of their daily existence outraged by the advent of sixty-three boats and a crowd of men, hilarious with joy at getting safely over the rapids, yelling and dancing in the exuberance of their animal spirits. It would keep a white man guessing to hold his own with his head piece, let alone an Indian. This will be an event for the Indians of Fort McMurray to hand down to posterity and tell of round the fire place while the wind howls down the chimney. This is probably the most peculiar and impressive sight that has ever taken place, or ever will take place, in the history of McMurray.

After having piloted boats and scows and greenhorns through the seventy-five miles of rough water from Grand Rapids to Fort McMurray, the pilots and rivermen, mostly Métis, hurried back upstream to bring others down. As the correspondent from Grand Rapids, who returned with one of them, said:

The pilots did not stay over more than an hour or two. I did not wait behind long enough to see the voyageurs off, but from information picked up since, I think they all got away within forty-eight hours of their arrival, which would be on the 25th of May.

The trip back to Grand rapids overland is an experience that will be uppermost in my mind for many a long day. I understood before leaving McMurray that there was a trail, but like a great many other trails in this north land, it is falsification pure and simple. We left McMurray on the afternoon of the 25th and reached here on the evening of the 28th. No person knows just how far it is because in order to get back from one place to another you cannot travel in a straight line and consequently cannot estimate the distance by the map. It is [a] case of zig zag, up and down hill, over muskeg and into muskeg and over miles of fallen timber, in itself no small feat. Burnt stretches of country are also met with, in fact every variety of obstacle is encountered. I had been brought up from childhood to believe that the greatest mosquito district in the world was Jersey. It is a mistaken idea. Henceforth, I remove my hat to the country between here and McMurray. In that favored region they simply travel in armies and to use a somewhat slang phrase they "don't do a thing to you." I can stop in the writing of this letter and count 100 marks on my hands, neck and face.

The time some of the rivermen make on the return journey seems incredible. They leave McMurray at sun-up, travel till sun-down, spell five and six times to eat and perhaps seven or eight short spells, pack their grub and blankets, and make the distance, nearly 100 miles, in from 24 to 34 hours actual travel. Clark and Kennedy are the fastest travellers by long odds. Clark has covered the distance in 23 hours and 38 minutes. Your correspondent tried to follow the men whom he was with, on the way back, and as a result he cannot now walk fifteen miles in that many hours and is waiting for a chance to get even on some one.

About the same time, McLellan, who operated a trading post, came upstream to Athabasca Landing and estimated that he met 150 boats between Fort McMurray and the Landing. He also reported that on May 5, a couple of weeks after the ice went out, some Indians found and buried the body of Patterson of the Hamilton party, who had been drowned the previous fall. McLellan also met some members of that party who were going down to the grave to identify the body.

A. D. Stewart from Hamilton heard the story of Patterson's death and stopped to see his grave. When he got to Fort Chipewyan he paid a carpenter to make a cross and to have it set up. On it he had inscribed:

WILLIAM KEITH PATTERSON

OF HAMILTON, ONTARIO

DROWNED AT GRAND RAPIDS AUGUST 31, 1897

The bulk of the Klondikers set out from the Landing as one large contingent and even when they reached Fort McMurray they all were more or less in a group. After a few more days, however, the space between the leaders and the laggards lengthened so that before long they were scattered along miles of the river. Similarly, when the ice had tightened its grip on the water course the previous fall, the many prospectors who were then heading north were strung out over hundreds of miles. When the ice went out towards the end of April those who had wintered along the Athabasca resumed their trip, but some of them were not many days ahead of the 1898 adventurers. By mid-summer Klondikers were to be found all along the great Athabasca-Mackenzie waterway, and in many cases those of 1897 vintage were mixed up with the 1898 crop.

At Fort McMurray, to add to the confusion, the stream of Klondikers received a small infusion of adventurers who came down the Clearwater from the east. Several small parties from the prairies and eastern Canada had chosen to leave the Canadian railway system in the vicinity of Prince Albert. While the total starting by this route was probably slightly more than a hundred, many turned back before reaching Fort McMurray, so that the flow of Klondikers down the Athabasca was only augmented by possibly seventy or eighty.

These seventy or so had followed the very old fur-traders' route from the North Saskatchewan River to Fort McMurray. They left the railway at Duck Lake near Prince Albert and, by means of portages, lakes and streams, headed northwest through Green Lake, Ile-à-la-Crosse Lake, the famous old Methy Portage, and finally the lower reaches of the Clearwater River. Some waited until the ice was out of the lakes and streams, but others set out over the snow with horses or dogs.

One of these was Eben McAdam's party of five from Montreal, which left Duck Lake about the middle of March 1898. They used a trail recently travelled by a convoy of twenty-one sleighs that had brought fur out from the Hudson's Bay Company post at Green Lake. As far as that post, which they reached on March 30, a freighter hauled their two and a half tons of supplies. When the teamster turned back, the party arranged to have its goods hauled by a new set of men. The next afternoon, with twelve single sleighs and three hired men, they advanced twelve miles, and five days later reached Ile-à-la-Crosse. After some revision of their crew, they left the Hudson's Bay Company post there on April 6, and McAdam's diary says:

> Left Isle a la Crosse at 8.30 a.m. with 13 single sleighs, 3 of our own and 10 toboggans, besides 4 loads of hay and fish for the dogs at Bull's House, head of Buffalo Lake – in all 17 loads and 7 men. Weight of supplies (less our sleighs) 6287 lbs. Camped at head of La Crosse Lake at 6.30. Distance 20 miles.

Thursday 7th: Broke camp at 6.45 a.m. Reached Deep River about 7.15 a.m. Had dinner 10.30 a.m. Had some refreshment at short portage 6 p.m. At this point Pierre Morin, one of the teamsters (the one who travelled with us from Green Lake to Isle a la Crosse) decided not to go with us any further as his horses were played out and the hay was not, he said, sufficient to see us through. After a lot of talk and waste of time he decided to go as far as the Narrows. We continued our journey from 6.30 till about 8.30 and camped. Distance 18 miles.

Good Friday 8th: Broke camp 6.30 a.m. and reached the Narrows about 10.30 a.m. Yesterday's trouble had been brewing during the morning travel, and on our arrival here Pierre again brought up the subject of not going farther. He said he could not go. As the rest of the men showed bad symptoms we asked them how far they proposed going, and they said they were in the same predicament as Pierre. They finally decided not to go any further. Fortunately, at this point, the H. B. Co. have two vacant buildings so we told them if they did not want to go any further they had better place our supplies in one of the houses.

On Saturday, May 14 they arrived at Fort McMurray and were pleased to hear that only four parties, presumably 1897 Klondikers from below Grand Rapids, had gone down the river ahead of them. McAdam, however, was not the only man who set out from Prince Albert to Fort McMurray. When, during June 1898, Inspector D. M. Howard of the NWMP patrolled that route and reached the trading outpost at La Loche, he was told of another adventurer and went to see him. This was a hardy lad of eleven by the name of Alexander McLeod, who had run away from his home in Prince Albert and joined a Yukon-bound party. After some weeks on the way that party had become worried about what to do with the boy and realized that it was a shame to encourage him to press on into the uncertain hazards ahead. With the men's acquiescence, Howard told the boy that he would have to take him back to his parents at Prince Albert, and in his report he said that young Alexander McLeod "seemed relieved."

From McMurray, Ernest Corp, who had come down from Athabasca Landing, found that

it was easy going to Lake Athabaska and Fort Chipewyan [which] was swarming with hungry, howling Indian dogs. Fish seemed to be the chief diet for both Indians and dogs. The Indians had nets out all the time, and would go out and bring in a boat load of fish when they felt like it and toss them out to the dogs. Between times, the dogs were more like a howling pack of wolves, and boats had to be watched all the time or the dogs would soon clean it out of anything eatable.

Leaving Chipewyan, our route lay across the end of the Lake, where a short river named the La Roche is found. This river, where it joins the

110

mouth of the Peace River, forms the Slave River, which runs into Great Slave Lake. The country between the Athabaska Lake and the mouth of the Peace River is practically flat, so that the waters of the Peace River coming from the South get to flood tide before the Lake has risen, causing the slow running La Roche River to reverse its flow and go back into the Lake for a day or two.

We had been told this by our guide, and, when the reverse flow started we got out and tracked our boat downstream to the junction of the Peace. Another party who were a few hours behind us happened to tie up for the night just before the reverse flow started. Next morning, starting out, they appeared to be going back upstream, and had quite an argument about it. Not knowing of this peculiarity of the river, they thought they were dreaming, so pulled ashore to figure out what was wrong. Soon another party came along and explained things, to their great relief. Here at the junction of the Peace River were great whirlpools. Our boat got sucked into one and was whirled round and round, and we had a hard time getting out of it.

Here at the mouth of the Peace River we came in contact with quite a number of men who had left Edmonton in the fall of -/97 to go overland to the Klondyke from there, some of whom we knew from Hamilton. It appears that the thrifty, wide-awake business men and storekeepers of Edmonton had hired a gang of men to cut a trail from Edmonton about fifty miles out into the country, supposedly in the direction of the Yukon, with a dead end, and called it the overland trail to Yukon. Many outfits started out with pack horses, or sleds, but few made it through, more turned back. I was told by several men who followed it through the winter that in the Swan Hills dead horses by the score lay across the trail. Those who got through to the Peace River, after a hard winter's trip, built boats and came down the river, where we met them.

While Corp's information was not wholly correct, when many of the overland parties reached Peace River Crossing they had endured all they could stand of pushing pack horses along tenuous trails. At that point during the spring of 1898 many of the parties split up, with some portions carrying on with horses and the rest, about a hundred men in all, making boats to go down the Peace. For instance, Dr. Brown, J. A. Grose, J. Bouret, T. G. Orchard and eight others, about half of the Brown-Morse group, went down the river. Practically all of the Willis party (Yukon Valley Prospecting and Mining Company) did so, as well as the Baudette party, G. W. Fugard and four men of his original large party and many others. By this time the Helpman party had split up also and five members, including Captain Hall, Dr. Hollwright and Messrs. Simpson and Bannister, went down the Peace. At Lake Athabasca or on the Slave River, the flotilla of the many hundreds who had recently left Fort McMurray was augmented by these boats that had come down the Peace. From the Slave River onward their boats and crews may be regarded as going by the Water Route.

To try to arrive at the number of Klondikers who passed through Fort Smith during 1898 we must first count all of the main contingent that left Athabasca Landing that spring and did not turn back – about 625. Then we must add three more groups: those who wintered along the water course above Fort Smith, some thirty; those who entered the Athabasca River at Fort McMurray, eighty; and finally the contingent of a hundred men who came down the Peace. In total these amount to about 835.

Eben McAdam's party reached Smith's Landing on May 27, but even though it was one of the leading groups, it experienced a long delay and had to wait its turn to get goods hauled over the portage. Furthermore, since McAdam decided to take the Hudson's Bay Company steamer as far as Fort Resolution, the party waited until June 20 when Captain Mills felt that conditions made it safe for his ship to proceed towards Great Slave Lake.

Meanwhile, boats filled with Klondikers arrived daily. On June 2, McAdam said: "Today 29 boats arrived. This is the largest number to arrive in one day. All came from Athabasca Landing. Anderson of Montreal arrived with his partner, nine men in three boats 'Rose' 'Shamrock' & 'Thistle.' The Anderson party & eleven other boats left to run the rapids after a rest of a couple of hours. There are quite a number of rapids to run – three have to be portaged. . . ."

W. Connors, a prominent trader, had recently left Edmonton for his trading post at Fort Smith and arrived there on June 8, just at the time when the press of Klondikers was trying to push its boats and supplies over the portage. During the next two weeks he and his staff took a hand in getting the larger boats across. Among these were the sternwheeler *Enterprise*, the Fargo party's screw steamer *Hendricks* and the *Manchester*. Then he set out for Edmonton once more and reported that the *Minne-ha-ha* and the *Garden City* were anxiously waiting to go across. On the way to Edmonton he met the Detroit party's iron propeller job on Lake Athabasca and the *Lillian B* and two of the Alaska Mining and Trading Company's boats at Sulphur River. The *Anna* and Wallwork's *Daisy Bell* were at Fort McMurray while the *Upas* was still at Athabasca Landing.

A. D. Stewart from Hamilton reached the Smith portage about the middle of July, 1898. From there he reported that Corporal Trotter of the NWMP estimated that since navigation opened that spring nine hundred to one thousand Klondikers had passed Fort Smith. The estimate appears to be too high.

Of the members of the Hamilton party, all busy at various tasks at Fort Smith, Stewart felt that one named Brock had suffered most, for he said: "Brock came in to supper that night with his face streaming with blood from the bites of the bulldog flies and presented such a sorry spectacle that we thought at first some accident had befallen him." While Brock had been troubled by insects, Stewart had his own grievances, for he said: "The native dogs which were continually prowling about were a source of great annoyance to us, and compelled us to keep a nightwatchman up to prevent our provisions being stolen. So persistent were these groups, that in spite of all our vigilance they succeeded in getting at our pork more than once, and actually stole two of our cooking pots to get at the drippings they contained."

Along similar lines is a comment of Alphonso Waterer, who had left the Pincher Creek country of southern Alberta and taken the Water Route. While his party was camped at the mouth of the Salt River near Fort Smith, he noted:

> The Indians had several nets stretched across the mouth of this creek. Their camp being about $\frac{1}{2}$ a mile up on the opposite bank and of course they had a large pack of dogs which were bolder than their half brothers the timber wolves and they were the most expert fishermen I ever saw. Swimming down the creek to the mouth they would stand on the bank and watch the nets and as soon as one of the floats went under water they would swim out, dive down exactly opposite to this particular float, take the fish out of the net and return to the bank with it, repeating the operation till their hunger was satisfied. I had bacon laid out to dry on a sail and they manoeuvred very skillfully to get some of it, but my shot-gun was rather too much for them.

While A. D. Stewart was at Fort Smith, he remarked that the Hudson's Bay Company steamer *Wrigley*, which had recently come upstream from Fort Simpson, had brought back from there "several broken-hearted men who had been up the Liard River prospecting, but who had found the work too hard and the discomforts too many, and were returning in desperation and disgust. Amongst them were two or three men suffering from the much-dreaded scurvy. They reported that one of their party, a man named Aitcheson [Atkinson?], from Saskatchewan, had died of the disease the previous February at Devil's Portage, and this, together with the fearful difficulties encountered on the Liard River, induced them to give up all further idea of gold-finding and get back to civilization as quickly as possible."

All unaware that he was foreshadowing his own fate, Stewart made these comments on scurvy:

> It is a complex morbid state, caused generally by long-continued privation of fresh, succulent vegetables or fruits or their juices. Symptoms – Sallow,

dusky hue of countenance and skin generally; swollen, spungy livid gums; foetid breath, disability; deafness; difficulty in breathing; sloughing of the gums; loosening of teeth; hemorrhage from nose, mouth, gums and stomach; swelling and stiffness of the legs; want of energy; great despondency; diarrhoea; dropsy; exhaustion. Treatment — Patient never to be left to himself; to be kept roused and interested; lime-juice, oranges, salads, fresh meat and vegetables, milk, wine or beer, iron, pure air, in recumbent posture.

It will be seen from the above what a frightful disease the miner lays himself liable to, and how difficult the cure must be with the crude resources at his command. The main thing, however, after endeavouring to get fresh meat and vegetables, is to fall back on liberal doses of lime-juice and keep the sufferer roused and away from himself to dispel the awful despondency which is characteristic of the disease, and which generally precedes the exhaustion which is followed by death.

Along with McAdam and Stewart and the steamboats, the hundreds of water-route Klondikers were held up at the sixteen-mile portage around the rapids to Fort Smith. Over this everything had to be hauled, and the long string of ox-drawn Red River carts, which had been adequate for the regular northern trade, was hopelessly overtaxed. The previous year the rate per hundred pounds for this service had been fifty cents, but the demand created by the competitive Klondikers had pushed it up to $1.50. That situation, however, was soon remedied. Billy Clark, the boatman, reported that "E. Nagle took down two teams of horses for use on the portage. The Alaska Mining and Transportation Company took two teams, Colin Fraser, of Chipewyan, bought two yoke of oxen and a team of horses from persons coming down Peace River, and the Hudson's Bay Company added 14 horses to their already large freighting outfit. Portage rates were reduced from a cent to half a cent a pound for the 16 miles."

Even then the Klondikers suffered vexatious delays. While their goods had to be hauled the whole distance, many of them ran their scows and boats down most of the rapids with the help of a pilot. When they came to the worst water at Mountain Rapids, however, even the boats had to be portaged.

Having brought the flood of 1898 Klondikers as far as Fort Smith and started them streaming down from there, let us now turn to the progress their colleagues of the previous year were making.

Gold washing with a "grizzly" at Edmonton, 1890

Gold dredges on the river at Edmonton, 1898

Mrs. Garner of the Fresno party

Some of the Garner (Fresno) party, 1897

The Fugard party
with toboggans, 1897-
pairs of poles in the
foreground are shafts

The Helpman or O'Brien party,
1897, camped adjacent to Fort
Edmonton—note Indian
tepees at the right

The Mason party on Jasper Avenue between 105 and 106 Streets looking east

The Ferris party, 1898-note packsaddle on the white horse

The Hastings-Crozier party

"Barrel" Smith's contrivance

To the Klondike with oxen—on Jasper Avenue between 103 and 104 Streets

Loaded pack horses in John A. McDougall's yard,
Jasper Avenue between 101 and 102 Streets

The Glen Campbell party, mainly
using toboggans, on the site of
the present Provincial Museum

Red River carts at Fort Smith, 1898

Athabasca Landing, 1898: the steamer *Boston*

Athabasca Landing, 1898: Jim Wallwork's paddle-wheeler the *Daisy Bell,* which he took to Dawson

Athabasca Landing, 1898: Klondikers building boats
—note Hudson's Bay Company steamer

The Jenner brothers' party, 1897

THE PIONEERS
OF THE WATER-ROUTE:
RETREAT, SUCCESS AND DEATH

Out of 106 Klondikers who were reported to have proceeded beyond Fort Smith in the fall of 1897, two women, Mrs. Craig and Mrs. Horsfall, and over eighty men ultimately reached the Dawson area. Sixty-two of these were actually seen in Dawson, while some twenty were reported to be speeding along the last easy downstream lap of their journey. Neither the NWMP, which had the responsibility for investigating rumours of accidents, nor anybody else reported these last as having any mishap. Of the remaining twenty-four who passed Fort Smith, eleven definitely returned to Edmonton or dropped out of the race and headed for civilization by way of Wrangell and a ship down the coast. Nearly a dozen others undoubtedly changed their minds and came back, but we have little record of them. Three died en route to the Yukon.

While these 106 were only a small part of the 860 adventurers who eventually took the Water Route, an examination of the ways they went, their struggles and their successes or failures, yields an understanding of what it meant to take the Edmonton route to the Klondike. Not only were they the vanguard of the much larger migration but their adventures or misadventures were typical of the trials and tribulations that lay in store for their successors. Studying the exploits of these 106 in some detail will provide us with a background of the perils of the route that would have to be faced by the 1898 contingent as well.

During the fall of 1897, twenty-three prospectors out of the 106 went up the Liard River from Fort Simpson. As they left that post, Chief Factor Camsell's sons Charles and Fred joined them, increasing the total of those bound up-river to twenty-five.

George Purches and George Filadeau spent the winter at Fort Liard, where they earned their keep by making thirteen thousand shingles for the Roman Catholic mission. N. Atkinson and P. de Wolf wintered at the mouth of the Nelson River and as far as we know stayed in that vicinity for some years trapping.

Several men were strung out in camps near the mouth of the Beaver River: Monty Velgue, who had been with Shand; T. H. Stephen, W. R. Howey, H. Woodward, A. Gibney and A. E. Lee, all of the Stephen-Howey party; Fred and Hal Jenner and their associates, A. S. Weeks and A. E. Schaefer. Shand had laboured along alone until he was at the hot springs where the modern Alaska Highway crosses the Liard. W. J. Graham and his associates, S. Schrieves of Edmonton, M. Meneely and Balaam (or Boland) of Sault Ste Marie, had all pushed on until they were near the Grand Canyon of the Liard. By the beginning of January the Graham group had split up, with Graham and Schrieves hurrying on ahead and Balaam and Meneely limping along behind. Because of either scurvy or freezing, one of Meneely's feet was intensely painful and nearly crippled him. As we have seen, the two men from Vernon, British Columbia, A. M. Pelly and D. W. Wright, the two Camsell's and Dan Carey and his son Willie were near Hell's Gate.

Of these twenty-five men, George Purches and George Filadeau, the two Jenners, A. S. Weeks, A. E. Schaefer, T. H. Stephen and W. R. Howey returned to Fort Simpson in the spring, while N. Atkinson and P. de Wolf remained near Fort Nelson for some time. This left fifteen men still working up the Liard.

Somewhat typical of the experiences of those who turned back was what happened to Stephen and Howey, who each had an interesting time before their return to Fort Simpson. After they went into winter quarters up the Liard, Howey made up his mind to head back to Edmonton by way of the Fort Nelson and Peace rivers. On October 16 he started paddling a pine bark canoe up the former but on the third day the canoe was so damaged that he had to abandon it and pack his supplies to Fort Nelson, which he reached on October 31. Then, setting out on foot with a sled and one dog on November 7, he tried to make his way up the dangerous new ice of the river; after a day or so he had to return to Fort Nelson. On November 12, with two dogs, he tried again, but after travelling upstream for two days he found the river open. He returned to the fort and shortly afterwards went back to where Stephen was camped.

After a few days both of them started out again with a train of five dogs and accompanied by two Indians with a team of three dogs. They reached Fort Nelson in nine days. When they got there Stephen was pretty badly used up by snowshoe sickness and a touch of scurvy.

While that alone might have been enough to deter them, they were also prevented from going farther because they could not buy any dog feed.

After a few days' rest, Stephen took three of the dogs, intending to go back to their old camp at the mouth of the Beaver River. In a day or so, his dogs played out because of lack of food. He shot them and started out alone, but even then was forced to return to Fort Nelson in an exhausted state.

Howey then decided to try the trip out to the Peace River alone. To save food he shot the two dogs he had kept and started out, hauling his own sled. The Beaver Indians, who kept an eye on any strangers wandering through their country, had told of some men who had spent a while fishing at some lakes between Fort Nelson and Fort St. John. Assuming that they were traders from Fort St. John and that if he could meet them he could accompany them home, Howey set out from Fort Nelson on February 8. After wandering around for over three weeks without finding either the lakes or the men, he came back to his starting point. Although he had not seen any white men, he did come upon a newly blazed tree on which Harry Garbett, Gilbert Velgue and W. P. Taylor had recently written their names. After resting at Fort Nelson for nearly a week, Howey spent fourteen days hauling his own supplies to the original camp at the mouth of the Beaver River. Stephen remained at Fort Nelson until the spring.

In this way, in exhausting and fruitless exertion, Stephen and Howey had used up practically all the winter. By winter's end they were quite resigned to waiting for the ice to go out so that they could float down the Liard to Fort Simpson.

During the winter, far up the Liard, scurvy had attacked Hal Jenner. By spring he had recovered somewhat and on May 9 he and his brother and the other two of the original party set out for Fort Simpson. They laid over for a few days at Fort Liard, where good meals, of which potatoes formed a large part, cleared up most of the scurvy. At Fort Simpson Hal, the only one of those who had been up the Liard to give up entirely, waited for the Hudson's Bay Company steamer to take him back towards Edmonton. His brother Fred, A. S. Weeks and A. E. Schaefer, went down to Fort McPherson where they became part of the contingent setting out over the mountains.

Stephen, Howey, George Purches and G. Filadeau, who also came back from the Liard, all went down the Mackenzie.

After accounting for those who turned back to Fort Simpson, we are left with fifteen men who in the spring of 1898 were still heading west up the Liard River. Of these, the Camsells, instead of going on to the Yukon as they could have done, decided to spend another year supporting themselves in the Cassiar country and did not return to Fort Simpson till 1899. Even though they did not complete the trip to the Klondike, their adventures in the Liard-Cassiar country illustrate the type of difficulty which the other Yukon-bound hopefuls endured.

Shortly after Christmas in 1897, Charles Camsell and A. M. Pelly had visited the Mud River Post at the mouth of the Kechika River and then returned to where their companions, Fred Camsell and Wright, were camped near Hell's Gate. On January 11 all of them took stock of their food supplies, which amounted to 1,050 pounds of flour, 300 pounds of bacon, 200 of beans, 100 of dried fruit, some rice, sugar and a few minor items. They also had a seven-foot whipsaw, a tent, stoves and blankets.

Early in February the four men reached the Devil's Gorge, some thirty miles upstream, camped there nine days and on February 22 got along as far as the hot springs. Once more they rested for a few days, worrying all the while about their supply of food and feed for the dogs and trying to augment it by hunting. On March 6, according to Fred Camsell's diary, "Wright went hunting and returned with five squirrels, 2 whisky Jacks and a partridge" – not a very satisfactory bag. Next day Fred Camsell went out and came back with one porcupine and a grouse. Although they were most capable frontiersmen, they killed only one moose all winter.

On March 17, Fred's diary recorded: "We now all have sleighs with runners, instead of toboggans. Charlie took 415 pounds, Wright 260 and myself 300, a total of 975 pounds. Pelly and Co. left for Klondike." "Co." in this case meant an Indian guide.

Pelly left the other three without any friction, for, as Charles Camsell said: "One thing. . . we never had to face, and that was quarrelling among ourselves. Certainly there was many an occasion for doing so, but we were all pretty experienced in this kind of life and realized the necessity for tolerance and self control. . . ." In that respect their temperaments were far more congenial than those of many of the other parties. At that point, as Charles Camsell said, all but Pelly had gradually come to the conclusion that there was not much use pushing on to the Klondike gold-fields because they felt that all available gold-bearing ground would have been staked by the time they reached Dawson. They decided, however, to try prospecting at Frances Lake.

The two Camsells and Wright with three dogs reached Frances Lake on April 29, 1898, and a month later, except for salt, tea and tobacco, had used up their stock of provisions. For the next six weeks they were forced to live on whatever they could get, and as Charles Camsell said: "During the interval of over two months we sampled every living thing that had flesh on it and could be killed with a gun; rabbits, ducks, geese, partridge, porcupine, squirrels, gulls, fish, fish hawks and finally wolf, all helped to keep us going. For the last six weeks of this period we never had more than two skimpy meals a day, and we had to work hard to get those. Occasionally we went a whole day without food and once in traditional style we had to eat stewed moccasins."

Failing to find either food or gold at Frances Lake, they made a boat and drifted back down to the Liard River. After being near starvation for weeks, they came upon two men cooking supper who turned out to be members of a Chicago group that had passed through Edmonton that spring. Pulling ashore, they asked the men for news of the outside world. Charles Camsell said of this occasion:

> They had with them a sketch map of this stream showing the location of the rich portions, a map which they said they had bought for some $300 from a man they had met in a saloon in the United States. Later we found several prospectors with copies of the same map, which the vendor must have sold to dozens of prospectors for the same amount. In one case the owner of the map told me he had got it from a friend while the two of them were engaged in shingling a barn in the Okanagan country in the State of Washington. The maps were no good, as these fellows found out later, and the person who sold them was probably never at the locality in his life.
>
> While this conversation was going on we watched the prospectors eating their lunch, but no invitation came to us to join them. When we offered to buy some food from them, they declined, saying that while they had supplies enough for three months in their boat they could not afford to dispose of any of it. . . . This was the first and only experience of my whole life in the north country, or among prospectors anywhere, that I was not invited to join in a meal when coming into a man's camp. I remember to this day the names of these two men, but the only excuse that I can make for them was that they were cheechacos. They came from Chicago and they had never been out in the wilds before. They did not understand the customs of the north country, and the spirit of hospitality that characterizes its people.

So the Camsells got into their boat and went downstream, where they soon met another group of 1898 prospectors who gladly fed them. These were members of the Patterson group from Collingwood, Ontario, and were men accustomed to the ways and the courtesies of the wilds. From that time on the Camsells worked in the Dease Lake and

Telegraph Creek regions until August 1899, when they descended the Liard to Fort Simpson.

The Camsells now drop from the race towards the Yukon, leaving thirteen men including Pelly who were still heading for the gold-fields. Eventually, after spending some months associated with the Camsells, D. W. Wright set out for the Yukon and got there. In due course, Dan Carey and his son also reached that destination, leaving a balance of only ten of those more stubborn Klondikers who had spent the winter of 1897-98 along the Liard between modern Nelson Forks and Watson Lake. These are Pelly, Shand and Velgue, Lee, Woodward and Gibney (originally with the Stephen-Howey party), and W. J. Graham and his companions, Schrieves, Meneely and Balaam.

Lee, Woodward and Gibney set out from the camp at the mouth of the Beaver River about March 1 and tried to work their way up the ice of the Liard. Conditions were so unfavourable that they returned to camp. A short time later, Lee and Velgue teamed up and went upstream until they fell in with Pelly. These three advanced till they reached the Mud River Post where, to lighten their loads, they sold most of their supplies. They felt certain that they could replenish these at one of Sylvester's posts at the mouth of Dease River. The trader there, however, had nothing left to sell. He did lend them two trains of dogs to go some one hundred miles up the Dease River to the post at McDame Creek, but it also was short of goods. Another eighteen miles up the river brought them to a Hudson's Bay post where they bought two hundred pounds of flour, one hundred of rice and a hundred of bacon, after which they turned downstream to the Liard. Along the Dease River they began meeting other Klondikers who had entered the area from Wrangell, on the coast, and from there on to the Klondike, Edmonton-based parties began to mingle with those who had started from Vancouver or Seattle. From the mouth of the Dease, Lee, Velgue and Pelly passed through the Liard canyon near modern Watson Lake and ascended the Liard about forty miles to the mouth of Frances River. Then they worked their way up its eighty-odd miles to Frances Lake.

Meanwhile, Shand had been pushing along alone, while Woodward and Gibney had kept each other company. At the same time, W. J. Graham and three of his original party, Schrieves, Balaam and Martin Meneely, had also been moving up the Liard. Before reaching the Devil's Gorge, however, Meneely had fallen behind and been left alone.

Eventually, Lee, Woodward, Gibney, Pelly, Velgue, Graham, Schrieves and Balaam reached the Frances Lake area as two or three separate groups, while Shand went on alone – nine men now. By this time some

120

prospectors from the coast had also reached Frances Lake. Finally, in several outfits, all left the lake by ascending the Finlayson River for some fifty miles to the height of land. Then, during the first days of June 1898, they descended Campbell Creek on their way to the Pelly. As soon as the depth of water permitted them to use boats, all stopped to whip-saw lumber and make them.

How simple it sounds to whip-saw lumber and make boats, and yet what a task! For hundreds of miles they had lugged along the awkward saws so that, when they needed a boat, all they would have to do would be to put up four posts six feet high, erect a platform and start to saw their own planks. After searching about for suitable trees, manhandling them to the platform, flattening each log on two sides with a broad axe and marking it for saw cuts, they could start sawing. For hour after endless hour one man stood on the platform drawing the saw up while, amid the flying dust, another stood below dragging it down. After days of tedious work they finally cut off enough two-inch planks for their boat. How simple, really – but what a hell of a job.

When this essential drudgery had been accomplished, the nine Edmonton-based Klondikers went whirling down towards the Yukon River, 280 miles away. Hoole Canyon, some forty miles down the Pelly, looked so dangerous that half the group portaged around it. Woodward, Schrieves and a man named Kennedy, who had come from the coast and had been weakened by scurvy, ran it in one boat, while Gibney and Balaam started out in another. Woodward's boat came through safely, but Gibney and Balaam were swamped and both drowned. Seeing the accident affected Kennedy so strongly that he dropped dead.

The remaining seven Edmonton-based men, including Shand, went on and about June 14 reached Dawson and disappointment. Within a few days Pelly returned to southern British Columbia. W. J. Graham, after looking around for a while, started a brickyard. All except one of the others had but indifferent success. That one was H. Woodward, who had secured a modest bench claim.

All of the ten Edmonton-based Klondikers who had reached Dawson – these seven, Wright, and Dan Carey and his son – had endured a difficult trip and some of them had been on the route from Edmonton since the previous August – over ten months. From November 7, 1897, until June they had been wandering in the wilderness from the mouth of the Beaver River a few miles below Nelson Forks, trying to complete that nine-hundred-mile portion of their trip to Dawson. At times they had been forced to turn back to await better weather or better ice conditions. At times they had spent weeks on end relaying their goods forward by three- or four-mile stages, and at times they had had to depart from their direct route to try to purchase more supplies. If ever men struggled on indomitably it was those ten who had ascended the Liard and who reached Dawson – those who led the way over the route which many were to use after them. And yet they were only ten out of twenty-five who had set out from Fort Simpson the previous year.

For those who failed to reach Dawson, the struggle had been even more fearful. It had been too much for Martin Meneely, who had been a member of Graham's party and who had been hopelessly hobbling along near the Devil's Portage. On December 28 he had energy enough for only a pitiful entry in his terse diary. "My partner deserted me and tried to cripple me further by taking my grub."

Alone from that time, suffering intensely and knowing what lay ahead of him, he kept on as well as he could and on January 5 made the last entry in his diary. "Walked eight miles on my awful foot and am crippled on an island alone. The pain in my foot is terrible."

At his last camp, twelve miles below Devil's Portage, he erected his tent, placed his goods in it and lay down, watching the streak of snow sifting through the flap of the tent and listening to the rustle of the wind as it bellied the canvas in and out – listening for the approach of help – listening for voices of succour – for voices that were to be nine months coming.

When they came, after the long winter had ended and another summer had gone, it was E. T. Cole of a party from Minnesota and Octave La Chapelle of Edmonton who looked into the tent. Piled beside the remains were the remnants of what had been some meat, a knife, compass, Martin-Henry rifle, twenty-five rounds of cartridges, twenty pounds of flour, matches, wood and a few scraps of paper. On them were the entries given above and an address, "Isaac Scott, Box 52, Sault Ste. Marie, Ontario."

The score for the twenty-five who set out up the Liard from Fort Simpson during the fall of 1897 was hardly auspicious. Ten got to Dawson, four remained in the Cassiar for a year at least, eight went back to Fort Simpson and three died.

Of the eight who returned to Fort Simpson, Hal Jenner made his way to Edmonton as soon as he could. The other seven went down the Mackenzie, although four of them ultimately gave up and came back to Edmonton. By the time the seven were ready to leave Fort Simpson, some of the group of sixty men and two women who had not been up the Liard but had wintered at or above Fort Simpson were also ready to start down the main river. Before long all of them had passed Fort Simpson.

Preceding them the fall before, of course, had been the nine-man Segers-Hardisty group, which, instead of going up the Liard, kept on down to the mouth of the Mackenzie, and the Pilon party which wintered on the North Nahanni. When these are included, a total of eighty-one men and two women of the 1897 vintage made their way to the Mackenzie delta. Of these, Mrs. A. C. Craig, Mrs. Horsfall and seventy men ultimately reached the gold-fields.

It would be tedious to follow the adventures of all these men and women in detail, even if we could. Of some parties and some individuals we know a great deal, but of others we know scarcely anything, except for occasional references. We do know enough to follow some of the main parties and to see how they split up, regrouped and then split up again, and to marvel at how various were the routes they chose to take below Fort Simpson.

West of the Mackenzie River the Mackenzie and Richardson mountain ranges constitute the height of land separating the Mackenzie from the Yukon River watershed. Of the dozens of streams flowing more or less northeast off these mountains, some of which could have been used as routes to the Yukon, all but a handful of the Klondikers became enamoured of four. The mouth of the first, the Gravel River (since renamed the Keele), was fifty miles upstream from Fort Norman, while the second, the Arctic Red River, discharged its waters about twenty miles above the Mackenzie delta. The third was the Rat River which flowed into the Peel River downstream from Fort McPherson, within a few miles of where the fourth stream, the Peel, spread out into the delta. Most of the bustle generated by the 1897 and the 1898 Klondikers, however, was concentrated in the triangle formed by the trading posts of Arctic Red River and Fort McPherson and the mouth of the Peel River. For this area, Fort McPherson was the focal point at which they got their bearings and made up their minds which of the alternatives they would use to cross the summit of the Richardson Mountains, some forty-five miles due west.

The Segers-Hardisty party had been the first to reach the Mackenzie delta. On arrival it split up and, as we already have seen, when the winter of 1897-98 set in F. M. Robertson, M. Sutherland, W. D. and M. Matheson took their supplies to LaPierre's House by dog-team, ready to go ahead at the first opportunity. The others, Captain Segers, F. A. Hardisty, S. A. McNeill, F. G. Taylor, Dr. G. Macdonald and A. Adamson remained at Fort McPherson where they remodelled their boat and waited for the spring break-up to float down the Peel to the mouth of Rat River, which they planned to ascend on the way to LaPierre's House.

F. M. Robertson and his associates reached Dawson weeks ahead of Segers and his men. The Robertson group spent all winter in an old Hudson's Bay Company shack, twelve by fifteen feet in size, at La-Pierre's House, which was the point at which the Bell River became navigable. By February they had cut enough logs for boats and before long whip-sawed them into planks. When on May 26 the ice went out, they floated down the remaining forty miles of the Bell River to the Porcupine River. In due course they passed the site of the modern Indian village of Old Crow and continued through the ramparts of the Porcupine.

There some driftwood struck Robertson's boat and sank it. He and Sutherland saved themselves by grabbing passing logs. Sutherland got to shore but when Robertson's log turned in the water he lost his hold. Fortunately he was able to reach the upturned boat and finally pulled himself onto a rock in mid-stream. There he spent twenty-four hours while his campanions went on to the Hudson's Bay Company's Rampart House and procured a long enough rope to rescue him.

A few days later, on June 1, the four men reached Fort Yukon at the mouth of the Porcupine. There they waited for an upward-bound steamer which landed them in Dawson on June 9, the first of those who set out from Edmonton to reach their goal. They had beaten Lee and his party, who came in by the Liard, by five days.

During the winter the remainder of the Segers party tried unsuccessfully to get enough dog feed to allow them to transport their outfit across to LaPierre's House. As a result of the delay, until May 29 they sat out the winter at Fort McPherson. Then, after hiring five Indians, they went the few miles back down the Peel to the mouth of Rat River and started manhandling their 31 by 5½-foot boat up its uncertain waters. Because the boat was still so large it was a slow, tedious process. On the way, six other boats of about twenty-foot length including those of the Langworthy party, which had spent the winter over a thousand miles up the Mackenzie at Fort Resolution, passed them. In many places they had to cut a channel and several times had to dam the stream to raise the water level. For a mile and a quarter at the summit they rolled the boat on skids. Although Segers's large boat was a severe handicap, he and his men reached LaPierre's House in July, nearly a month after their former colleagues Robertson and his associates had reached Dawson. Once Segers got to LaPierre's House, of course, his long, heavy boat was an advantage in descending the Bell and Porcupine rivers, and he and his group made good time to Fort Yukon. There they paid twenty-five dollars each for passage on a steamboat to Dawson, where they arrived on August 3.

Meanwhile, four of the Pilon party came back down the North Nahanni and thence floated downstream to Fort McPherson. It is likely that they had not gone far up that river because during the winter E. St. Jean came back to Fort Simpson. In the spring he teamed up with W. R. Howey and George Purches and went down to Fort McPherson where he rejoined the rest of the Pilon group.

That spring, four relatives of the Pilon party from the settlement near Fort Saskatchewan made a remarkable trip. They set out from Athabasca Landing about May 1, 1898, and reached Fort McPherson shortly after the Pilon group did. These four, Fred and Alex Lamoureux, Charles Lemire and his brother, actually reached Dawson on July 25, to make the fastest trip on record up to that time – eighty-six days. The Pilon party of five, which had been nearly a year on the way, and these additional four men all reached Dawson about the same time. Unfortunately one of the Lamoureux boys, we are not certain which, is reported to have succumbed to some illness there.

Both Stephen and Howey, who had come back down the Liard, went down the Mackenzie and attempted to cross by the Rat River route before giving up and catching the Hudson's Bay Company's steamer heading back to Edmonton. When Howey reached Edmonton, the *Bulletin* reported:

> In company with a man named Bond Mr. Howey attempted to cross over from the Peel to the Porcupine by way of Rat River. They had a skiff, with about 1600 pounds of cargo and an Indian guide. In the swift water they doubled with Purches and Filadeau. The latter two went through. Had Howey and Bond been more lightly loaded, say 1,000 pounds to the boat they could have got through. As it was they found the labor and delay greater than the value of the supplies. After returning down the Rat river Bond walked across the portage [Stony Creek] to La Pierre's house. . . .
>
> The ordinary charge for packing across the portage from McPherson to La Pierre's house was $12 per 100. Time, five to six days with loads of 50 to 100 pounds, and two to three days returning light. Of course much higher prices were paid by the prospectors. The principal cost was not what the Indians charged so much as what the miners gave away.

In addition to the men who had been up the Liard and who had come back to Fort Simpson in the spring, the 1897 parties that had wintered far up the Mackenzie began arriving at Fort McPherson. The Langworthy party, which had wintered at Fort Resolution and at Hay River, reached the mouth of the Rat River on June 5. These men ascended the short stretch of the Peel to Fort McPherson, where Woolley decided to try prospecting east of the mountains, threw in his lot with L. Graham of the Warmolts party and continued up the Peel. Eventually Woolley and Graham came back down the Peel and crossed the Rat River route to Dawson.

Three months later, when Langworthy returned from Dawson, he gave the *Bulletin* a good description of the route up the Rat River, saying that at that stage the "river was very rapid and shallow and tracking was most difficult especially with a heavy boat."

After toiling up it for twenty or thirty miles, Langworthy turned up a crooked, sluggish creek coming in from the west. It led to a chain of lakes lying in McDougall Pass. He packed over two small portages between lakes on the east side of the summit and another of two miles to the waters of the Porcupine. This portage was level and each party hauled its boats across. At this point the Pilon party, which had a very easily handled boat, caught up to him.

Beyond Loon Lake on the west side of the summit, a small stream led into Bell River, which in its turn fell into the Porcupine. The Langworthy party made a run of eight days from the summit to Fort Yukon. There, like Segers, it waited another eight days for a steamer going up the four hundred miles of the Yukon River to Dawson. The supplies with which it had left Edmonton were pretty well used up by that time.

H. Anthony, who had wintered at Fort Resolution, hurried down the Mackenzie in the spring and somewhere in the vicinity of LaPierre's House joined Purches and Filadeau and the Pembroke party. Writing back from a point near the mouth of the Porcupine River he said that, whereas he had persevered, several boats of Klondikers had found the Rat River rapids too hard to ascend, turned back to Fort McPherson and then crossed the summit by way of Stony Creek.

Following hard on Langworthy's group, the Duluth party set out from the vicinity of Fort Providence and reached the mouth of the Peel. Thereafter six of them crossed the Richardson Mountains, including Belleveau, who perished before he got to Dawson. One of the six, Charles Hall, did not get to LaPierre's House that fall but came back to winter near Fort McPherson and went on to the Yukon the next year. Two of the Duluth party came back up the Mackenzie to Edmonton in the fall of 1898.

For some time after the Duluth party reached Fort McPherson, other boats arrived daily. The water-route Fresno party, which had camped at Fort Simpson for the winter, reached the mouth of the Peel next. All five of its members crossed the summit, but Alex Holmes never reached Dawson. The Panet party from Montreal, which included Ransom, the correspondent for the *Montreal Star*, and to which Campbell Young of Edmonton attached himself at Wrigley, met with a misadventure. After reaching the mouth of Arctic Red River on June 5, its members became separated. Three went ahead in a canoe, leaving the rest of the party on the scow to come along in its own good time. That good time turned out to be several long days, because the scow missed the mouth of the Peel where it should have left the main stream and kept on down into the Mackenzie delta. The men did not realize their mistake until they reached salt water. The long haul tracking back to the mouth of the Peel was a laborious and vexing business, but eventually the whole party was reunited.

In getting up the Rat River each party had its vicissitudes, its successes and failures, its own methods and improvisations. Some made good time, others were disappointed. While other lighter boats were overtaking them, the men of the Panet party, for example, had a difficult time ascending the Rat River rapids. Finally they gave up and turned back down the Rat River, with the intention of trying to cross the Stony Creek portage. After purchasing three skin boats, making two others, and hiring some Indians to carry part of their goods, they started up the creek. On the way Panet's boat was swamped and the men lost a good deal of their supplies. As Ransom wrote to the *Montreal Star*:

> In five days work upstream they reached the point to which the Indians had packed overland in half a day. After taking on their full loads they made seven miles the first day. In some places they had to dig a channel to get through and cut away brush. On July 4th there was a heavy snow storm. They were then amongst the mountains twelve miles from the summit. On July 12th they reached the summit, 1,150 feet above Peel river.
>
> On July 15th they left the Summit lake to go down stream, and entered a small creek which had to be widened to let the boats through. On July 25th they passed Rampart House on the Porcupine at the boundary between Canada and Alaska.

A. H. Griffin and Ernest Crabbe of Edmonton and Neil Marshall of Sarnia wintered at Fort Resolution. Charles Griffin stayed at Great Slave Lake to prospect its shores. Eventually the remainder of the party tried to ascend the Rat River in company with Frasier of the Fresno party, a man named Short and Ernest George. Frasier, Short and Marshall went over the summit into the Yukon Territory, but A. H. Griffin and Ernest George gave up and returned to Edmonton. Shortly afterward, Charles Griffin also came back from Great Slave Lake.

The McKenzie brothers from Beaver Lake also crossed into the Yukon by way of the Rat River. When Rod McKenzie returned to Edmonton a year later, he gave a good description of the McDougall Pass to the editor of the *Bulletin*. It concluded:

> ... it will be seen that there is only one half mile portage which always has to be made on this route, with one quarter mile and one half mile that sometimes can be avoided, a mile and a quarter in all. The distance through the pass from Trout river on the east, to Rat river on the west is about twelve miles, and although the summit is crossed in this distance there is scarcely any ascent and the ground is level and not difficult in any way. Consequently the portages are easily made. The greater part of the labor and delay is in ascending Trout river. There are 301 small rapids in the 61 miles of its course to the junction of Rat river. The rapids are only small, but their number and the shallowness of the water make the difficulty of tracking loaded boats up very great.

No records seem to be available to show what became of the three men who were deserted by the famous Merriweather. Since no one commented on them after Inspector Routledge saw them at Grand Rapids, it seems probable that eventually they turned back to Edmonton. The other Chicago party, however, the one-time Warmolts party, which also experienced disappointment with its leader, fared better. At least seven of its members went on to Dawson by way of Rat River. These seven included the courageous Mrs. A. C. Craig and her husband. Before reaching the gold-fields, however, the party split into fragments which teamed up with other Klondikers. Five of the party reached Dawson about the first of August 1898 but Mr. and Mrs. Craig were delayed, spending the winter of 1898-99 along the Peel River before going on to the Klondike. So did Henry Card, a deputy leader of the original group. Of the men of this party who had spent the winter of 1897-98 along the Mackenzie River, only R. M. Springer, J. H. Cantner and E. Buck definitely returned to Edmonton. Like Mr. and Mrs. Horsfall, the others who are unaccounted for most likely reached Dawson without incident.

From the time the unfortunate Pembroke party left Fort Simpson until it was in the Bell River region it was closely associated with R. H. Milvain. Towards the end of April when his feet were healed enough to travel and before the ice became too weak to bear weight, Milvain and another man set out down the river. They intended to meet Garnett and go on, but, Milvain said in his memoirs:

> I found poor Garnett in a bad way. He had been taken down with scurvy a few weeks before and could only get about with difficulty. I was in hopes

that he would improve with the warm weather and it was with great anxiety that we longed for the river to break up, so that we might get him down to Simpson. The river broke on the 13th May. A few days later we carried Garnett on board our boat, one of our friends came with us. We started off in spite of the fact that the river was full of ice. It took us nearly 2 weeks to get to Simpson. We found the river jammed a few miles below camp and had to wait 4 days before it went out. If we have not been so anxious about Garnett, we should have enjoyed watching this jam. All night and day, an enormous body of ice was grinding into the jam, forcing enormous blocks of ice and huge boulders up the bank 20 feet above high water mark. All this time the river was rising. Finally, when the pressure got too great, the whole mass moved off with a roar that could be heard for miles. We were delayed several times by similar jams and were thankful to see Simpson at last. Garnett by this time was quite unable to move and was very weak. We soon had him in a comfortable bed, and on a diet of milk and raw potatoes he made a wonderful recovery.

Once Garnett got to Fort Simpson he remained there for two months recuperating. Milvain went on down the Mackenzie with the Pembroke group. They stayed at Fort McPherson for about a week and, Milvain continued, were

lucky enough in seeing the Indians arrive after their winter up the Peel. About 100 of them came down in 7 large boats made of caribou skins, loaded with dry caribou and furs. The tribe was much the finest lot of Indians we had seen. They are bigger men and more intelligent. They are meat eating Indians and the difference between them and the Slave Indians who live entirely on fish, is very marked. . . .

Mr. Firth, the Factor at McPherson, is a fine sample of the Company's servant. At the time I met him, he had been on the Mackenzie River over 40 years without going out. He was an Orkney Islander and had come out to the far north when he was 16 years old. . . .

In July, along with Moffatt, Ritchie, Irving and McPhee of the Pembroke party and two men from the Fresno and Duluth water-route groups, Milvain decided to cross the portage which went up Stony Creek. His memoir goes on:

One evening about 5 o'clock we started off – 7 of us and 4 Indians. Each Indian carrying 100 lbs. besides sufficient dried caribou to last them the trip, in all about 125 lbs. They carry the load well up on their shoulders, held on by a strap across the forehead. Each Indian had 2 dogs carrying from 20 lbs. to 30 lbs. each. The cavalcade was completed by my 4 dogs, for which I had traded my boat and what provisions were left over.

Our troubles began the first camp out of McPherson; one of my Indians wanted bacon and on being refused, turned sulky. Next evening when we got out, we found the Indian had disappeared, so there was nothing for it but for me to carry his pack.

We made about 15 miles a day, the trail was not bad. It crossed the Rocky Mountains, which are practically rolling hills at this point. The mosquitoes were bad and for a greenhorn packing is hard work. We used to rest 5 minutes every mile. We had several streams to cross, some of them very high and swift. One could not help but admire the Indians. At some of the crossings, they put the dog packs on top of their own, making close on 200 lbs. and walked across these raging torrents without any trouble. I had to have my pack carried across and even then had to get an Indian to help me, my toes bothered me a good deal.

We got to La Pierre House on the 6th day, and uncommon glad one of us was to see it.

When these men reached the Porcupine River all they had to do was to float down it, as so many other parties had done, and within a couple of weeks they would have been in Dawson. In fact, that is what Milvain and Irving did, and they reached Fort Yukon in thirteen days. Milvain said: "[We] had expected to make the trip in half the time, but the water was low and we had a great deal of trouble getting the raft through some of the shallows. We had nothing left but flour and not much of that for the last 4 or 5 days. We used to plan what a great feast we would have when we got to Fort Yukon, but alas, when we arrived we found there was nothing left but some very ancient bacon, sugar, flour and tea, so we did the best we could with that."

At Fort Yukon, Milvain said he and Irving "had plenty to amuse us 6 days we had to wait for a steamer. There were lots of duck and geese to watch and a constant procession of boats, loaded with disgusted people on their way out via St. Michaels. A lot of them had got so homesick and disgusted before they got to Dawson that they had not stopped at all. . . ."

When young Roy Moffatt reached the Porcupine River he was so jubilant at actually being in the Yukon Territory that he wrote home telling of his immediate plans. A couple of weeks later Irving mailed the letter in Dawson. It said:

My Dear Parents:
. . . We were in the mountains, on Rat river, and got up about 40 or 45 miles when we had to turn back as our boat drew too much water to go through, and the water was falling fast. We decided to go back to the fort and pack our goods across the summit, a distance of something over 85 miles, which we accomplished with the aid of 12 Indians and about 30 dogs. . . . After crossing the mountains we landed at La Pierre House, an abandoned H.B. post situated on Bell river about 40 miles from the Porcupine. It was quite strange to see the flowers in bloom on the moun-

tains and snow in some places 20 feet deep not 40 yards away from the flowers, but such was the case and under the moss in which the flowers grew was frozen ground not a foot from the surface. You would feel the ice when walking through the moss. We arrived at the Porcupine safely and all are quite well. Prospected the mouth and got plenty of colors, and think the indications good. We have nine dogs and will make them haul us up the Porcupine as far as we want to go, if we can get fish or moose enough to feed them. Ed. Irving is going to Dawson with another young fellow and will meet us there, if nothing goes wrong, which we trust will not. We propose ascending the river till we get something good and will then cross the mountains to the Yukon. We are still very hopeful and will stick to it as long as we can. Ed. Irving goes to secure provisions for the winter and attend to some mining matters. I trust you have felt no uneasiness on our account as we have never been sick a day since we left and no accidents have happened to us. I expect many people will come into this country this year and many go out sadly disappointed. No one who is not prepared to stand a great deal of hardship should think of coming. I never thought that mosquitoes could be so bad and they are only one of the many hardships to which I refer.

The report about gold on the Liard was bogus and the party who sent out that report was like the Liard minus the d. Nearly all the miners who went up it came down this spring and went around by Peel river. Address your letters to Dawson City and we will get them when we go there in the fall.

Your Loving Son,
ROY

Then Ritchie, McPhee and Moffatt, along with Belleveau, formerly of the Duluth party, and Alex Holmes, who had left Edmonton with a Fresno group, all set out prospecting up the Porcupine. For over three months they worked slowly up the river, panning here and there without success, and by fall were close to a tributary of the Fishing Creek. By the middle of August they had finished their small supply of flour, bacon and tea and from then on lived on what they killed – caribou, moose, geese and fish. In September there were thousands of caribou around them, but they delayed killing their winter food; the weather was warm and they intended to wait till it was cold enough to be sure the meat would keep. When they awoke one morning the caribou had disappeared.

By the end of October they began to worry. Rather than go back a greater distance down the Porcupine to LaPierre's House, the best prospect seemed to be to cross over the summit of the mountains and start down the Tadonduk River, which eventually ran into the Yukon near Forty Mile. On October 31 all five started out, but next day

Holmes broke through the ice and froze his feet so severely that he could not face the long trip ahead. He decided that his best chance was to return to the Fishing Creek, which had a good pool, where he hoped to live by catching salmon. He asked Belleveau to go back with him, which his friend was glad to do. The other three, the men from Pembroke, talked the matter over and, because Belleveau was known to be a very poor shot, Moffatt agreed to accompany Holmes and Belleveau. At this time they divided up their four or five days' supply of food and gave the bulk of it to the Holmes group.

Then Ritchie and McPhee, taking very little food with them, set out for the mouth of the Tadonduk with the four dogs by means of which they hoped to rush back more supplies to the sick man and his two companions. They were ten days reaching the mouth of the river and there, weak from starvation, they staggered into Lee Pate's cabin. They had barely made it. McPhee was suffering so severely with scurvy that he was weeks recovering. For two days Pate cared for them, feeding them small quantities at short intervals, and in a few days Ritchie was well enough to set out again.

Pate and one of his companions loaded up some food and accompanied Ritchie back to the relief of his comrades. They were nine days reaching the camp by the fishing hole where they hoped to find the unfortunate men. All they found was a note saying that they had finished the meat and eaten the dogs and had determined to travel down-river in the hope of meeting some Indians. Ritchie and Pate searched for them until for want of food they had to turn back. The following summer, a few miles from the camp, a party of Mounted Police found their bones.

Roy Moffatt, the young man who had written home so confidently and who, when the chips were down, volunteered to go back with the sick man, paid for his kindness with his life.

In these pages we have been giving the stories of those parties and individuals about whom we have considerable information. There were others among the 106 who spent the winter of 1897-98 north of Fort Smith whose experiences must have been very similar. From occasional references, sometimes in unexpected places, we know that some went on to Dawson and some came back to Edmonton. To trace the movements of every adventurer would be merely redundant, and it would, of course, prove impossible for the small number of prospectors who slipped down the Mackenzie without fanfare, and, therefore, without any record.

As near as we can tell, over seventy of the whole group reached the Yukon by way of Fort McPherson, while ten went to Dawson by ascending the Liard. Therefore, of those who left Edmonton in 1897 by the Water Route about eighty per cent reached the gold-fields safely. Along the main route there was only one death – Patterson of Hamilton, who was drowned in the Grand Rapids of the Athabasca. Three of the water-route prospectors who ascended the Liard died. These four casualties are not a large number considering the many men involved, the inexperience of some, and the situations they faced over a period of practically a year.

The trip down the Mackenzie itself was not difficult. If, of course, a group started rather late in the year, like most of those who left Edmonton in 1897, they knew that they would have to pass the worst of the winter in a shack somewhere. But as the year 1898 was to demonstrate, anyone who left Athabasca Landing at the time the ice went out had a chance of a relatively quick trip right through to Dawson. The main part of the journey consisted of coasting down the Mackenzie water system for five or six weeks. That part was easy. The strenuous work came on the 115-mile haul from Fort McPherson, across the summit of the Richardson Mountains to LaPierre's House. On that stretch the Klondikers had to push and pull and pack and drag everything up to the summit. But with reasonable luck, many of the parties got over to LaPierre's House in two weeks. After that, about two weeks of risky downstream navigation swept them on to the Yukon River.

Undoubtedly the Mackenzie route would not have seemed unduly arduous to the first score of Klondikers who took it because they were all Edmonton men and to some extent their experiences were mainly a repetition of many similar trials and risks borne on other trips out into the hinterland. Actually some fifty, or about half of the 1897 water-route Klondikers, came from Edmonton and its relatively small adjoining homestead area, while another half-dozen were from other parts of Alberta. Of the fifty, forty-two got through to the Yukon. Tackling the trip to the Klondike was evidently the type of thing they were used to. Of the remainder, about twenty-five came from other parts of Canada and twenty-five more came from the United States.

Some of the 1897 group remained at Fort McPherson even during the winter of 1898-99 and did not get to the Yukon till the summer of 1899. To confuse the picture even further, several who left Edmonton in the spring of 1898 got across that summer. Amongst these, of course, were the Lamoureux clan from near Fort Saskatchewan and G. M. Dyer, the one-time representative of a large New York life insurance company – but perhaps he was in a hurry.

Many of those who got through to Dawson had not originally committed themselves to go that far. They had started from Edmonton with the idea of enjoying the exciting possibility of getting far enough into the Cassiar or the Mackenzie or Richardson mountains to discover a gold-bearing stream and then to work it. No Klondiker anywhere could pass a stream without bending down to "try a pan." Among the hundreds of streams on the way to the Klondike they felt that many must be richly gold bearing. Each man intended that when he and his partners found that stream, no matter where, they would stop and work it, and, who knows? — maybe get rich. If, in spite of trying stream after stream, luck did not lie in their pans, they would press on. As one man writing from Dawson on August 27, 1899, said. "I was among the principal part of these people when they were passing the Athabasca rapids, as you know, and the destination of 70 per cent of them was not the Klondike, but the other side of the mountains, such as Peel, Gravel, Liard and Frances rivers. When nothing was found there the only remaining thing to be done was either to go back or get through the best way they could. And some came through the most outlandish routes possible. . . ."

Then, too, there were those men who, although hoping to find gold, would not have been too disappointed if they never did, so long as they could be on the move or could build a shack somewhere and pause for a year or two to trap or trade and do a little panning on the side. For even though in movies and other romantic trash the theme has been played to death, the North is nevertheless a vast region that stirs strong emotions. Men love it passionately or, rarely, hate it, but are never lukewarm. With its vast valleys, its great rivers and its unknown lakes, it calls men back again and again. As a result, somewhere along the way several Klondikers simply dropped out of the race and spent the rest of their lives in great contentment in the solitude of the North.

CHAPTER TEN

THE RIVER ROUTE
FROM FORT SMITH
TO FORT McPHERSON, 1898

Sweating, swearing and swatting mosquitoes, the 1898 Klondikers finally got past the delay of the Smith portage. Soon, along the 170 miles
from Fort Resolution to Fort Providence, in steamers, scows and stur-
geon-heads, they became a series of dots bobbing over Great Slave
Lake. Most of the scores heading west rowed their boats or steered
their steamers along the south shore of this long inland sea. Some
found its rolling waves too much for them and lay storm-bound for
days. Some found these waves washing the last gleam of gold from their
eyes and they returned to Edmonton. Yet all but a few pressed on.

The stormy lake dealt most harshly with the party from Sandon,
British Columbia, which included Joe Schneider, J. A. Hoffmeir, a
German girl named Rosie, Frank Hoffman and his pregnant wife. It
smashed their boat on a rock, carried away most of their supplies, and
drowned Hoffman. When the survivors got to shore and reorganized,
Hoffmeir gave up and started for home, but Mrs. Hoffman and Schnei-
der joined forces with another party and went on. Rumours among the
Klondikers spoke of a romantic triangle in the incident.

A. D. Stewart, however, met and felt sorry for Mrs. Hoffman. He
wrote: "The wretched widow is in a most deplorable condition. She
has lost nearly all her provisions and most of her clothing; her husband
and protector is dead; she is thousands of miles from her German home;
and her coming confinement stares her in the face. What will become
of her? What can be done for her? God pity and help the poor creature!"

Great Slave Lake's storms even exacted their toll from the handful
of steam launches, most of which are as hard to follow as the individual
Klondikers. Although there is little information about some of them,
thirteen out of all the steam-driven boats of one sort or another that
left Athabasca Landing were said to have crossed the Smith portage.

The *Chesrown*, owned by the Alaska Mining and Trading Company, was moved over the Smith portage but seems to have remained tied up there while the Klondikers swept on by it and went down the Mackenzie. The *Manchester* saw service on the lake, and the *Minne-ha-ha*, belonging to the Minneapolis party, puffed her way west into the Mackenzie. The fifty-foot steel-hulled, propeller-driven *Enterprise*, which at that stage was the property of a Detroit party, also completed the long crossing to Fort Providence. The *Lillian B* crossed the portage. For one little canvas-covered steamer, however, the waves of the huge lake were too powerful and wrecked her near Hay River.

One small sternwheeler, the *Daisy Bell*, Jim Wallwork's pride and joy, crossed Great Slave Lake without undue effort but not without an interesting incident. Below the Smith portage Jim had been towing a party which decided to hijack his *Daisy Bell* and leave him stranded. Fortunately two prospectors, Cadzow and Erickson, took his part. After he and the *Daisy Bell* escaped through the few shots that were fired, he agreed to tow his benefactors' scow and also John "Steamboat" Wilson's spoon-boat and York boat, hauling the lot down to the mouth of the Rat River. Crossing Great Slave Lake Wilson's party consisted of a marine engineer from Glasgow named Sandy McDonald, Charles Fowler, Chappie Jackson, Gus Breacher, and two men whom Wallwork described as ill-humoured helpers, Duncan McCallum and Tom Leo.

John Wilson, a remarkable man, was a lawyer who in 1895-96 had been mayor of Kalgoorlie, Australia, and had had occasion to go to London, England, on business. When passing through Canada on his way home, he was caught up in the Klondike Rush. Eventually, after reaching and leaving Dawson, he returned to Australia where he became an officer in a cavalry regiment that went to the South African War. When that affair was over he started a law business in Johannesburg but eventually went back to Australia and got married. Even marriage did not mute the call of adventure, for within a year or so he headed an expedition to Peru in search of Inca treasure. At Lima he died of food poisoning.

Like Wallwork's *Daisy Bell*, most of the steamboats made reasonable time along the long lake. In spite of having to pull into shore or to an island at frequent intervals to cut wood to fire their little furnaces, they puffed along. Those who manhandled their craft had no need for wood except for cooking but every night they too pulled in to shore to camp. With so many Klondikers stopping here and there all along the lake, it was no wonder that some of them cast a speculative eye on the surrounding terrain, and especially at the pre-Cambrian rocks of its islands and its north shore. Some spent a short while sniffing for minerals but most merely made a mental note to have a look at the area sometime in the future. A few who decided that prospects looked as good as any they might have if they continued to the Yukon stayed to study the strata of Great Slave Lake's shores.

One group that did this was the Willis or Yukon Valley Prospecting and Mining Company. Once this party of thirty men reached the lake, its leader decided that W. J. McLean, the one-time Hudson's Bay man, Willis and nine others had better see what prospects it offered, while J. M. Swigert led the remaining nineteen men off to the Yukon. The Willis party used the steamer *Lillian B* as a base for prospecting out into the northeast arm of the huge lake and located claims about two hundred miles from Fort Resolution.

Another group that decided Great Slave Lake looked much more promising than the remote Yukon consisted of Captain Hall, Dr. Hollwright and Messrs. Simpson and Bannister, who had split off from the Helpman party and had descended the Peace River. Since the area along the south shore of the lake west of Fort Resolution appealed to them, they spent the winter in that vicinity.

Some of the Holt party and a few other Klondikers also liked the looks of the Great Slave Lake area. Others, like W. A. Oliver and his companions from Edmonton, made a wide swing into the eastern end of the lake but decided to head for the Yukon after all. In all, about forty men fell out of the main rush to the Yukon and began investigating and staking quartz claims near the long, chilly lake.

The rest of the 1898 hopefuls, however, nearly seven hundred of them, made what speed they could to the outflow of the Mackenzie River. In a variety of craft and with a diversity of adventures or misadventures, the cheerful but thinly extended throng, keeping close to the marshy, forested or rocky shores of Great Slave Lake, hastened westward. Bobbing along in the boats sat the seven women who had had the courage to throw in their lot with the 1898 water-borne Klondikers: Rosie, the German girl, Mrs. Hoffman, Miss Jones, who had accompanied her brother from England, and Mrs. Lampman from Williston, North Dakota, Mrs. Le Francois from Woonsocket, a Mrs. Brown, cheerfully encouraging her husband in his venture, and Mrs. C. Westhead, who came with her husband from a homestead at Buffalo Lake, Alberta, and whose first name, Alix, was in due course given to a town in that area.

All of these women were associated with some party, large or small, that spent day after day rowing boats west. Even in favourable weather when the green water rolled towards them and rippled along behind in a languid succession of quiet swells, the 170-mile lake trip seemed interminable. Ever so gradually a headland that appeared as a misty blue haze in the morning came into focus and, if the Klondikers were lucky, became a reality of discrete trees and firewood and a spot to camp for the night. Camping was a kindly relief as with grunts and stiff muscles they tied up their boats, stretched their legs and straightened their backs. As they looked for level spots to lie on, they clasped and unclasped their hands, calloused and clenched like cats' claws from long hours of rowing. As they looked for firewood they rubbed their burning biceps, wiggled their blistered bottoms and stretched the cramps out of their sorely tried leg muscles.

Mile by mile they swept on past the marshes of the Hay River delta into the narrow neck of the lake near Big Island and continued west where the current beginning to slip out of the lake gave them a noticeable lift forward. Finally they reached Fort Providence and there were definitely enfolded in the huge river's embrace.

About April 22 the multitude of Klondikers had left Athabasca Landing more or less as one body. By the time the majority had reached Fort Providence, about two months later, Klondikers were spread out in a 1,300-mile sinuous line stretching from Fort Smith to Fort McPherson. The Baudette group, which had come by the Peace River, was the earliest to reach Fort McPherson, doing so on June 24. Milne and Gill were only one day behind them. At that time many of the laggards still had scores of miles of Great Slave Lake to navigate. The Chippewa party of Edmonton, for instance, did not reach Fort Providence until about August 15.

The Hudson's Bay Company's steamer *Wrigley* had towed some of the parties, including Eben McAdam's. It started down from Fort Smith on June 22 and reached Fort Resolution the next day. On June 25 it reached Hay River and during the evening of the twenty-seventh tied up at Fort Simpson. Other parties whose scows the steamer had pulled were the Springfield and Feltham-Mulholland parties.

Among the throng that had travelled by their own steam launches or rowed their way along were the Big Four and the Bourmans, the Clatworthy, Chippewa and Corp contingents, the Fugard group and the twenty-one members of the Chicago party, the Ferguson-Clutter party, the Spring-Rice group, the large Brown-Morse party and many others.

The Brown-Morse party, travelling by their own exertions, reached Fort Simpson two days ahead of the *Wrigley*. There bad luck awaited them, for as they nosed one of their boats into the shore, J. Bouret, their cook, underestimating the depth of water, stepped off the boat and sank out of sight. He was wearing hip rubbers and these, filling with water, kept him down. It was about twenty minutes before his body was found. He was the only fatality along the Mackenzie River that season, although Hoffman had drowned in Great Slave Lake and late in October a man named Wills was drowned at Fort Chipewyan.

As in the previous year, Fort Simpson was the parting of the ways, and once more, in spite of the advice they were given, about eighty out of some 750 who reached that point during 1898 started up the Liard. Most of them had a bad time, but, except for one or two interesting incidents, their experiences were essentially the same as those of the men who ascended that river the year before.

At Fort Simpson, A. D. Stewart, commenting on one of the 1898 men who had bad luck up the Liard, said:

> Edward Crundy from the state of Maine crept into our tent this morning begging us to assist him. He had ventured up the river getting almost as far as Fort Liard when his boat swamped and he barely managed to escape with his life. The unfortunate man had on a hat, an undershirt, a pair of blue overalls, and a pair of moccasins, and outside of these, with the exception of a little coffee, a pail of lard and a revolver which he had managed to save the poor fellow had not a rag left to cover him; not a cent of money to take him home, nor any means of going onward even if inclined to pursue his journey. The fact is we have heard of so many casualties, so many broken boats, so many damaged provisions, so many discouraged people that we pay little attention to anything we see or hear, but our precautions grow greater day by day, and we move more and more cautiously as our journey proceeds. . . .

When in July 1898 Ernest Corp of Hamilton saw some of the Klondikers start up the Liard, he was dubious, as his memoirs indicate:

> . . . another party of gold seekers were ready to start up the Liard River, consisting of several strapping young fellows and one old prospector who said he came along to show the young fellows how to do it. I'll always remember seeing them starting up the river, the young fellows on the tracking line and the old man on the boat handling the sweep and calling out in his shaky old voice, "Good-bye, boys, it's only the old timers will get through!"
>
> The upper reaches of the Liard River are very tough going, and I heard later from others who went that way that this party broke up, and the old man left his bones up there.

Included among the eighty or so persons going up the Liard were R. W. V. Vaudin, W. A. Oliver, and their associates from Edmonton; the Chippewa and the Big Four parties; the Minneapolis group of seven, which started up with the steamboat *Minne-ha-ha*; Mr. and Mrs. Lampman; and a party which included W. E. Keats from Montreal.

Vaudin and Oliver left Fort Simpson on August 18, exactly a year after the first of the 1897 adventurers had started up the Liard. Thirteen other men, including the Chippewa party, accompanied these two, and all pitched in to get each other over the worst stretches of the river and particularly through the first canyon, of which Vaudin wrote: "This place is a wide canyon about 15 miles long, and in the stage of water at which we struck it is one continuous shallow rapid. We found Clatworthy stuck here, camped on a ledge of rock about as wide as a table. It took us 11 days to get through this canyon, having to portage our goods most of the way, the water being too shallow to float a loaded boat. . . ."

At Fort Liard the Chippewa party disintegrated and three members joined up with Vaudin, who reached Nelson Forks on October 20. This was the main junction point where the water-route prospectors ascending the Liard met and merged with the various parties of overlanders. From that point westward these two groups were more or less indistinguishable and, like Vaudin and Oliver, spent the winter along the Liard.

The ice formed on the Liard when these two were past the Beaver River but still twenty-eight miles downstream from the mouth of Toad River. As Vaudin said: "When we got frozen in the only place in sight fit for camping was on an island. We managed to get the boats over there and pull them ashore. We then built shacks, using the boards of the boat for flooring, etc., and burning the remainder to get the nails out of them. The rest of the time we put in making sleighs and toboggans; also hunting and trapping. . . . We started up the river on 12th Dec. and left the shack on the 26th. We are moving our stuff by eight mile shifts, each man hauling 150 pounds eight miles each day; when the trail is good we can haul 250 pounds. . . ."

Little is known of the Minneapolis party's experiences but we can surmise that the *Minne-ha-ha* did not get very far up the river, probably not beyond the shallow water of the canyon which caused Vaudin and Oliver so much trouble about thirty miles above Fort Simpson. Mr. and Mrs. Lampman had also tracked up the Liard and spent the winter in a deserted cabin near a camp which the Klondikers christened Snyetown. W. E. Keats of Montreal, who left Fort Simpson in August, also wintered at Snyetown, which was near the mouth of the La Biche River a few miles upstream from Fort Liard. During the winter he went hunting, got lost and wandered for eleven days with nothing but a few berries to eat. Fortunately, L. L. Lampman found him in time to save his life.

About forty of those who started from Fort Simpson pressed on following the winding Liard. From Snyetown, however, an old, poorly defined Indian route ran west and by-passed scores of miles of fast water on that river. It started up the La Biche River and about twenty miles west of Snyetown crossed over to the Beaver and its tributary, the Crow. Following up the Crow River and crossing some low heights of land, it finally descended the Coal River to the Liard at a point near the mouth of the Mud River. Guided by an Indian, late in the fall of 1898, the other forty took this trail. When the native returned to Snyetown in the spring he reported the safe arrival of his party at the old Mud River Post.

The Lampmans remained near Snyetown and returned to Edmonton in the spring. When telling of their experiences, Mrs. Lampman was quoted as saying that "while the trip was not an easy one, particularly the 260 miles of tracking up the Liard, she did not find it particularly hard. She and her husband wintered comfortably in a deserted Indian camp, and being used to North Dakota winters, felt no inconvenience from cold. There was no sickness in or around their camp. . . ."

So, like their predecessors, the 1898 contingent of Liard-minded Klondikers ground to a halt for the winter. The following spring about a third of them returned to Fort Simpson and while most of these came back to Edmonton, a few went down the Mackenzie. Since those who went up the Liard or took the Indian trail mingled with those who had gone out from Edmonton with pack horses, we can now drop them from the roster of water-route Klondikers and discuss them later along with the overlanders.

While the 80 had gone up the Liard, the remaining 670 Klondikers of this category continued down the Mackenzie. Like a host of others, including Rosie, Miss Jones, Mrs. Brown and Ernest Corp, Eben McAdam had not been tempted by the Liard. He bought a large York boat for forty dollars from some prospectors who were ready to turn back to Edmonton and had an easy trip down as far as the Gravel River, as indicated in his diary:

Left Fort Simpson at 2.30 p.m. Caught up to Springfield about 6 p.m. Grose with two Indians & the Hx. [Halifax] boys caught up later. Floated down stream together all night. Had music in the evening.

Thursday 30 June 98: Arrived at Nahanni River at 2.30 & found four (4) boats there. Did not stop long. Separated from the Springfield in the morning & did not couple up again till evening. Put in shore at 11 p.m. owing to heavy rain storm & remained there till 1.30 a.m. Mosquitoes very bad all night.

Friday 1st July 98: Dominion Day. Passed Wrigley at 11.30 a.m. Did not stop as landing is very poor. Jack Grose caught up to us at 1 p.m. and remained with us all day & night. Reached Blackwater River at 11 p.m. & anchored till morning.

Saturday 2 July 98: Charlie McGinnis, Henry & myself & Dick Feltham, Dave Dench & Dave Mulholland went up Blackwater to prospect & returned about 12 a.m. I panned out a couple of times & saw colors for the first time. River very bad to go up & we decided not to try it. Left for Gravel River at 1.30 p.m. & arrived 11 p.m. Anchored for the night.

Although not even the Gravel River (Keele) could tempt McAdam, it looked good to some. It was said to rise over two hundred miles away in the summit of the Mackenzie Mountains at a point where a good pass would carry the adventurous over to the headwaters of the Macmillan River. By descending its tributary and main stream another 250 miles they would come to the Pelly River seventy-five miles upstream from the Yukon River. Thus, from the mouth of the Gravel River, which was some sixty miles above Fort Norman, the distance to the Yukon was a mere five hundred miles, with more than half it downstream navigation.

According to the local Indians it was a practical route and, furthermore, they had seen "white miners working there, who took out pieces of gold as large as a watch. They had built two houses and had been there several summers, going away in the fall and returning in the spring."

To ascend the Gravel two approaches were possible. One, of course, was to start at its mouth and navigate upstream, and about forty miners did this. The other, which appealed to the remaining fifty-five Klondikers who planned to take this route, was to strike out from Fort Norman on foot after freeze-up and head up the valley of the Little Bear River. For about sixty miles a vague trail followed this tortuous valley and then struck off across a shoulder of the mountains to reach the Gravel River about the mouth of Nailin Creek. Rosie, Miss Jones and her brother and the Spring-Rice party went on to Fort Norman and set out some months later by this short-cut route.

The forty who did not go down to Fort Norman but stopped when they came to the mouth of the Gravel included the Phillips party made up of E. Corp, Dr. Dillabough, Charles Krugg, Alf Willis and Vic McFarland. Along with them were Dr. Buck and his company of five from Great Falls, Montana, another nine-man party from Hamilton, and several others. About a month later, J. M. Swigert of the Yukon Valley Prospecting and Mining Company also started up the Gravel River.

About July 12, 1898, a dozen boats, which included Ernest Corp's, set out up the Gravel River, leaving others to follow later. Here, Corp said, "We soon found that pulling large boats up a swift river was a man-sized job, and that our many pleasant days of easy floating downstream were a thing of the past." A few days of the uphill struggle was enough to convince the crews of four boats to turn back and go farther down the Mackenzie. It took until September for Corp and the parties who pressed on to help each other up the first hundred miles of alternating rapids and flat, gravel-strewn stretches. In that distance the river dropped a thousand feet. Corp, in telling of those days, said:

> At times, where the water was very swift, it would be difficult to cross over from the head of the island we were on and catch the lower end of one across the channel. Once we missed, and so had to do it all over again, so we adopted the plan of two of us crossing over in the dinghy to be ready to catch the bow line from the big boat when the bowman threw it. The gravel banks of the islands were usually from three to six feet high and straight up, and a man leaping ashore from a boat was quite likely to go into the river if the edge of the bank crumbled with his weight.
>
> On one such occasion, two of us crossed over in the dinghy and stood ready to catch the bowline. The bowman threw the rope, but unfortunately for him he dropped a coil of the rope, which caught around his ankle. We caught the end of the line and held on, but he, poor fellow, was dragged into the water as the boat swung away from the bank. Unable to release himself, he held on desperately to the rope with both hands, but instantly went out of sight for a moment. Coming to the surface, he yelled, "Hold her, boys!", and then again disappeared. Coming to the surface again, the same frantic yell was repeated, "Hold her, boys!" By this time we had managed to drag man and boat to the bank, and hauled him out. As soon as he got his breath he grinned, and said, "Oh, I know it must have appeared funny, but I was afraid you would let go the rope, and then I would surely have drowned!"
>
> During the warm weather it was easy to dry out our wet clothes overnight ready for the next day, but as Fall weather approached we had to get into wet clothes in the morning, as we could not get them dry overnight. This was very disagreeable, to say the least, but miraculously neither of us caught a cold, even after shivering in an early snow flurry soaking wet.
>
> Now it was October, and too cold to continue tracking, so we decided to camp, build cabins, and wait until the river ice was safe to travel on. My party camped at the mouth of a small creek, with plenty of good timber.

About this time R. T. Kusch of the Yukon Valley Prospecting and Mining Company froze his feet so severely that for the rest of the winter he could not walk. The remainder of the party took turns hauling him along until he could be loaded into a boat on the Stewart River. After he reached Dawson his feet gradually recovered and he went to work.

143

Nearly a hundred miles up the Gravel, near Nailin Creek, Corp and his friends camped for a few weeks.

> We built a large cabin, 15 feet by 30 feet. The other Hamilton party we had been travelling with built cabins across the river on an island. Later two of them came over to visit us on the first ice, and spent the night with us. During the night an ice jamb [sic] occurred lower down, backing up the water several feet, and our visitors had to stay until the jamb broke two days later. I decided to go with them, and see how their mates had fared during the high water.
>
> When we got to the island, a desolate scene met our eyes. The island was covered by huge blocks of ice stranded when the jamb broke, and their large wood pile had floated away, but the cabin still stood. It had been flooded half way to the top, and they had piled their goods on the upper bunks and cut a hole in the roof to climb out of if it became necessary. Fortunately, however, the water had receded before reaching the roof.

While they waited for the ice to firm up they fashioned sleds, but because of their inexperience made the runners too narrow. All the while they kept in touch with other parties camped within ten or fifteen miles up or down the river. On one visit Corp broke through the ice and was soaked to his waist.

> Just then, luckily, I saw a column of smoke going straight up above the treetops not far away. With a shout, "There is a cabin!" I started straight for it, through thick brush, as fast as I could go in my now stiffly frozen clothes. Reaching the cabin, I banged open the door. A welcome sight met my eyes — a large fire in an open fireplace and a friendly greeting from my hosts. . . .
>
> One day we had visitors. Five Norwegians arrived overland from Fort Norman, a distance of about fifty miles [more likely seventy-five]. They too were going to Dawson by way of the Gravel River. Seeing their sleds, we knew at once the kind needed, and proceeded at once to making them — about six feet long, with runners three inches wide. They camped with us a while, and helped us in making suitable sleds. They were followed shortly by several more parties over from Fort Norman, where they had spent the early part of the winter — about thirty men and two women [Rosie and Miss Jones].

This was the group that had stayed at Fort Norman until October 22, when it hired an Indian guide and cut across country to intersect the Gravel River. According to J. M. Swigert of the Yukon Valley Prospecting and Mining Company, each of them

> had about 800 pounds of supplies. He could only haul 150 pounds at a time on his sled, so that the distance was made in stages of about ten miles. The same ground being doubled over from camp to camp until each man had all his supplies forward to the next camp. The party were

two months making the 78 miles from Fort Norman to the Gravel river and six months in making the 300 miles from Norman to the Stewart river. Counting the doubling back, they travelled 2,700 miles to make 300. Their guide who was engaged to take them to the Macmillan turned out to be unsatisfactory, and on reaching the Gravel river he was discharged. Afterwards the party followed their judgment, and their coming out on the Stewart instead of the Macmillan may have resulted from their having taken the wrong fork of the Gravel.

Before it started west from its camp the Corp party split up. Recalling this event, Corp said: "I might mention here that hardly a party that started out together from home but split up later on. Some quarrelled so bitterly that they even sawed their boat in two. Many others split up amicably and joined others for their own convenience. Our own party split up just before we started on our winter sledding. Two of us, myself and Alf Willis, decided to go on our own, and the others of our party joined in with various outfits."

On December 22 Corp and his companion started dragging their supplies about a hundred miles up the valley towards the height of land. They put in all the rest of the winter relaying their goods forward and on this portion of the trip were very near the route which the Canol Pipeline was to follow some forty-five years later. While travelling was difficult, it was nevertheless a task that could be overcome by extreme patience and stamina. Their sleds were a problem, and Corp's memoirs explained a method by which they improved them.

> The sleds, having no shoeing, and being made from green lumber, often got roughened up, which made them very hard to pull. One day, by accident, we found out how to remedy this, by turning the sled over and icing the runners by a quick swipe with a wet cloth when we came by an open water hole. However, this was too haphazard, and we made a practice of taking a can of hot water along, well wrapped up, on the sled. One day I met a little Irishman, Johnny O'Hara, on the trail. I said to him, "How is the sled going to-day?" He replied, "Well, Ernie, I'll tell you. It was pulling like a cat by the tail. I kicked it, cussed it, and turned it up and peed on it, and it ran beautifully!" So he, too, had discovered the water cure.

Breaking through ice or wading through places where water overflowed the ice were dangerous hazards. "The men had their feet wet frequently. Some had their feet more or less severely frost bitten and one man Chas. Geilds, of New York, lost his life. After a hard pull through one of these overflows he sat down on his sleigh to rest and was frozen to death. His body was found next morning by the men doubling back. As a grave could not be dug the body was wrapped in blankets and placed on a scaffold. . . ." Moreover, scurvy afflicted some of those who, not being aware that they should do so, did not watch their vitamin intake. Two of the aggregation going up the Gravel River died of this disorder, but their names have not been recorded.

Inevitably they ate into their supplies. As Corp said:

> As the weeks passed by, our supplies were gradually getting lighter, and we could move the entire outfit in three loads, two trips with about 300 to 400 pounds each, and one for the camp outfit – tent, bedding, stove, etc. At noon we often had our lunch on the open river, where we built a fire and boiled water for tea or coffee. One day it was forty below zero, and a fair breeze blowing and the coffee pot sitting at the edge of the fire with steam coming out of the spout, when I noticed a small icicle about an inch long hanging from the spout lip. I drew the attention of the others to it, and they said if they hadn't seen it with their own eyes they would not have believed it could happen.

Most of the Klondikers practised a culinary trick that Corp's memoirs recall. "After supper I would set to with two or three frying pans, making pancakes on top of the box stove. After three or four hours, I would have a pile of pancakes eighteen inches high, enough for two weeks, which, when frozen, were handy to pack and easily thawed out, and very healthy and palatable."

As Corp's associates approached the divide, the depth of snow increased until it was five feet. When, about the middle of April 1899, they reached a small stream trickling down to the west, they believed it to be a tributary of the Macmillan. As it turned out, they missed that river by a few miles. The stream they followed was a branch of the Hess River, which in turn ran into the Stewart. The west slope of the mountains was considerably steeper than the east slope which they had ascended. Even though going downhill was far more encouraging than creeping up, the steepness presented its own problems. Nevertheless, Corp reported that in one day a man unburdened with supplies could walk from the summit to where they found the stream large enough to use boats. At that point the men stopped to whip-saw trees and made twenty-three boats with which they set out down the river.

> Here again many new partnerships were formed. My partner and I joined up with a young doctor [Dr. Buck from Great Falls, Montana] and his father whom we had met, and liked, on the trail. We whipsawed lumber and built a boat, and as soon as the ice went out were ready to start. Now, when the ice broke up and moved out, what had appeared to be a good-sized river showed up for what it was, just a swift, shallow, rocky stream. But we now had to take things as they were, so we loaded up and cast off into a swift, swirling mass of water and foam. We had gone perhaps half a mile when the boat was lifted up and crashed on a rock, making a hole in

the bottom. We pulled ashore, unloaded and turned the boat up and patched and recaulked it. Next day we were ready to make another start. We now had better luck, and emerged into a much larger stream, which, while good for short distances, had rapids and canyons on and off for two hundred miles. This was a daily hazard to parties drifting down an unknown river, but we were lucky, and came through without mishap, while several others suffered damage to their boats and goods.

The rapids wrecked some of the twenty-three boats and battered the others about. The Spring-Rice party lost all three of its boats but the other parties divided up their supplies to ensure that they and other unfortunates had plenty to eat.

During the first hundred miles of their descent they still believed themselves to be on the Macmillan River, but one day they came to a blazed tree on which was written the names of two men and the date August 18, 1897, with the added information that this was the Stewart River and that it was 321 miles down to the Yukon. On June 6, while running a rapid, a sweep knocked Victor McFarland of Hamilton off the boat. His companions found his body about a mile downstream and all went into camp while they dug a grave in the frozen gravel. They lined it with evergreens and, with reverence and such ceremony as they could muster, laid the body in the grave.

When they had descended the Stewart to what is now Mayo, the group began to disperse. Rosie and Miss Jones and her brother, all of whom had pulled sleds along the way, reached Dawson safely. Corp went about forty miles farther down to the mouth of the McQuesten River to see what luck he would have.

Corp estimated that seventy-five men reached the gold-fields by way of the Gravel River, but that opinion may be a little on the high side. Out of the whole aggregation, however, only four had lost their lives: one man by freezing after becoming wet and exhausted, one by falling off a boat, and two from scurvy. Perhaps the fact that three doctors were among those Gravel River adventurers kept the death rate low.

At one time, rumours reached Edmonton of ten deaths along the Gravel River, but early in September 1899, when J. M. Swigert returned to Edmonton, he announced that several of those reported dead were in Dawson and very much alive. Speaking of the hardships of the route, he said: "Of course the hardships of the trip were very great, but they were undertaken with a knowledge of what they were, and with the belief that they could be overcome." In the same vein, the editor of the *Bulletin* added: ". . . men of energy and endurance can go nearly any where they want to, and pass through great hardships without being much the worse. The man who undertakes to prospect for gold expecting not to undergo hardships is simply under a mistake. If gold were easy to get it would not be worth getting. By the time its existence has been demonstrated in any locality, some one else has got it."

Many of those who passed on the news of the death of various Klondikers did so in the sincere belief that they were so ill that they would surely die. Ernest Corp told of meeting a man he had given up for dead and added some details of scurvy from his own experience.

> Thinking they might be someone we knew, I walked up to their fire, and, to my surprise, found the man at the fire was one we knew on the winter trail, but thought must have died months ago, as when we last saw him he was almost helpless after having his frozen toes amputated by a doctor during the winter, then later he had scurvy. He told me the story of his survival. He had finally got so weak he couldn't eat, and spoke only in a whisper. One day, just as his partner had camped for the night on a bar, a moose walked out. They shot it, and, being practically out of grub, proceeded at once to cook some of the meat in the frying pan. The aroma of this floated to the helpless one, and they noticed his trying to attract attention. Putting an ear to his mouth, the partner heard him whisper, "Give me some." They took him a nice tender bit, which he ate, and wanted more, but they were afraid to give him but very little more, and he went to sleep. However, next morning he ate a frying pan full, and at every meal he was ready for more. Inside two days he was up and walking about. I can quite believe this almost miracle of fresh meat, as I have had a bad spell of scurvy or what is called "Canadian black leg." Your legs turn black in spots, and the flesh is like putty, with no rebound when pressed in. This occurred in the early summer of -/99, from lack of fresh meat and vegetables. I was not able to walk without awful pains in the legs, and sitting in the boat with my legs held up. One morning, drifting downstream, we saw on an island bar what looked like a stranded tree with its roots sticking up, but which on close approach we found to be a dead moose . . . we ate moose fried or boiled for every meal for a week, in spite of the unbled meat acting like an overdose of physic. Then, suddenly, to my surprise and delight, the pains all left me, my legs got all right, and in three or four days I went hunting. Fresh native meat evidently builds up the system and cleans it out at the same time.

Although the Gravel River route left much to be desired, nevertheless, about ninety-five men started to ascend it and perhaps seventy-five crossed over to the Yukon. There was also a small group about which all we know is that they wintered at Fort Norman after having tried their luck at Great Bear Lake. Among them were the Westheads from Buffalo Lake, Alberta, who came back to Edmonton during 1899.

Eben McAdam, who along with many other parties had left Fort Simpson on June 29 and reached the mouth of the Gravel River four days later, decided to continue down the Mackenzie and arrived at Fort Good Hope on July 8. Presumably he and his associates signed the register kept by the missionary there and were included in the 457 Klondikers who had done so by July 26, 1898. Undoubtedly several more stragglers checked in after this, so that we will not be far from the truth if we assume that in the 1898 season about five hundred Klondikers got to the Mackenzie delta. All who tried to keep any record of the number of Klondikers are in reasonable accord on this figure. The exception is Charles Griffin, a 1897 Klondiker who came back to Edmonton the following fall, who stated that up to September, 1898, between one thousand and twelve hundred men entered their names on the register kept at the Hay River mission and that a number had passed there without stopping. Information that the writer has received from Hay River indicates that this figure was greatly exaggerated.

Even though McAdam hurried past the mouth of Arctic Red River on July 13 at four o'clock in the morning, not all the other prospectors passed it by so casually. A small but cosmopolitan group consisting of B. H. Rollins of New Hampshire, Fugard and Raleigh of Los Angeles, who had left Edmonton in November 1897 planning to take the Overland Route, a man named Bennett of London, England, another by the name of Ford, from Quebec, and Messrs. Johnson and Hawkins, who had previously formed part of a group from Hamilton, decided to try it. They worked upstream during the early fall and wintered about a hundred miles above its mouth. In the spring of 1899, Fugard and Rollins went on almost to its headwaters, but returned disappointed. In the meantime, Johnson, Ford and Hawkins had a brush with scurvy but recovered. Finally, all seven men returned to the Mackenzie River and joined the relatively small contingent that caught the Hudson's Bay steamer *Wrigley* for the long trip back to Edmonton.

While Fugard and Rollins were tracking up the Arctic Red River, Eben McAdam and his companions were floating farther down the Mackenzie. What with travelling all night and dozing half the time, McAdam allowed the boat to get into the wrong channel, which by-passed the mouth of Peel River and began to sweep them along towards the ocean. They had to track back until they could enter the left channel.

On July 14, when they were pulling the boat up the Peel River, they reached the mouth of Rat River, where they

> Found several parties . . . most of them busily engaged reducing the size of their boats & building small boats for work on the portage to the Porcupine. We remained all night.
>
> Saturday 16th July 98: Favorable wind began early in the morning & the

149

Huron sailed out early. Springfield, Halifax & ourselves started out at 9 a.m. & made the run of 12 miles in six hours reaching McPherson at 3 p.m. About 12 boats here.

At this point the prospectors had to face up to crossing the mountains and decide which of three routes to take. If the Klondike, and only the Klondike, was still their goal, they had to pick one of two choices, starting up the Rat River for McDougall Pass and LaPierre's House, or portaging the goods up Stony Creek on the short cut to LaPierre's House. If, however, they were not irrevocably committed to the Klondike but were inclined towards prospecting as they went, the Peel River was their logical choice. Along it those who had always felt that they were not necessarily going all the way to Dawson, but would stop when they found good diggings, would have their last chance. If the Peel River proved a disappointment, they would have to extend themselves, cross some yet unknown pass and complete the trip to Dawson.

After mid summer, 1898, and throughout the following winter, Fort McPherson was the busiest spot north of Edmonton. During the fall of 1897 only the Segers-Hardisty party had reached the area and these men had remained in the vicinity till they could start across in the winter or spring of 1898. In 1898, however, some five hundred Klondikers descended on the post. Indeed, one man who tried to count the boats on the Peel arrived at a total of 180, which seems high. Some of these Klondikers, such as Dyer, the Lamoureux party that had left Edmonton that spring, and nearly two hundred more, hurried up the Rat River, disappeared over McDougall Pass, and reached Dawson that fall.

Nearly three hundred other adventurers were to remain in the vicinity of Fort McPherson for weeks and even months. Of these, about a hundred went up the Peel River and during the winter kept in touch with the old fort. The remainder were scattered either at Fort McPherson or within easy communicating distance, and there were special concentrations of them at two winter camps in the approaches to McDougall Pass which the miners named Destruction City and Shacktown.

Unlike the hundreds of Klondikers who had set out for the mouth of the Peel River and reached there, the three teams of horses which the Alaska Mining and Trading Company had loaded on the steamer *Chesrown* to take to the mouth of the Peel never arrived. The *Chesrown* did not get away from Fort Smith that year, so presumably the horses also stayed there. Perhaps it was just as well, for at Rat River the fodder situation left much to be desired.

150

CHAPTER ELEVEN

THE 1898
WATER-ROUTE KLONDIKERS:
UP THE PEEL AND RAT RIVERS

Eben McAdam and his friends formed one of many parties that chose the Peel River route. Some of the others were the Huron, Hopkins, Dr. Conley and Brown-Morse parties, as well as A. D. Stewart's Hamilton group. While parties of two or three left day after day, some chose to combine forces with others, so that at least every few days a group set out upstream. McAdam remained at Fort McPherson four days so that he could start out with a few groups that he felt would be congenial.

During the first two days when the boat ascended the relatively slack water, they travelled fifty miles and caught up with a number of parties that were cutting down the size of their boats. Many did this by cutting them in half amidships and building a new bow for one half and a new stern for the other. Since this required additional lumber, the men had rigged up a sawpit, and after days of hard, tedious work, they finally cut off as many two-inch planks as they needed.

Here, at about the mouth of the Satah River, the hard tracking began, as McAdam's diary for July 23, 1898, affirms.

> Up at 7 a.m., & began tracking about 8 a.m. Tracking very bad & had to wade in 10 inches of water most of the day. Struck a bad place 3 p.m. & after working till 8 p.m. decided to lighten boats to overcome difficulty. Distance 3 miles.
>
> Sunday 24th July 98: Up at 7.30 a.m. & made breakfast. We here unloaded & removed keel & we took out about a ton. Got boats over bad place about 12 a.m. Started at 2 p.m. & tracked till 7 p.m. Made probably about 7 miles.

On July 29, near the Trail River and about a hundred miles up the Peel from its mouth, McAdam's group caught up with part of the

Enterprise party, which prior to this time had sold its sternwheeler to the Hudson's Bay Company at Fort Norman. By the time the group had reached the Peel River it had split up and about half of the men crossed the Stony Creek route from McPherson. Feltham, Dr. Waterman and Mulholland went up the Peel.

At Trail River the Peel bulged out to the east in a semicircle with a radius of about thirty miles. As it swung back west through rapids and ramparts to a point about 160 miles above Fort McPherson, it became a most difficult river to navigate. In the roughest part, and about twelve miles from each other, two tributaries entered from the south, the Bonnet Plume and the Wind. To cut off much of this difficult stretch of river the Indians had a trail running south from the mouth of Trail River to the mouth of the Bonnet Plume.

While this crude trail was of no use to the Klondikers who were using boats, at least two men did travel it during the winter, with tragic results. Duncan McCallum of Kaslo, British Columbia, accompanied by an Edmonton Iroquois called Tom Leo, both of whom had come down the Mackenzie with Jim Wallwork and "Steamboat" Wilson, set out for Wind City along this cut-off. Eventually Leo limped into Wind City, where one of the physicians treated his frozen feet while others went out to rescue McCallum. When they reached his tent they found his frozen body. Eventually Leo went on to Dawson with a party from Hamilton.

McAdam and his party continued up the Peel, however, and his diary for July 29, 1898, says:

> Up at 6.30 a.m. Began the morning's work 8 a.m. with a very difficult piece of water – It was a rapid & we passed a rope across the stream & drew the boats up & across. Finished the job at 11.45. After dinner began again (at 2 p.m.) After a short run came to another rapid. We got all the boats through at 5.30 but the Halifax canoe met with an accident, & took water so rapidly that we had to discharge her load. We are arranging to carry part of the Halifax canoe load. Spent the evening with them and had some guitar music & singing. Distance for the day 2 miles.

Many other parties also toiled up, and on August 1 McAdam came "in sight of a considerable camp which turned out to be Huron Imisk Idaho, Brown & Peacock parties. The three former were two days ahead of us, the latter about a week. At this point all were either busy making over their boats or had completed the job. . . ." About this time his party cut its boat down and rearranged the loads "so as not to draw more than 9 inches of water."

McAdam's party took another month to ascend the next hundred miles, reaching the mouth of the Bonnet Plume River on September

1. Most of their time had been spent in taking half-loads up a few miles and then taking their boat back for the other half. Fortunately various hunters shot all the caribou they needed, so that fresh food was abundant. Finally at 8 p.m., September 5, they reached the mouth of Wind River. Although many others were still behind, the Brown-Morse and several other parties were keeping pace with them. Altogether over a hundred men were strung out along this 160-mile stretch of the Peel River.

On September 15, when the snow was four inches deep, McAdam arrived at a spot about eight miles up Wind River where a few of the men ahead had decided to camp for the early part of the winter. Just before he reached there, he said, "we saw the Skin boat party arrive from over the Divide. They all appeared thoroughly satisfied with the result of their month's work. They report no portage from one river to the other thro the mountains, but say that the Peel takes its rise in a broad valley, and that the river running the other direction rises close by. The guide's (Andrew) information given in advance proved correct in every instance. They found a fine color on this side. . . ."

Who the skin boat party members were we do not know, but at any rate they brought good news. On the other hand, Dr. Brown of the Brown-Morse party pulled ashore after the second fatal accident to afflict his party since they had left Edmonton. "Tim Orchard was drowned on the 8th inst. The bridle of the track line broke and the boat shot out into the current drawing Orchard in. He was in the water about 20 minutes and was dead when taken out. It is supposed the line hooked on to a stone and held him down. He was buried near where drowned. A small log house was erected over the grave. . . ."

While the McAdam men had reached the campground, they still had a few days' work to bring all their supplies that far. On September 20, 1898, they finished that task, for the diary says:

> Up at 7 a.m. Left for lower cache at 9.20 a.m. Back at 1.23 p.m. with last load. Have named this place Wind City. Expect about 10 shacks and about 40 men to put up at this place this winter.
> Thus endeth the Track Line, thank Heavens!

Next day they began building their shack on a part of the campground where a number of friends could be grouped together. "There will be four shacks in our group – Peacock and Barclay, Dench and Waterman, Feltham Crichton and Payzant, and our Party. We have a little fresh snow each day and the weather is fairly cool. . . ."

By October 9 they had finished their shack, and that day six Indians brought two canoes downstream loaded with fresh caribou meat, which they sold as follows: "8 skins for 1 carcass cariboo; 12 skins 1 carcass moose. (A skin equals 50 cents.)" By contrast, a party of Klondikers who had been out hunting for nine days came back empty handed.

All the other prospectors who continued to arrive from down the Peel decided to winter in what had been christened Wind City. At the time, they thought that they might as well remain there for about four months, until the first of February, before there would be any point in starting up the valley again.

Meanwhile, lower down the Peel River several Klondikers had found their progress impeded by ice and built isolated shacks here and there. About the end of September, the four-man Cadzow-Erickson party from Edmonton decided to winter about seventy miles upstream from Fort McPherson. Before they had put up their shanty ex-mayor A. D. Stewart's party, now reduced to four men, came along, and in spite of the fact that they had experienced a most difficult day, refused an invitation to build beside them. Stewart related how difficult that day had been:

> The wind was blowing bitter cold, and the man at the sweep could scarcely endure the hour during which, at regular intervals, he had to take his turn in the boat and stand motionless and frozen whilst his partners floundered slowly along the bank. The tracking was a fearful undertaking too, for so muddy and slippery was the ground that we could hardly keep our feet, and found ourselves constantly lying flat on our faces in a confused and draggled heap. Just after dinner, which was a meal of short duration that day, we came suddenly and unexpectedly on some swift water which, in the summer time, when the river is high, would probably be considered a rapid. Inch by inch we dragged our unwilling boat through the hissing water until at last by sheer brute force, and so exhausted that we could not have pulled another ounce, we got her almost to a calmer spot ahead; but, just as with a final heave and scramble we made our last effort, our tracking rope broke, down we fell flat on our faces, and away went our boat like a frightened deer down stream to the point from which we had brought her. Fortunately Skynner, who is the best boatman in our party, was at the sweep, he very cleverly managed to swing her around and finally run her nose into a safe and comfortable resting place in the bank without loss or accident of any kind. We re-tied our ropes and took every precaution against a repetition of this occurrence; but three times in succession the same thing happened, until our spirits sank within us and we began to think that after all the stories we had heard were all too true. But we had not come to this northern wilderness for fun. Nor did we think when leaving home that our journey was going to be easy child's play, so we tried again, straining like cart horses, pulling like galley slaves, covered with mud and perspiration, and this time successfully brought our boat through and were for the time at ease again.

About a week later, on October 8 and about thirty miles above the Cadzow-Erickson camp, Stewart said that "it was evident that we were nearing the beginning of the end, and that the time was close at hand when our boat would have to be abandoned for good. The ice was floating down the river in huge blocks, crunching her sides and bruising and cutting our legs as it dashed against us. We had to wade knee deep in the ice-cold water all day, and were so cold and exhausted that we could not have gone on much further; but we kept on till night came, and when we stopped at last, we realized that the old boat had made her last journey and that we should know her in her present shape no more."

So they put up a tent and began to prepare for the winter.

> Then we dismantled and broke the "Fearnot" to pieces, inspected our stock of provisions, mending and retieing the damaged bags and packages, and stored our goods on the river bank, above what we estimated would be a reasonably safe water line. Every bolt and screw and nail and scrap of iron in the boat was carefully saved, as well as all the hardwood ribs, seats, etc., which we thought would be needed in making our new conveyances. We had to burn the wood so as to get the iron, bolts and nails out, and then the nails had all to be gone over and straightened before they could be all used again. We rigged up a carpenter's bench outside our tent, and there made a big sled and two toboggans.

After making these they relayed their supplies farther upstream to the mouth of a stream that Stewart called the Beaver but which probably was a creek entering the Peel somewhere below the mouth of Snake River. There on November 7 they decided to make their winter camp. There for three weeks the four men lived in a tent while they built a shack. On November 29, a week after the Arctic sun had disappeared for the winter, and when the temperature was 46 below, they moved into their log home. It was sixteen feet long, twelve feet wide and seven feet high.

On December 19 Stewart met with a distressing accident, of which he said: "Fell in woods today by tripping on a hidden branch while carrying a heavy log on my shoulder. Was pinned to the ground by the neck. Hurt my right side badly, near lower ribs, and skinned the muscles of left thigh badly. I fancy a rib is broken."

Although this accident was causing Stewart considerable suffering, to celebrate Christmas the four men opened a carefully saved bottle of brandy and gave each other such presents as they could devise. The most interesting were the armchairs that Skynner had been making.

On January 1, Stewart "rested all day in bed, nursing leg, which is worse today." For the next eleven days he suffered severe pain, staying indoors all the time and in bed much of it.

While he was laid up, Stewart, a man of versatile mind, wrote two hymns which eventually reached Hamilton and were of such quality that it is said they were frequently used in Presbyterian services. Two stanzas from one of them indicate both their calibre and the writer's mood. On January 13 his diary had said: "Bad night on account of leg. No doubt now of acute rheumatism. Went on knees to light fire this morning. Could not get up again and suffered greatly." On January 15 he wrote:

> My soul is filled with wild alarms;
>   Ah! Bid each gathering shadow flee;
> Hold Thou me up, lead Thou me on;
>   Oh, Saviour, let me lean on Thee.
>
> Alone, I faint, I cannot stand;
>   But on the suppliant's bended knee
> I stretch my weary arms and pray,
>   Oh, Saviour, let me lean on Thee.

Two months later he died of scurvy.

During the depths of the winter with the thermometer sometimes dropping to 53 degrees below zero, the four men made the best of an unpleasant situation. While all were remarkably well adjusted men, who got along with each other, Stewart and Tallman were older than the other two and their age told against them. Skynner, the man experienced in mining, was the most adaptable, but Cresswell, who was twenty-nine years old, came through the dreary winter best of all. Much of their time was spent in bringing in firewood.

On January 16 Cresswell trapped a hare, and was "received with shouts of joy. Last fresh meat November 2." Three days later Stewart noted: "Sun visible at last . . . sun last seen November 22 – four months today since we saw a human face." Next day, "Tallman shows inside of right thigh completely discolored, red and black hue. He has had no bruise, and Skynner and I are much alarmed thereat."

Like many other Klondikers who were worried about the possibility of scurvy, Skynner and Cresswell subscribed to the opinion that one way to try to ward it off was to take plenty of exercise. Accordingly, early in February Cresswell put on his snowshoes and tramped out a sort of race track on an island and thereafter consistently exercised by making a number of turns around it each day, sometimes going eight miles. Stewart was too ill to do this, but Cresswell insisted that Tallman, with his symptoms of scurvy, should also exercise. For instance, on

March 11 Cresswell's diary says: "Temperature 19 below. . . . This has been a hard week, as Tallman is now off work, and it is with hard work that Skynner and I can keep him doing his two miles on the track. It is very trying on us, and difficult to keep one's patience. We are hoping for warmer weather, as it will help our invalids."

Then on March 13, when the weather had warmed up to 23 below, Stewart died. Next day the thermometer registered 24 above and Cresswell wrote: "Walked 5½ miles on track. Whiskey jack arrived and stayed round cabin all afternoon." A day later "three whiskey jacks outside made it feel like spring. . . . We feed them, as it is pleasant to see something alive after our monotonous winter. Very warm. Cabin door open all day."

On March 20 Cresswell "Caught a rabbit in trap, and later on in the day Skynner shot another with rifle. Rabbit for dinner and supper, which was very much appreciated, as we had had no fresh meat since January 16."

Besides doing six or eight miles of exercising on their track, Skynner and Cresswell kept picking away at the frozen earth until March 28, when the diary says: "This was a sad day for us again, as today we laid A. D.'s remains to rest on a high point on the side of the Beaver River. Tallman was unable to go, not feeling strong enough, so Skynner and myself had to do the sad work. We drew the body up on a toboggan, and had a steep bank to encounter, but managed successfully. Skynner read the burial service, and after filling in the grave we retreated slowly back to the cabin feeling that we had done all we could for our late partner."

From that time on the three men waited anxiously for spring. For the next month Tallman suffered severely from scurvy, while Cresswell repeatedly comments on pains in his legs, undoubtedly from the same cause. On April 26 he reported: "Tallman very weak today; almost fainted; walked 1¼ miles. Only hope is fresh meat. If not, I fear the end is not far."

Fortunately the fresh meat did come for their relief, for on April 28 some Indians who had killed two moose arrived. There was a royal feast in the cabin. Later other Indians turned up, and thereafter they had a continual supply of fresh meat.

A short time after this the three men set out up the Peel River to form part of the procession plugging along towards the Klondike. We will touch on their experiences later, but in the meantime we should pick up the story of Wind City.

Wind City's life span was short — from September 1898 to the spring of 1899. What it lacked in looks it more than made up in the comfort and relaxation that it provided some seventy Klondikers, who for two months had been straining every fibre to get their supplies that far up from Fort McPherson.

Although for Klondikers who were anxious to reach the Yukon time hung heavy, Wind City was nevertheless a busy place. Men came and went on hunting trips but, as a rule, had little success. The Indians who supplied the camp with meat assured them that their luck would improve when a little later deep snow in the mountains would drive the caribou into the lower country. Moreover, looking to the day when they would resume their journey, they made sleds either from native timber or from the remnants of their boats; the next stage of their trip was to be on foot over the snow.

Several of the men were experienced miners who could not rest until they had tested the adjacent flats, where eight or ten feet of gravel covered the bedrock. After they got their shacks up the old miners began looking about, trying to determine which of the old filled-in river channels was most likely to contain gold. Then they sank shafts to try to reach the bedrock below. Their work was wasted, however, because water seeping in made it impossible to dig deep enough.

Others went farther afield and prospected up the Wind River, up Hungry Creek and up the Little Wind River – always without success. But, being either miners or would-be miners, they could not resist the chance. Speculation about rich diggings far upstream filled most of their time and hints and rumours of mysterious gold-bearing creeks circulated freely. Among those with the most active imaginations was G. M. Mitchell, who had led a party from Toronto and whose experiences on the Wind River were to be presented some decades later in a highly dramatic book. In it, his adventures were magnified and distorted so as to show him as the hero of manifestly impossible exploits which a study of Eben McAdam's diary quickly disproves. During the winter Mitchell broke a knee cap. One of the doctors patched it up, but the injury rendered him unfit to go farther with the result that in the spring he had to return to Toronto. He seems to be the central figure in a story about a mysterious and rich creek that was said to be somewhere higher up the pass – a story that McAdam believed and that for some weeks caused him considerable concern.

Because it was not possible to test the truth of the rumours until the men could move on, they made valiant attempts to amuse themselves. Idleness and boredom, the curse of such camps, lead to bickering and brawling; therefore, by means of lectures and concerts the many educated men in the crowd devised what entertainment they could. McAdam's diary comments: "The bi-weekly concerts continue and show improvement as the season advances. Our last concert was the best so far. The singing was good and the programme was carried out without any hitch. My part in the concert was a short lecture on astronomy entitled 'Primary motions of the Earth and Moon.' Last Sunday we had a short concert of sacred music. It was held in our shack and it is intended to repeat each Sunday."

Meanwhile the Indians continued to bring in meat, although after one visit they never brought their wives near the camp again. For months all the prospectors had hungered for female company. Many of them, particularly but not exclusively the Americans, had a low regard for Indians and their overtures to the native women nearly led to a battle. In that area the Indians, the Loucheux, were a fine group whose contact with white men had been confined to missionaries and Hudson's Bay Company traders, who respected and dealt fairly with them. The Klondikers provided their first experience of run-of-the-mill white men and by and large they did not impress the Loucheux favourably.

Men like Mitchell, McAdam and others of a better calibre had a high regard for these natives. C. S. Coatsworth from Windsor, writing from Wind City to Sheriff Robertson of Edmonton, said: "They are more christianized than most of our white brothers. Mr. Stringer, Episcopalian minister, now at Herschel Island, has been at McPherson assisting Archdeacon McDonald, and the work they have wrought would make many of our church orators seem small in comparison. I have seen the Indians offer a blessing before sitting down to a meal of roots and fish, and when we gave them food they never failed to return the gift fourfold. Their word and promise is sacred. . . ."

Some weeks after he had left Wind City, McAdam spoke of them in the same vein. "At this point (Joseph's Camp) there are two teppees occupied by three families – six adults & about a dozen youngsters from six years of age down. Joseph holds services Sunday morning & evening, in his teppee, – Episcopal. Henry & Andrew attended in the morning & Andrew & myself in the evening. They have the bible printed in their own language, (Loucheux), also the prayer book & hymnal. Joseph laid down the law in grand style. By special request, the two of us sang, repeating each verse after them. Their teppees are different from any I have seen so far – at the base they are about 24 feet, and stand about 9 feet high at centre. . . ."

Most of the Klondikers remained at Wind City until after Christmas, and McAdam was one of these. On December 25, 1898, his diary says:

Christmas here again. What a change in a year – 4500 miles from home and not a cheering word for nine months. Where will we be twelve months hence? In this country? Will we meet with success during the next year? What I would give to see my two little darlings today! No doubt they are enjoying themselves and perhaps thinking of me. . . .

We had a visit from the Indians a week ago. Ten dog teams came down with meat and all here will have a good Christmas dinner. . . . We had three meals today: breakfast at 7 a.m., dinner at 12 a.m., supper at 6 p.m. Andrew brought out the plum cake made by his sister over a year ago and it went fine. Breakfast – Cariboo steak, potatoes and onions, bread and coffee. Dinner – Boiled ham, potatoes and onions, apple pie, plum cake, coffee. Supper – The remains from dinner.

He spent the next evening "at Mitchell's shack and had a good drink, first since I left Montreal. Did not remain late as Mr. McGruder from the lower shacks was here and promised us a spiritualist meeting in the evening at our concert. It began about 9 p.m. and lasted till 1 a.m. Besides our party Dr. Brown, Dr. Sloan, Judge Morse and George Dalgleish were present. McGruder called our meeting a fairly successful one. The spirits spoke quite freely. I was the only one who did not converse. . . ."

For Wind City had versatile talent, as one of its inhabitants eventually explained to the *Bulletin*. "Before its inhabitants deserted it Wind City was the scene of mirth and social enjoyment; Chess, checquer and euchre clubs were formed, dances were held, lectures given on scientific and every other conceivable subject, a code of municipal laws enacted and the months passed pleasantly and profitably away. Its inhabitants were taken from every walk of life: Almost every profession was represented and probably at no other point in the north was social life and friendly feeling so much in evidence as at Wind City."

Lack of mail from home bothered all the Klondikers and at Christmas several of them made a deal with an Indian who, on the promise of $100 in goods, undertook to go down the 160 miles to Fort McPherson to bring up any mail that might be there. He made the return trip in twenty-one days. McAdam said sadly: "The mail carriers arrived Saturday 14th inst. & my disgust was great when I learned that they did not bring one letter for me. My disappointment is great, but I suppose I must bear with it. It seems remarkably strange that out of at least ten or twelve letters that I expected to receive, not one came to hand. There must be somewhere along the rivers quite a number addressed to E. McAdam. . . ."

When about the middle of September the weary trackers had decided to camp at Wind City, they planned to stay there until about the middle of February. By early December, however, many of them were

160

so restless that they just had to start up the pass. At the time they left there was no evidence of sickness in the camp. As Coatsworth said: "We had four doctors in our midst and four lawyers, but no use for either."

But on December 31, 1898, McAdam's diary says: "Scurvy has broken out. Three cases in Wind City, and eight or nine below the ramparts with very serious prospects for a considerable increase of the trouble. The cause appears to be unknown. The doctors recognize the symptoms but cannot account for the sickness breaking out. So far, the health of our party has continued good. . . ."

When he wrote of "below the ramparts," he was referring to the camp well below the mouth of the Snake River at which A. D. Stewart died. Along the Peel that winter three others fell victims to scurvy: Captain Bourman from Ottawa and his brother Archie at Wind City, and Schurman Anderson from South Dakota at a camp up the valley from that place. Rumours reaching Victoria, British Columbia, and Edmonton mentioned several more deaths and these stories had a plausible foundation. They came about because men who left the camp when a number were sick with scurvy presumed the victims would die. The records are very clear, however, and only those four perished of the disability. When Dr. Brown, the leader of the Brown-Morse party, reached civilization he corrected the reports. Dr. J. B. Mason, W. C. Gooch and T. Greig, all of Chicago, had been listed as dead, but as Dr. Brown said, the first two had been ill with scurvy and recovered, whereas Greig had never been ill. The disease sapped the strength of these two victims so much, however, that they were among the six who decided to go back to Edmonton. Dr. Martin, a dentist, also had a touch of scurvy but he did not return to Edmonton. Along with William McGinn he went back to Fort McPherson and in due course the two of them boarded a whaling ship and eventually came home. A few other Klondikers from the Fort McPherson area took passage on whalers to Alaska.

McAdam and his men did not leave Wind City until January 22. A few days prior to that they began hauling, and to help them transport their goods were able to obtain the services of Enoch, an Indian, and his dogs. In the fall, the men had dragged their boats up the shallow stream as far as Wind City; now they had abandoned them and were to drag sleds for many a weary mile.

McAdam's diary for January 22 says: "Farewell, Wind City! We began our journey southward on Friday (the 20th) at 11.30 a.m. and reached the 9 mile point (the Brown party cache) at 3.30 p.m. It was our longest haul, but our loads were not heavy. Yesterday we made 4 loads each (5 hauling), in all 20 loads, and brought all our goods up from cache 1½ below. To bring our camp to this point we have travelled (I have at least) 60 miles loaded and 51 miles light, in all 111 miles. This is truly horse work but we must get there. . . ."

For many weeks the diary was to be concerned almost solely with accounts of each day's struggle through the snow. By February 25 they had reached the "Swedes' shack," where Anderson from South Dakota had died, and on March 7 arrived at the mouth of Bear River. To get to the summit they still had a weary hundred miles to go.

All the while McAdam had been fretting about a mysterious gold discovery. Weeks before, with winks and nods, Mitchell had hinted that he and some of his party knew of something good somewhere far up the Wind River. From then on the tale bothered McAdam. Before he left Wind City he confided to his diary: "Andrew gave me a strange piece of information today & it accounts for Judge Morse Patterson Merritt & Coatsworth going up the river which has always seemed a strange business to me. We are both hoping the information is correct & not a hoax & that their plans can be carried out. If the information given certain parties proves correct, & we get places as promised, then it is quite possible our fortunes may be awaiting us within a distance of about 100 miles."

On the morning of McAdam's departure, "Mitchell said he would probably write us & send letter up with Indians. Mitchell did not speak to me about the information Andrew informed me of although he is one of the parties in the secret. Is his letter to be the one for us to act?"

A week later, "It would appear that Mr. Campbell told McGinnis about the affair Andrew spoke to me about and tomorrow or the next day when Mr. C. & Mr. Mitchell will pass on their way up, Coatsworth said that they would stop & talk the matter over. We are all anxious to hear what is to be told & are hoping that the news is good."

A few days later still he gave a little more information. "Last evening had a talk with Coatsworth re matter referred to in late notes, & he informed me that the Indians have given proof of gold in this country. He has seen black sand sample shewing what he thinks would prove good pay. He also saw very fine sample of rich quartz. The Chief (Francis) has promised to show Mr. Campbell the ground & they (Mr. C. Coatsworth, Judge & Mitchell party) are anxious to have us join them & be benefited, should information prove of any value. . . ."

On March 1 he was still fretting about the mystery. "I wonder what will be the outcome of the trip to Bear River. Will the news be good & is our fortune awaiting us within 50 miles? I am hoping it is true, but am fully prepared for disappointment."

Finally, about a week later, as he neared Bear River, his diary says: "The report brought down was not by any means cheering, & the probability is that we will have to go over the pass to find gold. All the parties are passing Bear River & making for the pass which is 46 miles farther on. Campbell, Coatsworth, Morse, Merritt & Patterson are still at Bear River, & their object in remaining there is somewhat obscure. They promised to tell McGinnis full particulars first opportunity & as McG. & Maltby are up there will probably have some information for us when we get there. . . ." The whole business had turned out to be just another rumour.

McAdam appears to have been a most reasonable and patient man. In spite of that, the rigours of the trip were beginning to depress him and undoubtedly the disappointment of the Bear River rumour added to his depression. On March 14, 1899, he confided some more of his feelings to the diary:

> Idleness does not tend to improve a man's spirits, but rather to give him time to brood over past and future troubles with very often the result, that life for the time being is simply unbearable. I often feel that my disposition is changing very rapidly and much more so, since I left home. I fight against this feeling, but fear do not win very often. As a party we are not suited to each other and time is not improving matters. As a whole, I do not regret the trip, as it is too early to despond, but had I to begin again, I should certainly give more attention to the choice of partners.

By March 28 everybody was feeling touchy, and that day J. Millete, who had been McAdam's companion ever since they left Montreal, decided to leave the party and to go with the Brown-Morse group. McAdam regretted his action and commented "personally I am very sorry to part with Joe as we have agreed very well."

On April 2 McAdam's optimism had still not returned, for his diary said:

> Am trying to keep hopeful, but as we draw near the gold country, find myself less sanguine of the final result. Our provisions are rapidly disappearing and how we are to replenish our larder is becoming a serious question. At the present time we have only 500 lbs flour and about 175 lbs bacon – enough for about 3 or 4 months. It is a long time since I came to the conclusion that our trip has been a big bungle, and have decided that should we be fortunate enough to "strike" will take good care to see that our provision list is more liberally attended to. The trip so far, has cost us much more than most of the parties here, and in many cases they are better provided for than we are.

Then on April 10 the diary contains the joyous entry "The Pass." In the next sentence McAdam gave a summary of the effort that had gone into the 143-mile trip, which so far had occupied 78 days of almost unceasing toil, often in weather forty degrees below zero.

Mileage to date: with loads 412¾, without loads 269¼: Total 682 miles, actual distance travelled 143½ miles.

Number of working days (counting one day my cook week) 60, average total mileage per day 11.36 miles, average actual distance per day 2.39 miles. Greatest distance one day 20 miles. Greatest actual distance one day (with all supplies) 3½ miles. Average camp move 6.83 miles.

But even though they could now look west down a stream whose waters eventually reached the Yukon River, they were still six weeks away from their destination. Not until nine days later, on April 19, while going down the Rackla River on the way to join the Beaver River, did McAdam have any definite idea of what lay ahead. "A large camp ground where probably 5 or 6 parties have camped. On a sign left there we learned the joyable news, that we have only 14 miles to go beyond that camp to reach 'the large river and hot springs' and that the trail was good, and also that Dr. Brown and the Bay City party (the Swedes) were there building boats. What a relief it is to know something definite about 'the beyond.' Up till the present we have been in complete darkness as to how far we had to go down this river, now this miserable uncertainty has disappeared, and this work will be completed inside a week."

When a few days later, on April 28, they reached what they called the shipyard, the diary bursts out joyfully:

It is finished

This morning we completed the work we began last January – hauling toboggans, and if ever men earned a good rest, we have. We are now in the *gold country* (?). It has taken us nearly fourteen months to reach this place, and the next few months will tell what reward we are to have, as a company. We are all hopeful, and intend working hard for success – Washing and a general clean up is now the order of the day.

At the "shipyard" various parties were busy whip-sawing lumber and building boats. By the time McAdam reached there the Brown-Morse party had finished its boat and departed. By the middle of May there were eighty-five men at the place. McAdam and his friends went to work with a will but did not complete their boat till May 21. During that time he made an unexpected discovery: "In a bag supposed to contain two 50 lbs. sacks of flour that one of the sacks contained about 35 or 40 lbs. of sugar. Had we lots of flour on hand, the discovery would have been a pleasant surprise, but unfortunately, this is not the case.

164

It is quite possible, however that we may be able to exchange the sugar for flour or something else that is more necessary. We had sugar in our tea tonight – the first time for many months."

On May 25, with a cry of "Goodbye Spring City" they launched their boat. Two and one-half miles downstream they came to the wrecked scow *Maggie* owned by Peacock, Barclay, Payzant, Crichton and Felt-ham, saw several boxes and oars and picked up the latter's dunnage bag. At this late stage in their trip, when all they had to do was to float down to the Yukon, that party had got jammed in the ice and to save themselves the men floated to shore on an ice floe. Evidently this final blow had taken the heart out of them. "The party did not make any attempt to save their goods, but managed to get down to the camp below, where the people raised a small quantity of supplies and built them a boat. . . . None here can understand why the owners did not make an attempt to save their goods; it seems a case of complete dis-couragement. Think what its means – not simply a loss of a few dollars worth of goods, but eighteen months labor practically lost."

McAdam's party was now on the upper Stewart above Lansing, and here and there some of them panned out traces of gold. Opinion was divided; some wished to prospect and others to hurry on to Dawson. A remark in the diary illustrates an attitude prevalent with most Yukoners: "We have not travelled the distance we have to see Dawson, but to get gold, and if we are to get gold we must look for it."

About a week later they were overtaken by Frank Braine, who had started from Edmonton in the fall of 1897 with the Langworthy party, and Jack Garnett, from whom Milvain had parted at Fort Simpson when Garnett had been laid up with scurvy. For a few days the two travelled with the McAdam party.

Braine shed some light on the two mysterious white men of whom the Indians at Fort Norman had spoken as building houses far up the Gravel River and taking out plenty of gold. "It appears that a man the name of Power has been up there two or three times (he left his name and dates of visits on trees) and they cannot understand what attracted him such a long distance from the Yukon River, if he did not find gold. Braine intends making enquiries at Dawson regard-ing this man. They prospected the head waters of several streams with-out success."

On June 10 McAdam's group reached the Mayo River and sat around discussing what they would do now that they were in the heart of the Yukon, "Andrew and I saying that we should prefer going on to Dawson and closing out the business. . . . I am now indifferent to what we do, and shall be glad when the end comes so that I can begin something on my own account. I am tired of the party and everything connected with it. . . ."

On June 13 they reached Stewart City, which was almost deserted. "Last summer about 6,000 were there. We saw groups of shacks every here and there for quite a time before we reached the City. When the rush into this section occurred last year, about every yard of creek and river was staked and is still held."

At 8 a.m. two days later they reached Dawson. "Immediately on our arrival here went up to P.O. to get mail if any, but had to wait around a long time (till 9 o'c. and our time was 1½ hours too fast) before we got in. Am I ever to receive a letter? Where are my letters? Surely the folks have written to me. Not a letter and I so anxious to hear from home and my little daughter. Will my luck ever turn?"

Cresswell, Skynner and Tallman were several weeks behind McAdam's party, but with the coming of spring and the effect of fresh moose meat, they all recovered and followed the earlier parties up the Wind River and over the mountains. All three reached the Yukon in reasonable shape.

The Peel River route, with its weeks and weeks of eternally hauling loads had not been a fortunate choice. Nevertheless, by means of it over ninety men got through to Dawson. In comparison, those Klondikers who, whether by luck or good judgement, chose the route from Fort McPherson to LaPierre's House had a relatively easy time.

Of all the Edmonton routes to the Yukon, the Mackenzie – Rat River route, the longest, took the least time. It was also the easiest and by far the most practical. Over it the greatest number of successful Klondikers, some four hundred of them, reached their destination. Its key points were Athabasca Landing, Fort McPherson, LaPierre's House and the mouth of the Porcupine on the Yukon River. The 1898 prospectors floated down to Fort McPherson and then, following in the steps of the previous year's Segers-Hardisty party, climbed over the easy pass to LaPierre's House, seventy straight-line miles west, and then made boats on the Bell River and floated down to the Yukon. The 1898 Lamoureux contingent crossed by that route and their elapsed time from Edmonton to the Yukon was eighty-six days. Isadore Fix also hurried across and was on the Yukon River three months after leaving Edmonton. Many others made fairly similar rapid trips.

The critical part of that long route was the short, seventy-mile section from Fort McPherson to LaPierre's House, which could be crossed by two alternative routes. The first took the Klondikers up the

166

Rat River to McDougall Pass and then down the Bell River to La-Pierre's House. The second took them up Stony Creek from Fort McPherson, over the summit and down an unnamed watercourse to the same destination. Leaving aside blind guessing, two conditions governed the adventurers' choice of one alternative or the other: time of arrival at the mouth of the Rat River, and how heavily or lightly laden the party might be.

If a Klondiker arrived there before the first week in July, he would find the water in the Rat River high, and, therefore, could ascend it fairly quickly. Even if he arrived during the next couple of weeks and was lightly enough laden, he could still use the route and get across that season. If, however, he arrived late and heavily laden, he was in trouble. Many in that situation started up the stream and got caught by the freeze-up, but by that time they were committed and had to follow through.

Some of those who reached the Rat River decided that their supplies were too heavy to take up by water and simply camped and waited to take their loads across on the snow. As James Wilson of South Dakota explained when he returned to Edmonton, "the reason that caused so many men to winter on this side of the divide was the large amount of supplies they had, and which they could not get across, in any other way so well as on the snow."

The prospectors had no trouble ascending the first languid twenty-five miles of the Rat River. To get up the next thirty-five miles to the summit of McDougall Pass, however, they faced an ascent of some 1,200 feet up the river bed. In anticipation of this climb, therefore, at the twenty-five-mile point, the Klondikers spent some time cutting down their boats. Since this place soon became littered with discarded parts of boats, the men called it Destruction City. Prospectors who were late in arriving had to spend the in-between season at Destruction City and built a number of log shacks.

During the early fall of 1898 many paused there, cut down their boats and went on up the pass, only to find that the freeze-up prevented them from going farther. There was nothing they could do but wait some months and while they waited they built a second cluster of cabins, which came to be called Shacktown.

While the majority of the prospectors went up the Rat River and then camped at Destruction City or Shacktown, several others who took the alternative route from Fort McPherson were caught by winter on the Stony Creek Pass and built shacks in two or three groups which they never bothered to name. In this way another temporary, although dispersed, community composed mainly of members of the

Enterprise, Springfield and Toronto parties came into being. All of these hopefuls finally made their way to Dawson.

During the winter all of the Klondikers, whether at Destruction City or Shacktown, or at the community along Stony Creek, carried their supplies forward to LaPierre's House and reached it in time to make new boats with which to descend the Bell River in the spring.

Several observers estimated the population of Klondikers in the Fort McPherson area generally during the winter of 1898-99 at about 170 men and women. They were divided up as follows: twenty at Fort McPherson, twenty-eight in the camps in Stony Creek Pass, eighty-one at Shacktown and forty-two at Destruction City.

In all these camps, of course, everyone was merely marking time until conditions were favourable enough to start the move to the head of navigation on Bell River to be ready when the ice went out. Included among those who wintered at Fort McPherson and crossed the Stony Creek portage were Mr. and Mrs. Sam Brown of Detroit, who established a novel record for the Edmonton route to the Klondike. They left Detroit about the middle of March 1898 and twelve months later were crossing the portage to LaPierre's House. Before leaving Fort McPherson, however, they were blessed with a baby — sex unstated. This child held a unique distinction — not only was it born on the way to the Klondike, but it was also conceived en route.

One of the Klondikers who started to take the Stony Creek route was R. C. Rolt, who had been with the English Clatworthy party. This group had been riven with such dissension at Edmonton that it was split up by a court order. Rolt went downstream with Clatworthy, Austin and Truman of the original party. Rolt, Austin and Truman started up the Rat River but returned to Fort McPherson and gave some thought to ascending the Peel. Since they did not like the look of that stream either, they obtained a clinker-built boat and headed for Herschel Island, nearly two hundred miles away in the Beaufort Sea. About thirty miles from their destination a storm forced them to seek shelter on a small island. During the night the storm broke their anchor rope and carried their boat away. Fortunately they were able to hail a passing whaler, on which they were put to work. They found the work most arduous and the food almost intolerable. While Rolt and his associates were with the boat the crew caught a whale and then set out for San Francisco, where they arrived on November 4. From there the three Klondikers crossed to New York by train and caught a ship leaving for England.

Mrs. Hoffman spent the winter of 1898-99 at Shacktown. There is no mention of J. Schneider, with whom she teamed up when her husband was drowned in Slave Lake, but he may have gone ahead and left her, as he was not recorded in the list of Shacktown residents. Somewhere along the way she must have given birth to her baby, which presumably died.

A group which had come in along the route from Prince Albert and consisted of George Dunn, Edward Miller, A. B. Clegg, W. Brownlow and Hugh Stevens also spent the winter at Shacktown and went over in the spring. They became associated with Jim Wallwork and "Steamboat" Wilson who had teamed up at Fort Smith. While there was plenty of snow on the ground Wilson and Wallwork and the rest of the party combined forces with some Indians who supplied thirty dogs and dragged the *Daisy Bell* over the summit from Shacktown to the Bell River.

Late in April, and by way of the Hudson's Bay Company's mail service down the Mackenzie, Wilson received a message that made it imperative for him to hasten back to Australia. Before long, he and all those associated with Jim Wallwork were hurtling down the rapids of Porcupine River and reached Fort Yukon on June 8, 1899. Wilson, anxious to hurry on, took passage on a steamboat and reached Dawson on June 24.

The *Daisy Bell*'s gallant little eight horsepower engine met its match when trying to ascend the Yukon to Dawson. Jim Wallwork, however, stuck by his engine and, after deciding that the *Daisy Bell* was not worth any more repairs, put the boiler and engine into a York boat. Then, once more mobile, he reached Dawson on July 9. Unquestionably, the *Daisy Bell* had made one of the most remarkable trips on record and was the only steamer to cross the mountains into the Yukon.

Destruction City had some interesting inhabitants, including Mr. and Mrs. A. C. Craig of Chicago, who had left Edmonton in 1897 with the Warmolts party. They were still with Henry Card, who led the group after Warmolts's defection, and were also with Ernest Crabbe who had left Edmonton about the same time with the Griffin brothers. Why these four did not cross McDougall Pass during 1898 as they might have been expected to do is not known. Possibly they had spent some time prospecting the shores of Great Slave Lake or even Great Bear Lake, as Mr. and Mrs. C. Westhead had done. In any event, in the spring of 1899, all four crossed over to the Yukon.

Keeping Mrs. Craig company at Destruction City was Mrs. LeFrancois of the Woonsocket party. She and her husband had a distressing winter while she tended one of the party's original members, Joseph Meyer, who died of scurvy. Perhaps the experience was too much for her nerves, because even when so near the goal towards which they had turned their faces for so long, she and her husband returned to Edmonton. In the spring the rest of the Woonsocket party went on to Dawson.

One of the adventurers who spent the winter in the vicinity of Destruction City was Alphonso Waterer who, from his reminiscences, seems to have had a bad time in that area. On one occasion, a few days before Christmas, he and a partner went out on some expedition and got lost. Both of them were badly frost-bitten. They had nearly reached the end of their tether and were preparing to camp for the night when a young Indian and his train of dogs came along. Seeing the state they were in, he led them to his lodge. As Waterer remembered it:

We walked in front of the dogs in order to break the trail, my partner wearing the snow shoes and I drew our empty sled which I was soon forced to abandon. Night was with us, and a keen wind was springing up. Coming to a part of the river where the trail needed no breaking, we fell behind the load and after proceeding for about a mile I suddenly missed my partner, when I called upon the Indian to stop while I went back on the trail to search, and within about half a mile I saw by the dim light of the stars an object describing circles. This was my partner gone temporarily wrong in the head from the extreme cold. Going round and round like this and falling down means being frozen to death. I went up to him and shouted as loud as I could but he still continued on his round and beaten trail. I knew that if I could get him to speak without falling down that there was a chance of saving him. There is a saying that it is cruel to be kind, and as I could make nothing of him at all, I acted on it, went to the bank, picked a good stout stick from a bunch of dry willows and started clubbing him with it. This arrested his progress for a few seconds but on he went again and I repeated the dose with a little interest. This seemed to have the desired effect as when I spoke to him he answered me just as if nothing had happened. I got hold of his arm and led him on to the trail. He was quite rational and asked what had become of the Indian then I told him what had happened to him but he seemed to know nothing about it. . . .

The next thing which impeded our progress was an overflow caused by fissures in the ice through which we were obliged to walk causing our foot gear to become frozen solid and as a great thirst and giddiness had come upon me I took a copious draught of water in place of snow which I had been eating, but I did not travel after this but a very short distance before I collapsed and became insensible. Just before I fell I could see sparks rising from the Indians' camp fire on the bank which was scarcely a quarter of a mile distant when this trouble over took me.

When I gained consciousness I found myself in the Indian's teepee stretched out on the broad of my back with my feet towards a bright fire. The old Indian was rubbing my feet, the squaw my hands and their

170

little girl my head. I was quite puzzled at first and could not imagine how I had reached this place of safety but it happened that as soon as I fell the young Indian promptly unloaded his carry-all placed me inside and urged the dogs on at top speed.

In due course, Waterer and his partner made their way back to Destruction City to find that during their absence "a miner's committee had been formed, a chairman elected, and laws drawn up which were about the same as those in force in California in 49."

Shortly afterwards the committee called a meeting for the purpose of drafting two or more men "to visit and generally to attend upon and relieve sick men who were afflicted with the scurvy all along the line, and as no men could be induced to undertake this mission of mercy, my partner and myself volunteered."

They were assigned to look after two sick men at Shacktown who were in a cabin somewhat isolated from the rest of the community. Waterer said:

> The time we put in here was of the most sorrowful description as everybody seemed to think that the disease was of a contagious nature. We were quarantined in the strictest fashion and had the utmost difficulty as the time wore on to communicate with the committee who had portaged to the headwaters of the River. Nobody would come near us but all appeared to shun us as they would some loathsome animal. If we wanted to communicate with anybody we used to go to the trail on the river and place our messages in a cleft stick, and sometimes they would remain there for several days at a stretch till somebody who was still possessed of a little nerve should chance to take them along....
>
> When we first entered this cabin . . . I could clearly see that they were in a filthy and dying state and no wonder at it considering the piles of dirty rags that were strewn all over the floor and the evil smell which lurked about in the place. Although it was after 10 p.m. we set to work to get the place cleaned up.
>
> My partner who was my senior took charge of one man and did the cooking whilst I looked after the other one and did the outdoor work such as getting firewood. . . . We went to work and washed them all over with warm water, put clean well dried clothes on them, and gave them some hot tea to drink for which they uttered expressions of gratitude and seemed to regard us with astonishment....
>
> My partner and myself both contracted this disease in this cabin but it did not trouble us above our knees till later on when it attacked us in the mouth at Bell River....

The first one to die was G. W. Springer of Los Angeles, and Waterer and his partner buried him and eventually notified the miners' committee. Its action at this point is interesting. These men insisted that the grave be opened so that they could view the body and identify it in order to make an affidavit to the effect that Springer was dead. They did this in the interests of his family and in this way made certain that the man's life insurance company, having proof of his death, could pay his wife.

Scurvy claimed three others on the Rat River that winter: George Thomas of Chicago and a man named Fred Hauser, also at Shacktown, while Harry DeBier of Chicago died at Destruction City. These men died not because of lack of food but because of an improperly balanced diet.

Of the several hundred Klondikers who reached the end of the long downstream voyage at Fort McPherson during 1898, a total of eleven died from various causes. Except for these, about thirty persons who came back to Edmonton, perhaps a dozen who went to Herschel Island, and some ninety who crossed over by way of the Peel River, the remainder, about four hundred, eventually reached LaPierre's House and went on to the Yukon. Some two hundred of these crossed quickly and were soon in Dawson. The rest, about 170, were caught by the freeze-up and remained in the general vicinity of Fort McPherson during the early part of the winter, but went on to the Klondike in the spring.

During 1897-98 approximately 685 Klondikers went downstream from Fort Simpson, and of these some 565 crossed over to the gold-fields. About seventy-five did so by ascending the Gravel River, another ninety reached Dawson by way of the Peel River, and the majority, at least four hundred, crossed over to the Yukon by way of the McDougall or the Stony Creek passes.

CHAPTER TWELVE

THE OVERLAND ROUTE:
EDMONTON TO PEACE RIVER
CROSSING AND FORT ST. JOHN

Beside the old trail some six miles out of Fort Assiniboine stands the railing of a small grave. There, seventy years ago, sorrowing parents buried their three-month-old girl, who but for the Klondike Rush might be alive today. What little we know of the story indicates that she was probably buried without more than a small marker. Someone travelling the trail, perhaps her parents returning disgusted, put a fence around the grave and wrote on the railing:

> In memory of a little girl buried here by her father in the days of the Klondike Gold Rush 1898.

Within a decade homesteaders coming to farm noticed the grave and for many years kept the fence in repair. Then about 1930 a bush fire swept it away. A year or so later the Ladies' Club of Doris erected a new cross and painted the original inscription on it.

We cannot be certain whose child fell victim to the trek towards the gold-fields, but as far as we can tell, only one couple among the Klondikers reached Edmonton with a child. They were Mr. and Mrs. G. W. Larrabee, and beyond the fact that they arrived in town we know nothing. It seems probable that they joined the cavalcade heading north and the hardship was too much for the child. It seems probable, too, that before long they turned back to Edmonton, because although Klondikers went out of their way to note the presence of women at Fort St. John and all along the Overland Route, no one mentioned Mrs. Larrabee.

As far as we know, out of all the hundreds who took the Chalmers Trail to Peace River Crossing this child was the only fatal casualty. Human beings, subject only to their own wills, went on successfully or else returned safely. Horses on the Chalmers Trail, however, subject

173

to all the whims and cruelties of inexperienced or ignorant Klondikers, died by the hundreds. And this is no exaggeration. Every Klondiker who took the trail had an average of at least five horses, and since during 1898 about 775 Klondikers went this way, some four thousand horses started with them. About half of these got to Peace River Crossing, while the rest perished of abuse or starvation.

The overland Klondikers were mainly people from western Canada and the United States who thought in terms of horse transportation. With them, of course, went all those who were not particularly anxious to reach the Yukon so long as by taking the Overland Route they could reach the gold-yielding areas between Fort St. John and the Yukon.

As they were to discover, of all routes, the overland one was by far the most difficult. Along it the failure rate was very high and the mortality amongst horses, and even the few oxen which some of the Klondikers tried, was appalling. Like the Water Route, it had many alternative branches. Because of these alternatives and because so many overlanders either turned back or switched to a water route, it is very hard – often impossible – to keep track of those prospectors who went this way or that, doubled back, or shot off in a new direction. From records of individual parties, we can get a fair idea of what these Klondikers went through, but, like a snarled fishing line, the detailed picture is impossible to untangle and present.

THE CHALMERS TRAIL THROUGH THE SWAN HILLS

The Overland Route set out north from Edmonton as one trail, then flared out like a long, nightmarish highway overpass where traffic lanes of all sorts merge and diverge, cross over and spread out, and finally came back together in the vicinity of Watson Lake to proceed mainly as one lane leading to the Yukon River. The principal trails and most of the secondary ones are shown on the accompanying maps. Along the main route the first key point was Peace River Crossing. From there one prominent trail led northward to Fort Nelson and on to the Liard River which it followed westward to modern Watson Lake. From Peace River Crossing a second main trail led westward to Fort St. John and then, branching into two alternatives which came together again at Fort Grahame, swept north and west along the Rocky Mountain Trench in the direction of Watson Lake. From that point the main route ascended the Frances River, crossed over to the Pelly and swept down it to the northbound Yukon River.

While all sections of these routes were to test the Klondikers' stamina to the utmost, perhaps the most rigorous testing came on the first part of their trip – the 320 miles to Peace River Crossing, and particularly the 120-mile stretch from Fort Assiniboine to Lesser Slave Lake – the stretch which the Klondikers called the Chalmers Trail but which now, to the exclusion of all other routes, Albertans call the Klondike Trail.

As we have seen, Chalmers's party started cutting the road from Fort Assiniboine over the Swan Hills about January 1898 and finished it to the low standard that the available money permitted by the following July. After that, of course, the trail saw little service because the heavy traffic over it started in the first two or three months of 1898 and was practically all over before July. The Klondikers used whatever part of it was cut out and then struck out ahead of the trail-cutting party. The Edmonton people who had conceived the idea of this trail did what they could to get it cut out, but the Klondike Rush burst upon them so swiftly and subsided so suddenly that the great roads they had planned never let the light of day through the forests.

During the early months of 1898 the Klondikers and their horses set forth along the Chalmers Trail. The fact that nearly one hundred of these prospectors turned back before reaching Peace River Crossing is a small indication of the hardships endured by those who pressed on. Perhaps the best way to try to understand the conditions along the Chalmers Trail is to follow some typical parties on their way north, in chronological order.

Whereas during the fall of 1897 the Fresno group and some other smaller parties took the vague trail by way of Lac Ste Anne and modern Whitecourt, almost all the 1898 adventurers struggled over the Chalmers Trail. As was expected, those parties that started during the fall of 1897, the Fresno people and others, found themselves caught by the freeze-up and wintered here and there between Sturgeon Lake and Fort St. John. Then in the spring of 1898, before they really got into gear again, the 1898 Klondikers caught up with them. From that time on the adventurers of both years fused into one inseparable mosquito-swatting migration straggling on towards the Yukon.

Four large parties left Edmonton early in the winter: the Brown-Morse, Fugard and Helpman groups and the Yukon Valley Mining Company. They were some weeks ahead of the large rush that started after the end of February and all but one of them made reasonable time over the Swan Hills to Lesser Slave Lake. The exception was the Helpman party, which, because of inexperience and internal friction, dawdled along and did not reach the lake until late in the spring. When it did get there the leader fired seven men.

In addition to these large parties, scores of smaller ones set out during February and March. Hardly a day passed without some aggregation or other getting itself into marching order and heading north. Some days several groups strung themselves out on the first eight-mile leg of their trip to St. Albert. There were the Indian Head party of four, J. T. Montgomery's combined sled and boat party, a Buffalo group, the Owen Sound party, the Woonsocket outfit of nine with twenty-eight horses and flat sleighs, a company with nine horses pulling travois with six-inch runners and loaded with nine hundred pounds each, the Fair brothers of Elkhorn, Manitoba, and many others. As the *Bulletin* of March 3, 1898, noted: "At least 50 [men] left on Tuesday alone."

J. N. Lhote, whose party left Edmonton on February 20 and after a relatively easy trip reached Fort St. John, sent back a trip diary from there on March 30:

We left St. Albert on Feb. 21st, and found we were quite early enough. The following is a list of the outfits we have passed on the road:

Feb. 21 – Passed a Montana outfit, also one from Cincinnati, and made 16 miles.

Feb. 23 – Passed Captain Willis, of Chicago, and two other outfits and camped at Lake Lennon [La Nonne].

Feb. 24 – Crossed Pembina river and made the top of the big hill.

Feb. 27 – Crossed Athabasca river and passed to-day two outfits from Detroit, Michigan.

Feb. 28 – Passed O'Brien's outfit [Helpman] which left in January.

March 4 – Crossed the Swan Mountain and camped on Swan river.

March 8 – Reached Slave Lake and camped 10 miles further on. The next day we reached the end of the lake which is 40 miles across and camped near Hudson Bay Post.

It is our intention to press hay here by hand press, to carry with us on our way to Peace River. To-night the copper colored people are dancing to the music made by a piper who is with the Sloan party. When we left the big Chicago party they were losing horses at the rate of one or two every day. We have passed several parties whom we did not know. It may interest you to know that we are the first to get to St. John of all who left this winter.

Frank Walker of Fort Saskatchewan, leading a party consisting of his brother Albert, J. Carscadden, J. H. Reid, W. Hepburn and others, set out on March 8. As a means of transport the group had thirty-five horses and one white mule, to which we will refer later. When these men reached the Paddle River, about seventy miles out from Edmonton, T. Cinnamon was stricken with pneumonia, so they camped for a week. Then on the advice of another Klondiker, Dr. Nichols from

Ohio, they loaded him, bedding and all, into a sleigh and started on again.

Walker's memoirs give this description of the route:

> By the time we reached the Athabasca, several of the parties who had gone ahead of us had become very much disgusted with the route, and stated so in no uncertain terms upon blazed trees. Some excellent poetry was also composed and written there apropos of the route. I now regret that I did not copy some of it, as it would be, at this date, very interesting. I remember one of these outfits was composed of what was known as "The Big Four." They were engineers and conductors from the Big Four Railway in the U.S.A. They were very humorous fellows and always signed themselves "The Big Four" after writing interesting stuff upon trees. . . .
>
> The Hillside [north bank of Athabasca River] was littered with broken boxes, smashed sleighs and harness, and practically every tree on the lower side of the grade was blazed and the owners of the outfits gave vent to their feelings in epitaphs upon the trees. At the very top of the hill on a rotten tree had been nailed a piece of board, with a hand pointing in each direction. The one in the direction of the Klondike had written underneath "To Dawson City 2433½ miles" and underneath the other hand said "To Home Sweet Home." . . .
>
> Passing along the south shore of Lesser Slave Lake, we commenced to find dead horses in abundance, the majority of course dying for the lack of feed, and at one place in particular we found several horses dead tied to trees by their halters. I am afraid it would not have been well for the owners of them, if they had shown up about that time, as all our boys were great lovers of horses.

About the same time that Walker set out Joe McDonald, a famous old frontiersman who lived in South Edmonton, left to guide a small party led by C. P. Braithwaite. Early in June Joe returned and gave the editor of the *Bulletin* an earful about the Chalmers Trail.

> It was impassable to anything but pack horses, and in order to get through, the parties blockaded there – and they were numerous – had to turn to and cut their own road to Swan river. The trail runs over mountains and hills through a country absolutely devoid of feed and as the outfits on the road had made calculations on the time it would take them to get to Lesser Slave Lake, where they could get fresh feed for their horses, and had taken only feed enough to carry them through to the post, the result of the blockade, which lasted a week, was that they all ran out of hay and grain and their horses were on the verge of starvation. For days they had positively nothing to eat but the bark of the trees they were tied to and what little frozen moss they found. As a result horses dropped in their tracks every day till the trail was landmarked with their carcasses; and those that lived through it, till they could get on Swan river, were run down to the last extremity and unfit to carry their packs or pull their

loads. Near the mouth of Swan river, where it empties in the lake, grass at last could be found beneath the snow, and the ponies, by pawing, were able to get enough feed to prevent further actual starvation. At Slave lake post a rush took place for grain and all that was on hand was speedily sold to the first comers.

. . . Every party in the blockade lost some horses, some lost all they had, among the latter being the White and Grose party. Though the condition of the trail could not be blamed for all the losses that were sustained yet in many cases it was responsible altogether. Some parties were unqualified to make the trip and were losers on that account, others, who knew their business and did all that any one could do, were also heavy losers and through no fault of their own. The encountering of so many hardships at the commencement of their journey by the parties taking this trail did incalculable damage to the route at large, as they judged the future conditions of the trail by that which they were then going through, and wrote back to their friends accordingly. As a result of the hardships met with on the trail before reaching Slave lake many parties had no horses to continue overland after reaching Peace river crossing, even had they desired to do so, and so built boats at the crossing and went down the Peace to take the Athabasca-Mackenzie route. A number of others, about thirty parties, decided, however, to continue westerly overland as they had first intended, and, fortunately, as the result showed, their decision was a wise one for after passing Slave lake the traveller has no serious difficulties to face.

Dr. H. L. McInnis of Edmonton set out on March 24, but he did not go over the Swan Hills. With two men and twenty-two horses and sleighs, he went to Athabasca Landing and then followed the trail up the river and around Lesser Slave Lake. The hay he had brought from Edmonton lasted until the party got to the Hudson's Bay Company's Lesser Slave Lake post, and there for six dollars he purchased all the hay his horses needed to take them to Peace River Crossing. At the post the snow had gone, but he hired freighters to take his supplies to the river, which he crossed on April 11, the day before the ice went out. He remarked upon the number of freighters who were doing a good business at Lesser Slave Lake by charging two cents a pound for the eighty-mile trip over the wagon road to Peace River Crossing. Among these were: "W. Carson, late of the Sturgeon who has 16 carts and 3 wagons; C. Anderson, 4 wagons; Wm. and Geo. Taylor, 2 wagons; Roger Ferguson, 3 wagons; Mearon Bros. and others. . . ."

The Montgomery party from Toronto reached Peace River Crossing about the same time as Dr. McInnis. These men had left Edmonton around the middle of February with their much touted combined sleigh and boat, but along the way it had failed them and they had to buy pack horses to complete their trip to the Crossing.

178

One small party which circumvented the Chalmers Trail rather neatly consisted of W. Gifford and his partner Manley, who arrived in Edmonton with a Peterborough canoe. They had this hauled to the crossing of the Pembina and then paddled down it and the Athabasca to the mouth of Lesser Slave River. They ascended this, paddled west along the large lake, had their effects hauled across the eighty-mile portage to Peace River Crossing and reached there about the end of May.

Charles and William Parsons from Wales also circumvented the Chalmers Trail, but not so successfully. They hauled a boat overland to Fort Assiniboine and then floated down the Athabasca, rowed up the Lesser Slave River and finally got caught in the ice of the large lake. They had to abandon everything and for four days lived on flour and fish without salt. In the middle of June they returned to Edmonton to acquire another outfit and started back north.

One of the more enlightening accounts of the trip through the Swan Hills is that of Fred M. Ferriss, who led a party from Manitoba. These men bought horses and double sleighs in Edmonton, and on March 24, he wrote, "Pulled out about ten o'clock and reached the top of the hill [St. Albert] without much trouble but the freighter whom we had engaged to haul a load part of the way let his horses run away and upset the load took about half an hour or more loading again. Camped in good shelter for noon and found the trail very good except in two or three places some of the ponies got down twice by pulling off the road. Stopped all night at Qu Barre River with a Frenchman from whom we obtained 55 bus of oats for the trip. . . ."

Two days later, he said:

> Reached Lac La Nun about four o'clock excellent water and has fish in it bought or traded for two with some Half breeds or Indians. Reached the Pembina River and find excellent water and good camp ground are staying over Sunday, thankful for a day of rest. Another party we passed a few miles back in camp have come up and have broken down one sleigh.
>
> 27 [Sunday] I am trusting that the giver of all good will more than repay us for keeping His Command.

On March 31, after crossing the Athabasca near Fort Assiniboine, Ferriss related, they

> Started in good time and found the roads in much better condition than we had been led to expect as it was reported they were quite bare. Bob's sleighs broke and we were forced to put in new runners and had a stop of about four hours for the purpose. Caught the others at a creek about twelve miles out and camped for the night plenty of water but the grass was rather short.

April 1   Found the horses that had been turned loose had gone back during the night and Jack started back on little Nigger expecting to find them a mile or so down the trail so went bareback. It was nearly five hours before he returned having caught up to three about six miles down and the rest at the River where they had been stopped by Glen Campbell's men whom we had passed on the 30th. After feeding we got away shortly before twelve and made about fifteen miles for camp found an Italian watching a part of the supplies for an outfit that had been on the road since the 4th of March. The rest together with his wife who drives four or five sleighs had gone on to Deer Mountain near Swan River and part of them were to return in a few days for the balance of the stuff.

The Italian woman was Mrs. A. P. Toneilli who, with her husband and his companion, J. M. Favallini, formed part of a group from Chicago which reached Edmonton about February 15 and had been prevailed upon to take the Overland Route.

Before meeting Mrs. Toneilli, Ferriss and his companions had crossed Doris Creek at a point which in later years came to be a landmark. For there, along the trail, on the northwest quarter of Section 13-63-5, a small community grew up which the settlers who came to farm about 1910 called Klondike City. Inherent in the name was the idea that a number of Klondikers had built cabins there in which to winter. It is hardly probable that any Klondikers would have wintered at this point, since they could have reached it in a week or less from Edmonton. When about ten years later a Dominion Land Surveyor reported on his survey of this township, he noted the presence of the Chalmers Trail and stated that on this quarter section, beside a fairly good hay meadow, he found a "collection of Indian cabins." It seems likely that about the time of the Klondike Rush some Indians or Métis decided that this would be a desirable place to live and built several shacks. Neither Ferriss nor any of the Klondikers who left records made any remarks about the existence of these shacks at the time they passed. After the rush, however, a local trader operated a store, which stayed in business for a few years before "Klondike City" was abandoned.

Ferriss's sleighs were constantly breaking down and, between repairing them and looking for strayed horses, his group lost a lot of time. Before long it came to the end of where the Chalmers road gang had cut out the trail and then, like all other parties, it had to follow any trail it could find. We can get an idea of the exasperation Ferriss suffered by quoting from the diary which he had been too busy to continue keeping on a daily basis. About the middle of April it says:

The next morning we took two teams back for the load and left Bob repairing his broken sleigh we got back about ten o'clock but though we done our best found it about three P.M. before it was possible to start. Made about four miles over pretty rough roads and came to the first very steep hill and doubled up it and chained down the other side as it was apparently a ridge. After a mile more or further we came to a second hill and as it was very steep we concluded to camp until morning before trying it. This was the first night we had failed to catch the other boys so had quite a lot of work fixing up our tent as it had not before been used. In the morning we doubled up the hill and pulled up a second about half a mile further on within the next mile we caught up to the boys trying to go up a very long icy hill where their teams had stuck, we cut footholds for the horses on the worst part and had no great difficulty in reaching the top only a short distance on we found the Westmount party using block and tackle to go up a very bad hill. We were delayed probably three hours but got up all right and passed them on the top about two miles further on we came to a magnificent panorama as we looked far out across the banks of the Swan River none of us had the least idea that it would take us till the next afternoon to reach the real foot of the hill.

Bob had quite an accident before going more than half a mile down the hill the tongue came down and the horses got going pretty fast and upset on a turn but he held them. The other boys passed on ahead and we caught them long after dark camped in the road the snow so deep on either side that we just tied up where we stopped. On Friday after going down several hills and over a lot of very rough road we reached a creek where we found some grass for the horses the first since Sunday last. On Saturday we reached a point about ten or twelve miles down the River where we found plenty of grass. Sunday we spent at this point though it was thawing all day and we found the River in bad shape next day. I could not decide on Saturday what was best to do under the circumstances so did not say anything. I find the temptation to do work on Sunday very great, especially as it is getting so late in the season. Monday and Tuesday till near noon we continued on the river when concluded to try the bank and struck out through the bush in the hope of finding a trail that runs down the valley and struck it about a mile and a half from the camp. The next day we started and made a little over three miles before night. Thursday morning we went about half a mile and finding the trail very difficult to follow we decided to go ahead and locate a road.

Bob and I started about 11 A.M. and struck the trail where it had been travelled about a mile from camp however as it appeared to cut across the country we took up the wrong way but soon concluded it was a Indian hunters trail and circling to the right struck it again about a mile farther on. We found it went down the hill and followed the valley again until crossing the River at a point about five miles below camp. It was about three o'clock and we were very hungry with no apparent prospect of dinner before returning to camp when the Westmount party (who had passed our camp on Tuesday) came in sight and from them we got a good lunch. We tried to find a trail that the Helpman party were reported to be cutting on the East side of the River but failed and did not get back till near sundown.

Friday some of the horses were missing so as soon as I got up started to search for them and went back to where we had left the sleighs about two miles and found two old horses but on my return found that Bob had gone on with six horses packing and that three others were missing still. We hunted all day and did not find them till near evening so concluded to tie them all up and make an early start in the morning as one tent was ahead with the boys and one on the sleighs we slept out and did not find it uncomfortable. Were up at the first glimpse of daylight, and got an early start and got down about nine o'clock to where the boys had camped Friday night. After unloading we returned to the sleighs and found Bob and Frank whom we had met in the morning still fixing up made a start for camp about five o'clock and it was about nine when we got there leaving two sleighs about three and a half miles behind. Taking all through the past two weeks have been hard work and poor progress the horses have failed very much and we have had few oats for a week and but a few quarts left.

May 1st   It is again two weeks since I have found time to write so will go back over that time. On Monday the 18th one of the horses was missing and Jack failed to find him and as he had not looked in a certain point near camp I told him to go through it but he got angry told me to go myself and began to swear at me. I told him as he was starting on to stop that he could go no further with me this seemed to make him worse and he threatened to shoot me, as he had the rifle and was in a passion it seemed probable that he might carry out his threat. On his return he wanted to come to an understanding so we came to terms in the following manner, he to apologize for his conduct, and I would take him to Peace River give him some clothes to take him back to Edmonton it is a matter of extreme regret that he has turned out so badly. Since then he was reformed considerably and I have not heard him swearing for perhaps ten days.

On the 18th we made but 1½ miles to a steep hill that we used the pulleys on. The next morning I started back with two teams for the sleighs left behind and found the strayed horse on the road about a mile from our former camp got the load and after a number of upsets caused by the led horses pulling back and a number of minor difficulties as well as a lot of cutting, reached within half a mile of our camp of the previous evening. Here was obliged to stop and concluded to make the best of the circumstances and stayed all night sleeping in the tent and one quilt, fried some dried potatoes but could not manage them.

20th [April]   Was up about daylight and went ahead cutting the road to hill. Had breakfast on my return hardtack, and reached the hill about same time as Jack who had returned for some stuff they had failed to get to camp the previous day, we blocked up both sleighs with ease and started for camp about two miles ahead the road had to be cut for nearly half a mile to let the sleighs through and was pretty tired before reaching camp. Bob came back and met me about a mile out so got on better. It was snowing quite fast and melting as fast as it fell we stayed in camp all afternoon except Bob who went on to look for a road we were forced to cross the River and re-cross about two miles down, which we did the next day with all our stuff leaving two horses after the first trip to rest on the Bank of the River. On our return we found but one and could get no trace of him for four days except some Indians said he recrossed the River.

[On April 25] we came to a creek that it was possible to navigate with canoes so we took our canoe off and put it together to run part of the stuff down to the Lake. [We] returned to camp for night.

From that point it took them until May 10 to get all their outfit to Lesser Slave Lake post. During that time, sometimes taking loads in their canoe, sometimes dragging them along with their exhausted teams, their progress was one continual struggle. They spent from May 11 to 19 making two-wheeled carts with which to cross the eighty-mile portage to Peace River Crossing. As a result of so many parties discarding equipment at Lesser Slave Lake Post, Carson, one of the freighters, reported that every soul there had acquired an abandoned jumper (a horse-drawn sleigh with runners) and a yard full of toboggans.

On May 23, Ferriss and his companions started west from the Anglican Mission and a week later got their first view of the junction of the Peace and Smoky rivers. During that week they repaired wheels which broke off their carts, spent hours looking for strayed horses, and generally had a discouraging time. On May 28 the diary says:

Could not find two of the horses and I had started at it about sunrise we all searched near the camp for two hours or more. I asked the Lord to guide me and made a vow to give five dollars to missions over all other giving if He would help me find them. (Making in all Twenty Dollars vowed in this manner since leaving Edmonton) We all reached camp soon after and as we were tired took horses and rode in our further search I went up the road as far as Heart Creek three miles and found them a short distance from the Bank.

29th. We lost over half of yesterday looking for the two horses. . . .

On June 4 they arranged with a boatman to take their gear across the river and then faced the task of getting their horses across. A day or two later, "Having some difficulty finding all the horses it was rather late in the afternoon before we found a suitable place to start from and pushed off with the first lot. Altogether it was nearly a mile and a half to swim but we struck a bar that gave them a rest for a few minutes and they landed safely. It was about seven o'clock by the time the next lot were landed so it was decided to leave the rest till morning."

From about the first of March 1898 to the middle of June, Peace River Crossing was a busy place, with men camped on both sides of the river. Before the ice broke up some parties hurried over to the west side or, indeed, continued to Dunvegan on the ice, while others were busy felling trees and building boats because about a hundred men of several groups had decided to go down the river. Once the ice started to break up a couple of weeks ensued when no one could get across the river; some parties were caught half on one side and half on the other. In any event, the break-up period involved a serious delay to many who were heading westward to Fort St. John or northwestward towards Fort Nelson. Since most of the parties had reached Peace River Crossing with flat sleighs or double sleighs and had to prepare to go on with pack horses, many, like Dr. H. L. McInnis, spent a week or more at the Crossing making pack saddles and fitting up packs.

PEACE RIVER CROSSING TO FORT ST. JOHN

From the Crossing a good wagon road wound its way through the Shaftesbury Settlement and then climbed the hill and went on by Old Wives Lake to Dunvegan. From that point to Fort St. John the trails were nebulous. While the fur traders and Indians had a very sketchy trail well back from the north side of Peace River, it had seen so little recent use that it was almost impossible to detect. Moreover, the Klondikers' problem was complicated by the fact that the Indians who lived on the headwaters of Notikewin River had a trail leading south to Dunvegan, and it was much easier to find than the other trail to Fort St. John. Similarly, the Indians who lived a hundred miles north and east of Fort St. John had a trail from their area to the Hudson's Bay Company's post there. In order to get from Dunvegan to Fort St. John it was necessary to start north on one trail, then leave it, and strike off west and hope to hit and recognize the trail leading south into Fort St. John.

Before the Klondike Rush was over, however, the adventurers had made a good trail running from Peace River Crossing to Fort St. John. It was located much farther back from the river on the north side than the old wagon road to Dunvegan and was intercepted by a trail from Dunvegan. By taking in chronological order the records left by the Klondikers, we can watch the evolution of this cross-country trail and get a glimpse of some of the misadventures befalling the prospectors who hurried on to Fort St. John to catch up to the few who had reached that place during the winter by a different route.

184

For, as we have seen, the 1897 Klondikers had reached Fort St. John by way of Lac Ste Anne and Whitecourt, taking essentially the same route Inspector Moodie took. W. Inkster of Edmonton and his partner were one pair that set out for the Yukon along this trail. Although they merely paused at Fort St. John and then hurried on to spend the winter of 1897-98 at Fort Grahame, a few others, including many of the Fresno party, gradually assembled at Fort St. John and remained there until some other Klondikers had reached that point by working west from Peace River Crossing.

When that winter closed in on the Fresno people some of the original party gave up in disgust and went back to the United States. Out of the 130 horses with which their original party had started, all but thirty-six had died due to the hardships of the route or the inexperience of the drivers. During the winter the stragglers, including King and Mr. and Mrs. Garner, had made their way to Fort St. John and now in the spring of 1898 some eighteen of the original group were still in the mood to press on.

Two of the earliest parties of 1898 vintage to reach Fort St. John from Peace River Crossing were those led by J. N. Lhote and by Dr. Sloan, which travelled together and reached there during the last days of February. Whether or not their progress was speeded by the presence of Dr. Sloan's Highland piper is a moot question. Several other parties were more or less abreast of them because once the spring really opened up Klondikers began to flock in from Peace River Crossing. Until the end of July Fort St. John was busy with the comings and goings of the determined prospectors.

Some of the first to run into difficulties were a few of the members who broke away from the Fugard party when the main body decided to build boats and go downstream. Ed Smith and F. McCandless had set their hearts on trying their luck in the Omineca area, whereas F. E. Banks and A. L. Dominy wanted to head for the Liard River. The four travelled together along the ice as far as Dunvegan and then about February 10 Smith and McCandless continued west along the ice, while Banks and Dominy struck out overland, trying to follow the first half of the sketchy trail to Fort St. John. They planned to leave this after going about halfway and intended to strike out northwest direct to Fort Nelson. Their first problem arose when they realized that they had missed the trail, and before long they were trying to hack a way west through the woods lying south of the Clear Hills. Many miles west of Dunvegan and a few miles west of modern Worsley the two Klondikers began to look for an opening through which they could cross the Clear Hills and head north in the general direction of Fort Nelson. Finding such a gap after crossing the deep valleys of four small tributaries of the Clearwater River, they came to the Doig River, where it appeared to be heading north. After following it north and west until about the middle of April they became convinced that it was a tributary of the Fort Nelson River and at a point where there was good pasture for their horses they stopped to build a boat.

When Banks and Dominy had completed it, they left their horses and started down the stream. Because it was small, with some difficult rapids, they had several minor mishaps. Game was plentiful; they saw many moose tracks and killed four beaver. After travelling down about four days, and finding that the stream turned westward and finally southwestward, they concluded that it must be a branch of the Beatton and was not the Fort Nelson River at all. At a point on the north side the two men found a number of teepee poles and a trail heading north, which they concluded must lead to that river. They therefore walked back several miles across the bend of the stream till they found their horses and then brought them down to where the trail left the stream.

Leaving their boat they headed their horses north along the well-marked trail which showed signs of having been used considerably the season before. After travelling three days the adventurers struck the east side of a stream flowing north – possibly Katah Creek. So they built another boat and, leaving their horses once more, started down. At first the stream was comparatively small but at the end of the first day's journey a much larger stream came in from the west – undoubtedly the Sikanni Chief River. Even though the stream was now fairly large, navigation was difficult because of the low water. Prospecting as they went, they found colours of gold. At the end of their third day's travel, however, their boat grounded on a rock at the foot of a small rapid and upset, throwing the cargo into the water. They managed to recover their boat and about ninety pounds of flour and some bedding, but the rest of their supplies were lost. This accident compelled them to hurry back to Dunvegan to save themselves from starvation.

They tracked and rowed upstream, and in five days surprised the horses by showing up once more. Then they packed across the portage to Beatton River till they came to their boat. Abandoning their horses for good this time, they went down the stream to the Peace and floated on to Dunvegan. There Dominy joined the Sunny South party from Los Angeles and went to prospect on the Finlay while Banks came back to Edmonton.

In striking out from Peace River Crossing towards Fort St. John, Banks and Dominy were some weeks ahead of anybody else. About the middle of March, Joe McDonald, guiding the Braithwaite party, drove his teams west along the ice from the Crossing. About fifteen parties followed him and in due course reached Dunvegan. There he and a number of other prospectors clubbed together and hired an Indian to guide them along the disused trail to Fort St. John. When they reached that old post Joe had a difference of opinion with his employer and came home. On the way back he retraced the party's steps until he was north of Dunvegan and then headed due east for Peace River Crossing. When he reached Edmonton he talked to the editor of the *Bulletin*, who printed the following information.

> From the Crossing to Dunvegan is a well beaten trail, but to follow it into Dunvegan is making an unnecessary detour of about thirty miles in and back. By following the trail about half way to Dunvegan, at a place called Old Woman's lake, a fairly well beaten trail made lately by travellers leads in a westerly direction. By travelling on this trail for six or eight miles and about a mile beyond Island lake, a big trail cut out like a surveyors' line can be seen due north. By taking notice they will see a trail just there running to the left which they will follow and just on top of a little hill as they pass through some poplar they will see "OK" marked in pencil on a blazed tree. This is the trail to follow to St. John. On the north can be seen the clear sky hills which they will travel parallel to, keeping some distance to the south. After going about eighty miles they will come to a well beaten trail. The Clear Sky rivers are passed on this trail, which is the one Mr. McDonald followed on his homeward trip and he found no difficulty in travelling on it, excepting one muskeg about 50 miles from St. John which might be troublesome in summer. On the road out Mr. McDonald blazed the trees "OK" for the benefit of those parties following, as he travelled on the snow which was rapidly disappearing and obliterating his trail. So many parties have since followed that the trail should now be plain.

Like Joe McDonald, Frank Walker led his party over the ice as far as Dunvegan and then climbed the hill above it with thirty-five pack horses to take the trail to Fort St. John. Describing the view as he looked back towards Fort Dunvegan, Walker said: ". . . it was a wonderful sight to behold . . . horses, pack saddles, flour, pork and beans were scattered all over the hillside. Our horses were not accustomed to pack saddles, and on the long uphill climb (which was terrible, even for experienced pack horses) our horses laid down, rolled, broke their cinch straps and did everything possible to get our boxes off. We kept the main bunch moving until we got to the top. . . ."

Also keeping their bunches moving and intermingling with the Klondikers who pressed on west from Peace River Crossing came the Jones and Lang cattle parties. Three such parties had left Edmonton driving cattle towards the gold-fields: G. W. Lang of Texas, H. Y. Jones of Swift Current, and the Geddis-Harris group from the United States. From Edmonton all three went by way of Athabasca Landing and Lesser Slave Lake to Peace River Crossing. At that point the Geddis-Harris party decided to follow Taylor's Trail to Fort Nelson, but Jones and Lang headed west towards Fort St. John. While both batches of their cattle reached that destination early in June, the trip proved too strenuous for the one-time sturdy old cowboy G. W. Lang, who died of dropsy where the north trail crossed the Clearwater River. After burying him, his party, now led by J. P. Mansfield, herded the cattle on to Fort St. John. Somewhat later, Jones of Swift Current worked his herd on to the old fort without losing a single beast. Before starting to ascend the Halfway River he sold twenty-six of his steers at a profitable price.

Dr. H. L. McInnis was another who towards the end of April set out west from Peace River Crossing. Before leaving he counted about a hundred men who were making boats to descend the Peace, some sixty who were going by trail to Fort St. John and about forty who were heading northwest for Fort Nelson "taking Taylor's trail." His trip west occupied about a month, although his actual travelling time was only fifteen days. Commenting on the trail, he said: "At the time these parties were passing over it the new grass had not yet started well as the spring was very dry, and fires carelessly let out had burnt off considerable stretches of the old grass. In one case the burnt country extended for 25 miles. This fire had burnt four packs and two horses. This made the trip very hard on the horses and slow progress was made. . . ."

After Dr. McInnis reached Fort St. John he returned to Peace River Crossing by boat and came on to Edmonton. On his way downstream about June 10 he met seven boats tracking upstream between Dunvegan and Fort St. John. When he reached the Crossing he found another ten or twelve parties ready to start up the river.

Whereas Dr. McInnis when making his way up to Fort St. John had left Peace River Crossing about the end of April, F. M. Ferriss and his associates were there during the first week of June. Ferriss arranged with the Westmount party to take part of his supplies up to Fort St. John by water, while he and his companions took the trail. They had bad luck when they came to the Roman Catholic mission in the Shaftesbury Settlement on June 10, because dogs there stole about seventy pounds of their bacon. Pulling on to the Anglican mission, they had the further misfortune of having "a sack of flour half destroyed by cows." In spite of the reception both missions had given them, they

188

were very much impressed by the country and went on and spent Sunday at the Rev. Brick's farm at Old Wives Lake. "It is a very fine country on the upper banks of the river from the Crossing to Dunvegan with splendid feed." Ferriss, of course, was seeing the country at a very favourable time, and perhaps because of this his trip of twenty-five days to Fort St. John was uneventful.

J. Livingstone, who seems to have been a Jack-of-all-trades, and who had an interest in the stopping place at Fort Assiniboine, with its stable which would hold forty horses, left Fort St. John on July 30 for a trip to Edmonton. He set out from the fort on a raft with 150 pounds of mail for Klondikers, and in spite of staying at Dunvegan for a day, reached Peace River Crossing in four days. Taking horses there, he arrived in Edmonton nine days later. He reported that at Fort St. John he had seen "the Sunny South party of six men bound across the mountains; the Kilgour party, of five, bound for Fort Graham [sic], and two of the same party coming back. Jones, of Maple Creek, with 75 head of cattle bound for Fort Graham. They had seven work oxen under packs and they worked well. They had not lost any cattle so far. Lang's cattle herd which had reached St. John in May had gone on to Fort Graham." Between Fort St. John and Dunvegan he had met five parties totalling twenty-five men, including an eight-man Philadelphia party. While at Peace River Crossing he found four or five parties camped.

Even that late in the summer, Klondikers were still heading for Fort St. John. When coming across the portage to Lesser Slave Lake, Livingstone met about twenty-five men, and at the Hudson's Bay Company's post there heard that "Harry Mehan, D. James, F. Urinberg and another called 'Fritz' had gone to prospect the Smoky and on to Fort St. John by way of Sturgeon Lake. McCarthy, McKay and another from Montana, had taken the same course. Also a party of six, names not known. Also Capt. O'Brien's wing of the Helpman party, who would prospect the Wapiti a tributary of the Smoky."

Between Lesser Slave Lake Post and Fort Assiniboine he met nearly fifty men heading north, including

> Chas. Smith, who started in the spring with his freight loaded in barrels, was at the Athabasca, with two carts attached together and three horses hitched tandem.
>
> The ferry across the Athabasca had been stopped from running by high water, which had torn the cable loose at one end. The Dibble and McFee parties were held up there for eleven days and finally got across by rowing the scow across. The cable was in place when Mr. Livingstone crossed.

Livingstone's budget of news touched on many interesting items, including some government survey parties sent out to day-dream about railways, and some members of the Helpman party. Not the least interesting was the news about our friend Texas or "Barrel" Smith. Although his idea of barrels had been a failure, he was still persisting in using an unorthodox approach to transportation. Our main interest in Livingstone's news, however, is that even as late as the middle of August 1898, several parties were still on the move on the first leg of their trip to the Klondike.

This was corroborated about the first of September by a group of eleven prospectors who returned to Edmonton from as far afield as Fort Grahame. On their way to town they had met "about fifty men going in with pack horses, carts and wagons." While the main push towards the north had taken place during the first four or five months of 1898, men continued to dribble north all through the summer. Among these was a party of five experienced men from Saskatchewan who had ridden into Edmonton along the old Winnipeg trail with an outfit of forty horses. This cavalcade included Ernest Rose and his father, who were both well versed in travelling with pack saddles. The group reached Edmonton towards the end of June and hurried north to Fort Assiniboine accompanied by Dan Noyes and his son Bob.

As we have seen, the movement was not all out-going, and during the summer the trails between Edmonton and Fort St. John were busy with two-way traffic. Starry-eyed northbound hopefuls met an increasing number of hollow-eyed, homeward-bound prospectors as some 120 who had taken the Overland Route returned to Edmonton.

CHAPTER THIRTEEN

FROM PEACE RIVER
TO THE LIARD-CASSIAR AREA
VIA FORT NELSON

Each of the parties that reached the Peace River or travelled along it to Fort St. John had its own idea of the best way to go north. Four main routes, each some four hundred miles long, leading from the Peace River to the Liard River bore the brunt of the Klondikers' curses, three starting at Fort St. John and one starting at Peace River Crossing. Two of these headed for Fort Nelson, one out of Fort St. John and one out of Peace River Crossing. Which route a Klondiker chose depended to some extent upon the destination he had in mind. If he were determined to reach the Yukon, one or other of the routes by way of Fort Nelson was a logical choice. But if he left Edmonton with the idea of trying his luck in the Omineca or Cassiar gold-fields, or at some other point along the way, and considered going to the Yukon only as a last resort, then he would pick one of the routes leading to Fort Grahame.

PEACE RIVER CROSSING TO FORT NELSON

Of the two routes aimed at Fort Nelson, the more easterly followed the trail which on March 17, 1898, W. P. Taylor started to blaze from Peace River Crossing. His trip to lay out the trail, though somewhat futile, was nevertheless accomplished with commendable celerity. Having had the mission of being the gateway to the Yukon thrust upon it and not yet perceiving that its career in this role was to be very brief, the town of Edmonton felt it imperative to get a proper road cut through to that area. For a time during the previous fall Edmonton's businessmen thought that through Inspector Moodie and his federal government effort they were to start getting their road. But Moodie had not led his party along the route which Edmontonians thought the proper one. Moreover, by mid winter he appeared to be more or less indefinitely bogged down at Fort Grahame. Writing Moodie off as a

191

bad job, they arranged with W. P. Taylor to blaze a trail from Peace River Crossing to the Pelly River and to hurry back and report. Taylor hurried and fairly flew on towards the Pelly. After reaching the Liard River on his return trip, he came back by a different route which brought him home by way of Fort St. John.

By the time he got back to Edmonton early in August and took his report to the town council, he found that everyone was beginning to be touchy at the mere mention of the route from Edmonton. He rushed enthusiastically over to his sponsors, the town council, prepared to give his report, only to discover that, while its members were polite and amiable, none of them wanted to hear it. All the glamour had gone out of Edmonton's route to the Klondike. That boom had bust.

That, however, was not Taylor's fault, and because his trip illustrates how rapidly such a venture could be carried out by a man not encumbered with a heavy load of supplies, it is worth following.

On February 25, 1898, Taylor set out from Edmonton with a train of dogs and reached Lesser Slave Lake Post in short order. He found the Chalmers Trail cut out only as far as Deer Mountain in the Swan Hills, but from there followed an old pack trail. At Lesser Slave Lake he hired an Indian to accompany him, as well as Harry Garbett, an adventurous Englishman, who, during the previous fall, had gone with Jack Graham from St. John to the Liard River. Taylor and his companions left Lesser Slave Lake with seven dogs hauling two sleds, and reached Peace River Crossing on March 17.

Then the three headed northwest in what was as near a straight line as possible until they reached Fort Nelson, about 260 straight-line miles from Peace River Crossing. In passing, Taylor noted Cardinal Lake near modern Grimshaw and the headwaters of the Whitemud and Notikewin rivers, and on March 25 crossed the upper Chinchaga River. Somewhere on the divide between that stream and the Fontas River, which flows to the Fort Nelson River, he abandoned his sleds and packed the loads on the dogs' backs. He then followed the Fontas River to its junction with the Sikanni Chief, but, instead of descending it and making his way through miles of deadfall, he struck off northwest, keeping to the higher land. Before long he came to an Indian trail that approached Fort Nelson from the southeast and, following it, reached the temporarily unoccupied fort on April 8. Next day he crossed the main river and set out up the Muskwa for about fifty miles along much the same route taken by the modern Alaska Highway. Along this stretch he followed the route that Harry Garbett had taken the previous fall. Then turning north, Taylor crossed a high divide to Toad River, which he followed for twenty miles to where it runs into the Liard at the old Toad River Post. After ascending the Liard from there for four miles, he and his companions made a raft and crossed to the mouth of the Grayling River.

There he met a band of Indians and engaged one to guide him through a cut-off which ran parallel to but well north of the Liard. Leaving Garbett and his Lesser Slave Lake Indian to hunt and accumulate food for use on the homeward trip, Taylor pushed on.

After going up the Grayling River and crossing to the headwaters of the Crow and thence to the high reaches of the Beaver River, Taylor followed his new guide across the valleys of the Rock, Coal and Hyland rivers and reached the upper end of Frances Lake on May 19. He pushed on west and on May 21, nearly three months after leaving Edmonton, stood on the shore of the Pelly River, upstream from Pelly Banks. Taylor made a raft and went down the Pelly about forty miles, on the way noticing traces indicating that a couple of white men had descended the river a short while previously.

Turning back at this point some nine hundred straight-line miles from Edmonton but over 1,100 miles by the route he had travelled, Taylor retraced his steps to the mouth of the Grayling River, picked up the men he had left there and followed his previous trail to a point on the Muskwa River some fifty miles above Fort Nelson. At that point he decided to investigate the route running more or less directly south to Fort St. John and started out on July 2. In due course he crossed the Prophet and the Beatton rivers, and on July 11 reached Fort St. John with six of the seven dogs he had when leaving Lesser Slave Lake on the way north. From Fort St. John he floated downstream and reached Peace River Crossing on July 15. There he switched to horses and took eight days to reach his home at Lac Ste Anne.

Taylor had made a remarkable round trip of some 2,200 miles in 157 days, an average rate of over fourteen miles a day, which illustrated how fast the trip could be made under the best available conditions. All he and his party had carried with them was enough food to take them from one fur-trade post to another. Unlike the Klondikers, they were not burdened with supplies enough to last for nearly a year after they got to the Yukon area. On the first part of the trip from Edmonton to Peace River Crossing Taylor had used lightly laden pack horses, but from there on with commendable versatility had switched to dogs. Taylor was the sort of traveller that Edmontonians expected frontiersmen to be and undoubtedly enjoyed the trip and the sense of accomplishment it gave him.

The value of his trip to Edmonton, however, is open to question. He had actually seen the country and could report that travelling through it presented no unusual difficulty. Nethertheless, rushing along at the speed he did, he could only blaze trees to indicate where he had passed; if he ever found that for a certain stretch he would have been better off if he had chosen a different route, he had no time to retrace his steps and pick out a better one. While his trip did demonstrate that men could travel where he had led, his blazes upon trees did not necessarily mean that anyone following them was taking the best route.

By the time he reached Fort St. John on the return portion of his trip, he was convinced that the best route to Fort Nelson was really the one starting at Fort St. John and not the one he had taken when outbound from Peace River Crossing. Perhaps an element of irony was added because, while he was still far away along the Liard and long before he came to the conclusion that the best route lay north from Fort St. John, scores of Klondikers, trusting to his prescience, set out from Peace River Crossing to follow Taylor's Trail to Fort Nelson.

Even though the Klondike boom was dying out, the editor of the *Bulletin* gave a detailed account of Taylor's trip and, looking ahead, advocated doing some work on a trail from Fort St. John to the Pelly River. With thousands of miners in the Yukon, it would be advisable to send at least their food supply in from Edmonton. He said: "We have the beef in the Territories. They want it in the Yukon. If a cattle trail were cleared from St. John to the Pelly, 700 miles, this important part of the trade of the Yukon would be assured to the Territories. Even if a trail were well blazed people would take chances on getting through; as they are doing this season, finding and cutting their own way."

Approximately 150 Klondikers with some eight hundred horses set out from Peace River Crossing to follow Taylor's Trail. Among the first to leave were A. D. Osborne of Edmonton and his four colleagues who reached Fort Nelson on May 24. Others who took this route were members of Captain J. H. Mason's Philadelphia party of fourteen, Geddis and Harris the cattle drovers, John and James Fair, the Richardson aggregation from Kansas, the Fraser-Stanley group from Calgary, J. Cluthe and his friend from St. Albert, the Crooked Five, including Peter Simonson of Edmonton, the Big Four, J. L. Secord and many others.

All of the parties in this contingent left Peace River Crossing as soon as they could cross the river and get organized on the west side, and most of them did so during the space of a month, starting about April 15. They bunched themselves into groups of parties embracing about

194

50 men and 250 horses. Most of them crossed the Chinchaga River about three weeks after leaving Peace River Crossing, and the majority described the terrain through which they pushed as easy to travel. All of them arrived in Fort Nelson before the middle of August.

Plugging along also came the Geddis-Harris cattle party, which left the Crossing with some fifty cattle and twenty-six pack horses driven by six men and reached Fort Nelson during the first week of August. At the crossing of the Chinchaga the two Harris brothers decided to go back to Edmonton. Out of the lot of cattle, a few had become so lame that they were turned into beef, but the party arrived in Fort Nelson with forty-six beasts in good shape.

The Philadelphia party made reasonable time, enjoyed the trip, and reached Fort Nelson on July 28. On July 11, young John Rudolph Smith of that party, all unaware of what tricks the trail to the Klondike held up its sleeve, wrote a letter which his parents in Philadelphia received on October 8. Amongst other things, he said:

> We all live in hopes as we expect to reach the Liard river in about 20 days and as that is supposed to be the new Klondike, we hope to send you good news. So you see it will take us very near till fall before we reach the fields therefore coming home this fall is nearly out of the question, as it would be useless, to turn around without gaining anything except some experience. You see this trail is not what it was supposed to be. It has been one continuous fight all the way up from the mission on the Peace River, but not the fight the 49'rs had in California. One does not hear the crack of the pistols from the hand of the Indians, in fact we have not seen an Indian since we have been on the trail, but we hear the steady "crack," "crack," of the trail cutters' axes as they cut away trees and build bridges across streams and valleys; making a road so our pack horses may pass through this portion of the great Northwest, where no white men ever set foot before. So if we succeed in getting through, of which I have not the slightest doubt, for there are some 60 brave hearted men on this trail, we should surely be entitled to the name of the "Pioneers of the Northwest Territory."
>
> There are about 18 parties with about 60 men and some 250 horses. We are the largest party. There is the O. H. Gedis party taking through 45 of the finest steers I ever saw. As the most of the parties keep in a bunch, we visit one another and have many a jolly time together. One party has a fellow with them who has some Sankey hymn books and we have quite a good quartette, so we spend the evening singing such hymns and songs as we can remember, and we are always called upon to sing "Home Sweet Home," "Where is my wandering boy to-night," &c., &c., thus we enjoy ourselves twixt all our trouble.
>
> I presume you heard some very sad news from some of the would-be gold seekers, and from the newspapers, but let me say to you "Let no man's

news scare you; don't believe anything you read in the newspapers about hardships." The only hardships we have are the flies and mosquitoes and, great scott, they do torment us. As for the other hardships don't take any stock in them. . . .

The brothers James and John Fair of Elkhorn, Manitoba, seem to have made good progress to Fort Nelson. They reported that the general group with which they travelled started out from Peace River Crossing with about three hundred horses, but owing to accidents or straying, fifteen per cent of the horses dropped out before reaching Fort Nelson.

Joe Birchner of Edmonton and his companions left home around March 1, crossed the Peace River about April 16, and reached the Chinchaga River three weeks later. From there on they seem to have strayed from the proper route and wandered in a wilderness of muskeg and forest for nearly three months before becoming one of the latest parties to reach Fort Nelson.

When the Richardson party from Kansas reached the Fontas River, the members decided to leave the trail the others had taken; they made a raft and floated their supplies down to Fort Nelson. At the same time some of the party drove the lightly loaded horses along the bank. Their progress was slow, but when they reached Fort Nelson on August 20 their horses were fat and in fine shape to go on.

Glen Campbell's party of five from Brandon, Manitoba, also set out for Fort Nelson but added a variation to the route by rafting its sixty horses and dogs down the Peace to the mouth of Keg River and then using its pack horses to ascend that stream. The party spent the winter trapping near Hay Lakes and in the spring set out, intersected Taylor's Trail and followed it to Fort Nelson. The Chatfield brothers of New York wintered near Campbell but one of them froze his feet so badly that he had to be taken out to Edmonton. Still another party of three men, whose names we do not know, went farther down the Peace River, and about a dozen miles below Carcajou struck across northwest till they reached the Hay River and then descended this to Great Slave Lake.

The Strathdees from Brantford, a father and son partnership, drove their sixteen horses over Taylor's Trail but in the fall somewhere near the Sikanni Chief River the son, W. H. Strathdee, went missing. The last his father saw of him was one morning when he got up, took his rifle and started out to look for game. For eight days the father searched fruitlessly but finally, because his horses faced starvation, he had to move on. The following spring the Indians in the area found what everyone presumed was the son's body.

Thus with the loss of only one human life and without too much hardship, those who took Taylor's Trail reached Fort Nelson. There they mingled with those who came in by way of Fort St. John, and either prepared to set off north or west or decided to settle down for the winter.

FORT ST. JOHN TO FORT NELSON

The more westerly of the two routes to Fort Nelson started out of Fort St. John and went up the Beatton River. This was the one which W. P. Taylor thought the better of the two he had travelled. Unfortunately his opinion came too late for most of the Klondikers to hear. Regardless of his assessment of this route, however, relatively few Klondikers took it. That it was practical is confirmed by information he received about June 26, 1898, when he met Gilbert Velgue, Duncan McFarlane and "Milo" of Edmonton on the Liard River. Whereas Taylor's party had headed north from Peace River Crossing, these three men starting from the Crossing three days after Taylor had gone around by Fort St. John and thence north and reached the Liard River on June 20. Velgue, of course, had been over the route once before, for during the summer of 1897 he had accompanied Jack "Cayuse" Graham and Garbett along part of it. On that occasion, which was before the Klondike Rush through Edmonton had started, Graham and Garbett had left Lesser Slave Lake in March 1897 with a band of horses which they planned to take through to the Liard River.

Five men who had left Edmonton as part of the Fresno overland group took this route up the Beatton River. Although the fragmentation of the Fresno party had begun soon after it left Edmonton, all but one or two of the members eventually straggled into Fort St. John and spent part of the late winter there. Early in the spring of 1898, C. Hoag, W. Hoag, T. J. Kelly, B. F. Sears, R. C. Wigmore and W. Bisson hired H. Burbank, a man who had been trading at Fort St. John for nine years, to guide them to Fort Nelson. In the deal they made he was to take possession of their horses when they reached that point and was to supply them with boats to descend the Fort Nelson River.

A few other small parties also picked their way along this route up the Beatton River and crossed over to the Fort Nelson River. Two or three of the latest of these groups, which included Wm. Bevan from Butte, Montana, Henry Tottenham of Kamloops, and a man named Nolin, started north so late that they decided to winter along the Sikanni Chief River. The total number of prospectors who used this route from Fort St. John was insignificant, but at Fort Nelson those who did so mingled with the Klondikers who had come in over Taylor's Trail.

From Fort Nelson the Klondikers used two alternative routes to head for the Cassiar country. One ascended the Muskwa River, while the other lay down the broad Fort Nelson River some 110 miles to where it flowed into the Liard at what was called Nelson Forks. Klondikers could float down it and, if they wished, drive their pack horses along its valley. Perhaps the earliest to float down to that point were the Hoags and their associates of the Fresno group, who seem to have hastened west from there up the Liard well ahead of any other 1898 Klondikers.

John and James Fair decided to leave their horses at Fort Nelson and floated downstream. They left the fort on August 18 and reached the Liard on August 24, but by that time they had endured all they wanted of the trip to the Klondike. Next day they turned around and worked their way back upstream to Fort Nelson, climbed astride their horses and set out for Edmonton. By October 13 they were back at Peace River Crossing. At Fort Nelson, or when they reached the Liard, several other prospectors also closed their eyes to the gleam of gold and returned to Edmonton.

The majority of the Klondikers who passed through Fort Nelson, however, were still optimistic and pressed on at least to the Liard River, and generally much farther. The men of the Richardson party, for instance, who floated down the river system to Fort Nelson, kept floating till they reached the Liard and then went west from there.

The Philadelphia party, about which J. R. Smith had written home so cheerfully before it had reached Fort Nelson, began its streak of bad luck below there. At that post the men built rafts and floated downstream, horses and all. On August 24 at the mouth of the Fort Nelson River both of their rafts got hung up on separate sand bars some distance apart. Their leader, Captain J. H. Mason, remained alone on one of the rafts, undertaking to lighten it by driving the horses off it into the shallow water while all the rest of the party worked at the other raft. They saw that he was successful in getting the horses off and was riding one of them through the water to shore. They went on with their work, expecting the captain to join them shortly, but when he did not, became alarmed and searched for him. They found the horses all right, including the one he had been seen riding, and after searching the river as well as they could found his hat, but no other trace.

198

The Philadelphia party's bad luck had only started and now that it had lost Captain Mason's leadership, misfortune really set in. At Nelson Forks the party fell in with a number of Klondikers who had just ascended the Liard River and entered into an agreement with them which proved disastrous to both sides. The Philadelphians, who had thirty-five horses,

> offered to pack their supplies over to Sylvester's Landing, a distance of 175 miles, stating that they had a trail across and were doing a packing business. On the strength of this, three parties gave them in all 1,050 lbs. of provisions to carry over, and 35 pack horses started out. In six weeks they returned, not having been able to strike a trail, and having eaten the provisions. Considerable dissatisfaction arose and the miners convened a court and tried them on the charge of obtaining goods under false pretences. The jury found them guilty and awarded their horses to the men whose provisions they had secured. As the Philadelphia party were out of supplies, and by the award were deprived of horses, the party split up, the members, except three, being taken into other expeditions. The three who were left out went up the river themselves. Had it not been for the delay caused by waiting for the pack train to return and take their supplies the men state they would have pushed on over the divide in the fall, easily. As it was they waited until it was too late to go by boat, so some forty went across with an Indian guide in the winter. The others returned this spring, coming out at different times.

Except for the earliest, like Hoag and his companions, all these overland parties were amongst those which Vaudin and the other water-route Klondikers who came up the Liard met near Nelson Forks. Since by that time the ice was beginning to form on the river, both the water-route people and the overlanders were forced to camp on a relatively short section of the stream below Hell's Gate. In that vicinity all spent part of the winter and pushed on during the early months of 1899, and thereafter in their common laborious struggles up the Liard much of the distinction between the overlanders and the water-borne ceased.

The other route out of Fort Nelson lay west up the Muskwa River and across the mountains. For some fifty miles it followed the trail Taylor had taken, but whereas he had turned north on a route paralleling the modern Alaska Highway, eventually struck the Toad River and descended it, these overlanders crossed that stream. Then they continued west until in the Rocky Mountain Trench they reached the Kechika and followed it to the Mud River Post on the Liard.

Among the overlanders who went this way was A. D. Osborne of Edmonton, who teamed up with the two Jamieson brothers of Griswold,

Manitoba. Accompanying them were Murphy and O'Neil of Chicago and several other men. All of them left Fort Nelson during the first week of August 1898 with a total of sixty horses. For the first forty miles they had a good trail, but after that it was of a most sketchy description. Having no guide, they experienced grave doubts at times about where they were. They nevertheless got through without undue difficulty and on October 5, 1898, reached the Mud River Post. They lost only two horses. These became footsore and had to be shot.

Geddis and four men herded his band of cattle along a slightly different route but reached the Mud River Post about the same time as Osborne. All the cattle survived that portion of the trip and, after looking around, Geddis decided to drive them over to McDame Creek on the Dease River for the winter.

Thus in due course Geddis and his cattle, as well as those other Klondikers who had headed west out of Fort Nelson, reached the upper regions of the Liard River. During the fall of 1898 a few of the earliest to arrive went on to Frances Lake or even, as in the case of the Hoags of the Fresno party, as far as the Yukon. The majority, however, were late in reaching the Kechika River in the Rocky Mountain Trench, where they began coming in contact with the overlanders who had headed north out of Fort Grahame. By that time, for all but the earliest arrivals who had already gone much farther, it was time to camp for the winter.

CHAPTER FOURTEEN

FROM PEACE RIVER
TO THE LIARD-CASSIAR AREA
VIA FORT GRAHAME

When the Klondikers who had surmounted the difficulties of the Chalmers Trail reached Fort St. John, they were grateful for the excellent pasture surrounding it. Farther up the Peace at Bear Flats they found another pasture in the open rolling country, about twenty miles wide and extending up the Halfway River. For some generations the Beaver Indians had grazed large herds of horses in this area and wintered them there. Many of the Klondikers who were planning to follow Moodie's trail or else were hoping to continue west up the Peace River did not tarry at Fort St. John but hurried on to this other area of luxuriant fodder. For the mouth of the Halfway River was where the two routes to Fort Grahame diverged, the more easterly ascending that stream, while the other went up the Peace River to Hudson Hope.

Before long the Beaver Indians, who were normally quite friendly with all strangers who trespassed on their lands (which they had not yet yielded to the white man by way of any treaty), began to resent the Klondikers' intrusion. Without even the courtesy of asking the Beavers' permission, the Klondikers began pasturing their horses with the natives' herds and were not above stealing a horse or two that took their fancy. A large number of the prospectors were Americans, who depised all Indians, and their attitude added fuel to the Beavers' resentment. With no respect for the Indians' rights they abused the natives, killed their game, let campfires get out of control to start forest fires, and generally made themselves unwelcome. In a letter written in May 1898 from Fort St. John, J. Carscadden of Frank Walker's Fort Saskatchewan party said that someone in one of the parties ahead of his "shot three of the Indians' stallions and one dog."

Barney Maurice, who for many decades was a respected businessman of High Prairie, Alberta, spent some time at Fort St. John and Fort Grahame during the Klondike Rush. His own relations with the Beaver Indians were good, but he reported:

> In Fort St. John there was an Indian scare. The Beaver and Dog Rib tribes did not want the white man to come and stay in the country which they said was theirs. Some miners stole caches of food, snowshoes, etc. which were hidden in trees. On top of the hill at Fort St. John there were about seventy-five buggies, wagons and Red River carts left by miners. The Indians put the whole works down the hill and I could see afterwards broken wagons and equipment for about six hundred feet down.
>
> All of the white men, with the exception of the doctor, myself and our partner, left at night. We had to stay, but the Indians didn't do any harm to us.

One cause of acute resentment came about when a party of Klondikers were heading up the Halfway River. Suddenly a log fell on the lead mare and nearly killed her. She had blundered into one of the Beaver Indians' bear-traps. In another half mile the same thing happened again. After that, the Klondikers walked ahead and incensed the natives by destroying five of these laboriously made traps.

FORT ST. JOHN TO FORT GRAHAME

The route up the Halfway River crossed Laurier Pass and finally came down to Fort Grahame on the Finlay River. It followed an ill-defined Indian trail and was the way that Inspector Moodie of the government road-blazing party had chosen. Along it during December 1897, W. Inkster of Edmonton and his partner had been more or less in step with the police party until both of them went into winter quarters at Fort Grahame.

Another party that started for the Laurier Pass early in the spring of 1898 was the main body of the Fresno group. As we have seen, most of that party eventually reached Fort St. John, but it had split into three units. Two men decided to go to Fort Grahame by way of the Peace River canyon, five had set out for Fort Nelson with H. Burbank, but the remaining eleven crossed the Laurier Pass. Jack Graham, who is always appearing and reappearing in the tales of the Klondikers and who had recently returned from Hell's Gate on the Liard, led them away from Fort St. John so early that they had to camp in the pass and wait until enough snow had melted to make the crossing possible.

Frank Walker's Fort Saskatchewan party, accompanied by its lone white mule, Sophia, set out by way of the Laurier Pass. Walker and his companions reached Fort Grahame on July 2, but while the party was

202

starting up the Halfway River Sophia's sentence of hard labour for life was commuted.

In her day, Sophia had been a character. Undoubtedly she and her male team mate, also white and also of the long-eared braying breed, had reached Edmonton as an inheritance from the building of the Calgary and Edmonton Railway line in 1891. For years after that, Donald Ross, one of Edmonton's earliest pioneers and an old Forty-niner as well, owned Sophia and her companion, and in his service the team of white mules became well known to Edmontonians. Then, just as the Klondike Rush was well under way, her mate died and Donald had little he could do with a team of only one white mule. So he sold her to his friend Frank Walker, and Sophia entered upon the last of her varied careers by bearing a pack saddle and turning her big ears north.

But the years were telling against Sophia, though she performed creditably till she got past Fort St. John, and they finally overtook her. As Walker told the story:

> We just got to the top of a very steep hill, coming up from a creek, when Sophia's hind legs gave out, and she started down the hill backwards, not like an ordinary animal would do by rolling, but end over end like a cart wheel. There was an old rotten tree about half way down, lying horizontally about four or five feet off the ground, kept up by old rotten branches. This tree was fifteen inches in diameter, and Sophia went through it like a knife, and disappeared down among the trees about 150 feet below. We hastily unpacked two of the animals, and went down to bring up Sophia's load of flour and beans and riding saddle which was on top. When we got down there we found Sophia right side up, but wedged in between two fairly good-sized trees. The pack saddle was smashed to pieces, but the food was first class, not even a tear in it. We had to cut down a tree to get Sophia out and then pull off her load. She then shook herself, got up, and walked to the top of the hill, apparently all right, but she died about two weeks later. She had been hurt internally.

Although Sophia never saw Fort Grahame, hundreds of other beasts did as every few days all summer parties crossed over to the Finlay River. In addition to William Inkster and Frank Walker and the Fresno people who reached Fort Grahame early in the season, these parties included Mrs. Nansen, who, when she reached Fort Grahame with her husband, was the first white woman to be seen there. They also included Mr. and Mrs. Heizer and Mrs. Allen and her husband. The Lang and Jones cattle parties also reached Fort Grahame. Lang's beasts grazed for a while on the excellent pasture at the mouth of the Halfway River and gradually worked up that stream and over

Laurier Pass and reached Fort Grahame during the first week of July. Some time later Jones of Swift Current drove about fifty of his cattle over the same route.

Many of this 1898 crop of Klondikers spent the winter along the Finlay River. F. M. Ferriss, who crossed the Laurier Pass on September 5 and reached Fort Grahame on September 23, was one who decided to stay in the area. He spent a few days looking for a good hay meadow and went up the Finlay a few miles, but finally decided to cut hay for his animals and build a cabin about twenty miles up the Ingenika River. About this time he met Dr. Pelly (no relation to A. M. Pelly who accompanied the Camsells) and his partner White, who were mining a few miles farther up that river, and during the winter he ran into several other Klondikers who were trying their luck in this area.

All the way from Peace River Crossing Ferriss had been in close contact with the Sunny South and the Westmount parties, and in fact the latter helped him by taking his canoe from Fort St. John to Fort Grahame. They did so along the more westerly of the two routes between the posts, that is, across the portage from Hudson Hope to above the modern Portage Mountain dam, thence up the Peace River to the mouth of the Finlay, and finally up that river some forty miles to Fort Grahame.

Several score Klondikers, including two of the original Fresno party, used this route. Some did so with the intention of continuing to the Yukon but many had the idea of trying their luck along the upper Peace and the Finlay or in the nearby Omineca field, which had seen miners working near the old gold-rush towns of Germansen and Manson Creek ever since 1868. When they left Edmonton many of the so-called Klondikers had always intended to stop in this area. During the winter of 1898-99 about a hundred prospectors were scattered about the old Omineca field or stretched along the Finlay and Peace Rivers from Fort Grahame to Hudson Hope.

Not all the men camped in that area that winter were miners. C. F. K. Dibble had his camp on the Black Canyon of the Omineca some ten or twelve miles above Finlay Forks. Dibble was in charge of a Dominion government survey party seeking a route for a railway up the Peace River to Finlay Forks and thence westward towards the coast.

That winter, in spite of the availability of considerable hay in the Fort Grahame area, some three hundred horses died. On the whole, the men wintered well but nevertheless scurvy with its subtle approach and scathing aftermath got in its deadly work.

During the spring, reports began to trickle into Edmonton telling of sickness and death among this group, the nearest large aggregation of Klondikers. While it is likely that the complete toll was never known, the lists given by two or three men who returned to Edmonton must have included all but an occasional victim. As a matter of fact, the toll was not high. The few deaths had been due to scurvy or accident and, while they certainly occurred among the Edmonton-based Klondikers, it is a moot point whether or not they can be blamed on any failing of the routes chosen. Because there appears to have been plenty of food available in the Omineca — Fort Grahame area, starvation was generally out of the question. Scurvy is of course due to vitamin deficiency; while the Klondikers did not know it, the onset was caused by the diet they followed and to some extent seemed to hit the more slothful who simply denned up in little shacks and did not bestir themselves to try to obtain fresh game. In those days an occasional bachelor or home-steader in the Edmonton area succumbed to this sickness. On the score of accidents, men travelling over the terrain and under the conditions met by the Klondikers were bound to encounter death by accident occasionally, but its incidence was only slightly higher among them than among individuals settled on homesteads within forty miles of Edmonton. Even some physical weaknesses, such as hernia or appendici-tis, caused the death of a few Klondikers.

The best record of scurvy's effects in the Fort Grahame area is in-cluded in a report quoting C. F. K. Dibble when in June 1899 he returned to Edmonton.

> Two men, named Walker and Calberg of the Dikeman party, were ill with the disease at Grahame; four men were laid up at Hudson's Hope and are now at Peace River Crossing being brought down; another was affected at Peace River Crossing; and at the mouth of Clearwater creek, eighty miles above Hudson's Hope, on the 10th of May, Mr. Dibble's party on the way down, came across the cabin of a party of six from Sault Ste. Marie, Ont. The leader of the party, Capt. Geo. W. Pontine of Sault Ste. Marie, had died on the 27th of April from scurvy and his five companions were so weakened by the same disease that they were not even able to bury the body. Mr. Dibble's party interred the remains, and brought the other members of the party down with them. Wm. Ormiston was left at the Episcopal mission at Peace River Crossing. He will probably recover. Walter Raines died at the Crossing and was buried there. The remaining three men are recovering and came in with Mr. Dibble. Their names are: I. S. C. Ironsides, Sault Ste. Marie; W. B. Moore, Kingston, and G. S. Cotter, formerly in the Hudson's Bay Co. employ.

While Dibble reported only two deaths, a group of Klondikers return-ing from the Fort St. John — Fort Grahame area who arrived in Edmonton somewhat later reported: "A Dutchman, name unknown, was supposed to have been drowned while crossing the Pine river. Another, name unknown, died from scurvy at Grand Prairie. An elderly man named Dewie is reported to have died on an island in the Peace river this spring, and another man, unknown, is said to have died from rupture at his camp some miles north of St. John. . . ."

The Dutchman to whom they referred was undoubtedly Hinkle of Matoon, Illinois.

> Hinkle and his partner J. R. Peters were coming down the river from Mount Selwyn at the junction of the Finlay and Parsnip rivers, where they had staked out quartz claims. They had reached the crossing of Halfway river and camped. On August 2nd Peters went back to a stream called Red river to look for some of their horses which had strayed. While he was away Hinkle was to try the ford across the Halfway on horse back. When Peters returned he found the fire burning at the camp, and a meal partly prepared. Not suspecting any mishap he ate his dinner. Some time after he noticed one of the horses with a pack saddle on, and apparently having come out of the river. He then began to search for his partner, but without avail. . . . He searched, and found where the horse had gone into the river, and also where he had come out on the same side further down. He had gone in where the river was narrow and therefore deep, and where there was a cut bank on the opposite side which the horse could not climb up. . . . A Montreal party, who were coming down the river on a raft, also landed at the Halfway on the same day. All hands searched again and found where the horse had come out of the water on the east side, and then returned to the west side, leaving no doubt as to Hinkle's death. Peters then gave up the search and came down to St. John. But there he hired another man and went back to search, but without avail. . . .

In due course Hinkle's body floated down the Peace nearly to Fort St. John before some prospectors found it on a bar and buried it.

FORT GRAHAME TO THE LIARD-CASSIAR AREA

The first to leave Fort Graham to strike out for the Liard River, of course, were the very few who had left Edmonton during the fall of 1897 and who either reached Fort Grahame at the end of the year or had pushed forward from Spirit River or Fort St. John during the winter or late spring. Of these, the first were the lightly loaded W. Inkster and his companion who had enough cash to enable them to buy six months' supplies whenever they reached some point where they could do so. On April 4, 1898, carrying their guns, bedding, thirty pounds of flour and nine pounds of bacon between them, they set out on foot from Fort Grahame. Of all the Klondikers, these two pioneered this route along the Rocky Mountain Trench to the Liard

River. They ascended the Finlay to the mouth of Fox River and then followed that stream up to Sifton Pass, some 110 miles from Fort Grahame. After they crossed the height of land, another hundred miles of travelling brought them to Sylvester's old outpost at the mouth of Turnagain River. From there they seem to have cut across country to Lower Post at the mouth of Dease River. Not being able to obtain supplies there, they shouldered their packs again and walked up the Dease River without benefit of any trail to the post at McDame Creek, which was also called Sylvester's Landing. Since the people there were also on the verge of starvation, they headed for the post at Porter's Landing, only to find that to support themselves there they had to set to and catch fish. Summer not being too far advanced, they soon left there and headed for the Yukon by way of Teslin Lake.

The next group to leave Fort Grahame were nine of the Fresno party under the guidance of Jack "Cayuse" Graham, who about the middle of June set out up the Finlay River. While this group included Mrs. Garner and her husband, two of the former members of the Fresno party had stayed behind at the fort and planned to follow eventually. Because no one had cut out a pack trail and because the forest was dense, they made slow progress in chopping their way along. It was not long, therefore, before several of the 1898 parties overtook them and helped in the work of clearing a way. Within a week or two, members of the Montana party, a Minneapolis party, Adsitt and Mc-Callum of Edmonton, and several others took advantage of the trail they had made and in turn took their places in pushing it ahead more rapidly. By the middle of July there were the remnants of forty-five other parties all forging slowly ahead. But even if chopping out a trail was strenuous and slowed them all to an average of a few miles each day, they had no worry about which way to go. For all of the 260 miles to Lower Post the great wide valley of the Rocky Mountain Trench kept them heading along a line that always trended about thirty degrees west of north.

From time to time various groups dropped out. The Good Hope party went the few miles to the mouth of the Ingenika River and waited there for some of its members to come back down from where they had been prospecting along that stream. After a few more days the Mansfield party gave up and turned back south towards Fort Grahame. Then, a day or so later, Ingles and Stevens of the Fresno group decided to stay and work a stream flowing into the Finlay, which left seven of the original Fresno party pushing on.

Even they were beginning to weaken, for Jack Graham and Howsley started showing symptoms of scurvy. Finally, on July 24, 1898, at a point which they estimated was 160 miles upstream from Fort Grahame the bulk of the Fresno prospectors turned back. It is about 110 miles from Fort Grahame to the summit of Sifton Pass, and in spite of their estimate it is unlikely that they got any farther than that. At whatever point it was, however, Walton, Howsley, Boot, Mr. and Mrs. Garner and their packer Jack Graham gave up. By then, out of the original twenty members of the Fresno overland party, nine only were left to push on: the five who had chosen to go by way of Fort Nelson and W. R. King, A. S. Cagwin, K. Emerzian and H. Rustigian, who continued chopping their way forward along the Rocky Mountain Trench.

Six other discouraged prospectors joined the returning Fresno people and they brought Graham and Howsley back as far as Fort St. John, where Dr. Bennett's attention and a better diet soon put them on their feet. Jack Graham stayed there until he felt better and then set out north again and reached McDame Creek before winter set in. Howsley was able to go on to Edmonton with the members of his original party. That group reached Edmonton during the first week of September 1898 – a few days over a year since the Garners and their optimistic associates had been photographed, bidden Godspeed, and with high heads had ridden north towards the Yukon.

When on September 5, 1898, the editor of the *Bulletin* went to see Mrs. Garner, he admired her pluck, and wrote:

> Mrs. Garner, who accompanied her husband, and had the distinction of being the first lady to leave for the Klondike overland from Edmonton, has borne the long, hard trip bravely and shows no signs, beyond the inevitable tan, of the hardships of the journey. Among the experiences of the trip was a winter spent in a cabin on the Smoky, which to one who had never seen snow before, was an experience decidedly novel. Mrs. Garner, though realizing that the trip was more arduous than she had ever expected, regrets the circumstances which compelled her husband's and her own return and was anxious to keep on and if necessary go through to Dawson.

While the Fresno people had been dozens of miles up the Finlay River cutting a trail, Inspector Moodie, the official federal government trail-blazer, had been having his problems. Like the Garners, he had left Edmonton around the first of September 1897, but unlike them had got as far as Fort Grahame before he bogged down. He had arrived on January 18, 1898, and in some uncertainty of purpose left his party wintering there while he went off on a wild-goose chase which took him to Stuart Lake and to Quesnel, far south on the Fraser River, and other places before he returned to Fort Grahame. When he did come back with supplies and horses and got his party moving again, it was July 14 before he set out to continue the trail-blazing function. By that time many of the Klondikers who had left Edmonton seven months after he did were busy trail-blazing up the Finlay far ahead of him.

The editor of the *Bulletin* and the Board of Trade in Edmonton had never been enthusiastic about Moodie or his route, and most of the Klondikers who fell in with him during his fourteen-month trip were critical of his performance and ability. Some of the criticism levelled at him probably was rooted in the tendency of local men to run down an outsider – in this case an easterner who had been foisted on them – but undoubtedly many another man would have made a better job of leading his expedition. With respect to the detailed report of the creeks, muskegs, hills, valleys and fords he crossed, few could have done better. In that report, however, one senses some embarrassment that the Klondikers were so far ahead of him. What references he made to them were usually to record their failure and their turning back. Before he set out from Fort Grahame, the prospectors had already cleared out a trail for a long distance towards Sifton Pass and he was thereby enabled to make fair time forward. Occasionally, as on July 27 when he was about fifty miles beyond Fort Grahame, the report mentions the fact that his men were cutting trail. This could indicate that previously the trail had been cut out that far. The Klondikers were never given credit for the fact that from the fort on they were working with or ahead of his men.

In any event, on August 2 Moodie reached and named Sifton Pass. Thence, following the route the Klondikers were taking, he descended the Kechika River almost to the mouth of Turnagain River and then followed the existing pack trail from Sylvester's old post there to the Hudson's Bay Company post at McDame Creek, which he reached on August 19. Five days later he headed down the Dease River for Lower Post and the Liard, and before leaving commented: "All outfits which arrived from Grahame before I left abandoned the idea of going on to Pelly River and went out by way of Glenora."

Trailing along behind Moodie's party from Fort Grahame to McDame Creek were several other groups of Klondikers who had been even later in starting than he had. Besides these, the two cattle parties were also behind him. Lang's cattle, now in charge of Mansfield and his men, appear to have been right behind the NWMP party and they reached Mud River Post on the Liard without any losses. Jones had sold twenty-six of his cattle before leaving Fort Grahame, but brought the rest up through the Rocky Mountain Trench route a few days behind the Lang cattle and wintered them at the Mud River Post.

Except for J. Carscadden, who turned back a short distance beyond Fort Grahame, Frank Walker with his party of neighbours from Fort Saskatchewan was also behind Inspector Moodie all the way to McDame Creek. His memoirs confirm the fact that Moodie and the Klondikers were able to follow "an old pack trail, which was in very good condition" from Sylvester's old post at the mouth of Turnagain River to McDame Creek. There, however, his party split up; Hepburn and Albert Walker had had enough of the business of going to the Yukon and like many other Klondikers decided to take the easier course of going west to the coast by way of Telegraph Creek and Glenora. Frank Walker, T. Cinnamon and J. H. Reid, however, decided to push on along the route they had always intended to follow.

While Walker's party seems to have advanced fairly successfully, many other prospectors were bedevilled with bad luck. As the ice began to form in the streams, the M and M party (Maine and Minnesota) decided to cache some eight hundred pounds of provisions and then to push along the Kechika River to a point where they built a winter camp. Several weeks later they went back to relay their provisions forward but found that work unnecessary. Some party had opened their cache and vanished with the supplies.

Far more in tune with the unwritten laws of the North were three men who came hurrying into the Cassiar from Fort Grahame and found a similar cache. For several days they had been near starvation and finally had eaten the last vestige of their food. All the next day they plodded on, but luck was with them. Towards dusk at someone's abandoned camp they found a discarded package. They opened and devoured the contents with gusto if not relish, for it contained three boxes of yeast cakes which they said were "mouldy – but good." The next day the three men reached the cache from which they extracted a bare minimum of food and left a note giving their names.

Some parties that respected their pack horses, and to whom travelling with them came naturally, pushed on north and west more or less unobtrusively, making little fuss but good progress. Such a group was the Rose party from Saskatchewan which overtook and passed many Klondikers who had left months ahead of them. Although they left Edmonton about the beginning of July, they reached the Dease River valley in good time to go into winter quarters, with the loss of only one or two of their forty horses.

With all these Klondikers arriving from so many routes, the Liard valley from Nelson Forks west 260 miles to Lower Post (Watson Lake) saw men in numbers it had never witnessed before and was not to see again until after a lapse of forty years. For Edmonton-based Klondikers

210

had poured in from Fort Nelson and from Fort Grahame and up the Liard from Fort Simpson. Moreover, other Klondikers who had started from the coast or from Ashcroft had come up the Stikine River, over to Dease Lake and down the Dease River to Lower Post. As fast as more came in – the laggards from Fort Nelson or Fort Grahame – others who had reached Lower Post and the Dease River previously were pulling out, either heading for Wrangell and home, or heading for Frances Lake and the Yukon.

In this vortex which the Pacific Coast newspapers dubbed the "Spectral Trail" we must leave them for the time being while we follow the fortunes of some of the few parties who pushed on beyond the Liard during 1898. On August 19 that year, Moodie, the pathfinder, bought a large boat at McDame Creek and sent a load of supplies down to Lower Post, while ten days later, travelling with the horses, he reached the Hudson's Bay store there. From there he ascended the Liard to the vicinity of what is now the town of Watson Lake and set off up the Frances River. From time to time he met or overtook a few Klondikers, including some who had come up the Stikine from the coast. By following up the west arm of Frances Lake he reached and ascended the Finlayson River to the lake of the same name and on September 30 started descending waters running down Campbell Creek towards the Pelly River and the Yukon. Next day he reached the Pelly River and assembled the two portable canvas canoes, twenty feet by four feet beam, that he had purchased from C. S. Watson at Frances Lake. In going down the Pelly he met various men who were preparing to winter along it, and on October 12 ran through the Glenlyon Rapids.

Half a mile below the mouth of the Macmillan River he found evidence of a recent camp. Such a camp presents problems to the chronicler. The obvious explanation is that this is where a contingent of Klondikers coming down the Macmillan from the east had stopped to reorient themselves but none of the records we have show any such group coming over the mountains at this time. It may have been a sort of base camp for Klondikers ascending the Pelly and going up the Macmillan to prospect, but it also may have been merely a campground for Klondikers working into the Yukon and preceding Moodie along this route. In any event, its inhabitants had left a sign blazed on a tree calling the place "Humbug Camp."

A mile or so below the mouth of the Macmillan River, Moodie found three parties of in-going Klondikers wintering, with the intention of prospecting out from their camp. Among them were a man and his wife, presumably a couple who had come into the area from the direction of Telegraph Creek.

Finally on October 24 Moodie reached the mouth of the Pelly where Lt.-Col. T. D. B. Evans of the Yukon Field Force had recently built Fort Selkirk. There he learned that if he were to get out of the Yukon that fall he would have to catch a boat which was expected shortly. Consequently he terminated his trip there, gave a report to Colonel Evans for transmittal to Superintendent S. B. Steele, who was in charge of the police at Dawson, and hurried away. Leaving Fort Selkirk on November 2 and travelling by steamer and train, he reached his former headquarters at Maple Creek, Saskatchewan, eighteen days later.

Moodie was a Mountie and probably a good one who, when directed to carry out a mission, went and carried it out. During his rapid trip back to Maple Creek he must have wondered why it had been necessary to take pack horses, dogs and canoes, to slug his way through deadfall timber, up or down cascades and over untravelled passes for thirteen months to blaze a trail to the Yukon when by conventional means he could make the reverse trip to the prairies in eighteen days. Nevertheless, he had blazed the trail he had been sent to mark, and, like his long-dead biblical predecessors, Joshua, the son of Nun, and Caleb, the son of Jephunneh, he had searched out the land and reported on it, listing the streams to be bridged, the side hills to be graded, the areas of good pasture, and a host of other information, and in due course compiled all of it into a good report.

Unlike Moses, to whom Joshua and Caleb had reported, Moodie's superiors filed his report and forgot it. For during the year and a half since his expedition had been conceived, the situation had changed. The apparent desperate need for such a road as he had laid out had died, and even if it were to be built, no one would have tried to travel it.

Perhaps a better organizer or a man better versed in travel in the northwest or a leader less autocratic with packers and guides could have accomplished what he did in much less time. Most Edmontonians and most Klondikers were apt to speak slightingly of his efforts, but though their reactions were probably natural, they were tinged with a parochial intolerance. The fact that someone else might have excelled Moodie's performance does not detract from the fact that he carried a major expedition through to a conclusion.

On his way from Lower Post to the Yukon River, Moodie met several Klondikers or observed signs of their passing. Several reached the Yukon River that fall, some who had come in from Edmonton and others who came up the Stikine River. Among those who pushed on beyond the Liard during the fall of 1898 were W. Inkster, King of the Fresno party, Frank Walker, and A. D. Osborne from Edmonton.

Because they were two men on foot, packing a minimum of supplies on their backs and depending on their guns for their food, W. Inkster and his partner made very good time. They reached the Yukon in the fall of 1898, well ahead of Moodie, and from Sylvester's Landing onwards followed a route different from the one he took. Inkster and his companion set out across the hundred or so miles of mountains which lay between Dease Lake and Teslin Lake. In doing so they crossed over from one route to another – from that by way of Lower Post to the Pelly to that from Telegraph Creek to Teslin Lake and on down the Lewes or Yukon River. The latter route was the one favoured by Klondikers who came up the Stikine as far as Telegraph Creek, as well as those who had left the CPR at Ashcroft and made their way north along the telegraph line – a route which came to be called the Ashcroft Trail.

In any event, the partners reached the little settlement of Teslin Lake late in the fall, about the same time that Lieutenant-Colonel Evans and his Yukon Field Force did. They found the town to be dotted with log shacks and tents with Klondikers occupying all the available accommodation, while a large overflow of prospectors slept out in the open. Inkster and his friend joined this group. The next day after he arrived, he got a job at five dollars a day and continued at this employment until the beginning of September when Colonel Evans and his men set out to build Fort Selkirk on the Yukon River at the mouth of the Pelly. At this time his partner decided to team up with another Klondiker and Inkster bought a boat and eight hundred pounds of food and supplies and set off down the Yukon River from the site of Fort Selkirk.

In the van of those who had passed through Fort Grahame and the Dease Lake area were the four remaining members of the overland Fresno party, W. R. King, A. S. Cagwin, K. Emerzian and H. Rustigian. When on July 24, 1898, the largest remnant of the original party gave up and started retracing their steps towards Edmonton, these four were farther north in the Rocky Mountain Trench and kept pushing on. They seem to have made good time as far as Dease Lake, but there Emerzian decided to quit and headed for civilization by way of Telegraph Creek, Ashcroft and thence by railroad. At some similar point Cagwin dropped out.

Rustigian and King, however, decided to go on to the Yukon, and reached there and prospected various valleys, including the Stewart River. Finally, deciding that their chances of success were better in Fresno, California, than in the Yukon, they took passage on a steamer down the Yukon River and eventually returned to San Francisco.

During the fall of 1898 Frank Walker, who had reached McDame Creek along with Cinnamon and Reid, pressed on across the Liard River. At McDame Creek, like others, they bought a boat and floated their freight down to Lower Post while they drove their horses along lightly loaded. About the end of September they set off from Lower Post along Moodie's trail, but the pasture was so poor that most of their horses died.

By this time a man named Shahaun, who had come in from the coast, joined the trio, and after several misadventures they shot the last three of their horses and built a cabin on Frances Lake at the mouth of Finlayson River. There they fell in with another twenty Klondikers who also built cabins.

During the winter Walker met some Indians, and according to his reminiscences:

> We tried to make a deal with the Indians for moose meat but those worthies had heard of the high prices in the Klondike and asked $1.00 per pound. Not having any money, we were "up against it," but a happy incident happened at this time for us.
>
> The son of the old chief, Smith by name, who could speak a little English, (and all of us could smatter a little Chinook) informed us that his squaw was sick, and wanted to know if we had a medicine man with us. Knowing the peculiarities of the Coast Indians in regard to medicine, and remembering the wonderful medicine chest which Reid had brought from Chicago (Reid had taken a course in medicine), we informed Smith that we had a doctor, and next day we rigged up this medicine chest on a toboggan in the most beautifully-colored blanket that we possessed, and while Cinnamon and I took the rope to draw it, we told Jack that he was to walk behind and give the appearance of being a man with wonderful knowledge of medicine, and order around Cinnamon and myself as his willing slaves. It worked fine. We were not in the Indian camp (just a short distance across the river) more than half-an-hour before every blessed one of the tribe was coughing and had an ailment of some kind. They were simply mad about medicine, and believed that the white man's medicine could cure anything. We told Jack before going over to give them all kinds of medicines, but for heaven's sake not to give them any poison. They received quinine and sulphur in abundance and even pink pills for pale people. After spending almost the entire day while Reid was compelled to feel the pulses and endeavour to locate imaginary ailments, we returned that evening well-satisfied with our day's work. Two days afterwards, the Indians, true to their traditions, came over to our camp in a body with a potlach each to the medicine man who had done so much for them (as they thought). The biggest gift from the great hunter Smith was the ham of a moose, and every Indian, according to their station or size, had a chunk of moose meat down even to the little papoose in arms, whose contribu-

214

tion would be about three pounds. We were now living on the fat of the land.

While several of the others camped nearby began to feel the onset of scurvy, Walker's colleagues seem to have remained in reasonable health. On March 17, 1899, they started up the Finlayson River and reached Pelly Banks early in April, where they

> settled down and made a boat and shot squirrels, as our meat supply was exhausted, and for the balance of our grub we were on half rations. We had a long wait here, the ice not going out of the river until the 23rd day of May. We left the following day, six boats in all, and had an easy time on the last leg of the journey. The difficulty was portaging around Hoole Canyon, a very dangerous and treacherous bit of water. One boat did really run the canyon light without any load, with four men at the oars. The pilot was Jack Russell, a man who was for some years pilot on the Athabasca for McDougall and Secord. This daring bunch of fellows joshed and dared one another to make the trip until finally they ventured forth. We took posts on the top of the hillside or canyon side, and watched the attempt. Their boat filled with water twice; the second time it filled was when they went over the cascade. The onlookers thought then that they had seen the last of those fellows. However, they came out safely but pale from the fright. Russell remarked afterwards: "No more of that for me."

Having got past Hoole Canyon they continued to Dawson, only to face up to the same disappointment which ninety-nine per cent of all Klondikers faced whether they came by the Edmonton route or any other. Before long they returned to Edmonton, poorer perhaps financially than they had been before they set out, but infinitely richer in the satisfactions they had derived from their adventurous trip.

Similarly, a number of others who had followed Taylor's Trail to Fort Nelson and the Liard River got through to Dawson. Some, like the Hoags and four others formerly of the Fresno party, did so during the fall of 1898. Unfortunately B. F. Sears of this party was drowned en route.

All these adventurers, the Hoags of the branch of the Fresno party which went by way of Fort Nelson, and King and others of the Fort Grahame Fresno party, Inkster, Frank Walker and his Fort Saskatchewan friends, and several others are typical of some of the Klondikers who reached the Cassiar country by way of either Fort Grahame or Fort Nelson and who pushed on to the Klondike during the fall of 1898 or the next spring. A significant number of others, enough to bring the total of 1898 vintage to fifty, also succeeded in reaching the Yukon that fall. The majority of those who set out from Fort Grahame or Fort Nelson, however, were not so successful and, like

215

Jack "Cayuse" Graham, spent the winter of 1898-99 along the Liard in the Cassiar country. The following spring about a hundred of them, including A. D. Osborne of Edmonton and the Roses from Saskatchewan, went on to Dawson.

The proportion of these overlanders who got through either during the fall of 1898 or during the next spring was fairly small. Some failed because their endurance gave out. By the fall of 1898, however, word had worked its way out from the Klondike that only one man in a hundred was finding gold and that hundreds who had reached there had turned around and gone home. Scores of those who had reached the Liard and Cassiar country and who could have gone on realized the futility of doing so and headed for the coast and home. Others were too ill, too disabled or too discouraged to go on.

CHAPTER FIFTEEN

THE SPECTRAL VALLEY

During the fall of 1898 Klondikers by the score had poured into the wilderness of the Liard River watershed. Its devastating maze of tributaries, whirlpools, canyons and cascades became the sinkhole of their hopes and the sepulchre of their friends. For the hardened and the experienced, fighting their way along presented a succession of rather routine problems. For the others, worn out by six, eight or ten months' hardship and poor diet, the struggle was so severe that they gave up their quest and in a few cases their lives. All along the way from Edmonton the less fit had fallen out and turned back: in the Swan Hills, at Fort St. John, or along the lower Finlay or the lower Liard. But even after that the weeding-out process went on. Even at Fort Grahame or Fort Nelson some pressed on who should never have done so. Even at these places the ranks of the Klondikers included the fit and the foolhardy.

Throughout the winter many suffered severely and emerged in the spring disappointed, hungry or scurvy-ridden, while twenty-six Edmonton-based Klondikers actually died in the watershed of the Liard. Of these, scurvy, which with complete impartiality fell alike upon prospectors who had come in from the coast, or by way of the Ashcroft Trail, or along the perilous route from Edmonton, claimed about half. Once they got into the Liard watershed, into the valley of the shadow, regardless of which entry had enticed them, their main concern was to get out alive.

But their getting out was long delayed and meanwhile, as some of their memoirs show, they had much to endure. Some of the last to arrive in the valley had set out from Edmonton, and these remnants of two or three original groups spent the winter on the Sikanni Chief River above Fort Nelson. Scurvy stalked their camp, and on March 30, 1899, William Bevan of Butte, Montana, died, and was buried behind his cabin, while a man named Nolin also succumbed. When spring came some of these winterers pressed on north, but ten decided to return to Edmonton and to carry an ailing companion, Henry Tottenham of Kamloops, with them. Tottenham had been taken ill about the beginning of March and on June 8, on the way out, died. Among his papers which friends turned over to N.D. Beck, Q.C., of Edmonton, was a letter of credit on the Hudson's Bay Company for $1,000 and other records indicating that he had $5,147 in a Kamloops bank.

Joseph Birchner, an Edmontonian who spent the winter of 1898-99 at Fort Nelson, was more fortunate. In August, about the time he reached there, many parties, including A. D. Osborne of Edmonton and the Jamieson brothers, had just left or were on the point of moving on, several up the Muskwa River and several down the Fort Nelson to the Liard, leaving 120 of their horses behind. Birchner and a few other sometime Edmontonians, including J. Secord, Hans Danielson, F. Tagen and W. Fay, undertook to run the horses with their own and to watch them during the winter.

They put up a few tons of hay but expected the horses to obtain most of their living by pawing the snow off the rich grass in the area. Most of the animals died early in the season, not from lack of food but apparently from some illness. All but seven of the remainder died of starvation when the winter turned out to be a very severe one. As soon as the ice went out of the Fort Nelson River, Birchner and his companions made rafts and floated down to the Liard with the seven horses.

At Nelson Forks they were told that the trail up the Liard was impracticable for horses, so they sold them to McLeod, the Hudson's Bay officer, for $2.50 each. Then Birchner went on to Snyetown, whence several of the party started up-river, while others, including Birchner, decided to return down the Liard to Fort Simpson and Edmonton.

On December 26, Vaudin, Oliver and Brooke, who had tracked up the Liard in the fall of 1898 and camped near the mouth of the Beaver River, set out west up the Liard. They had such heavy loads that they made little progress and somewhere along the way Vaudin and Brooke went on ahead. By April 5 Oliver reached the mouth of Trout River. Today the Alaska Highway, sweeping north from Muncho Lake to where it crosses the Liard near the hot springs, follows Trout River. There Oliver and some associates built boats and, on May 25, started up the Liard during a snowstorm. They made reasonable time, passed old Fort Halkett, and in due course reached the Brulé Portage around Whirlpool Canyon — some forty miles above Trout River and fifteen miles below the Mud River Post.

When eventually Oliver talked to the *Bulletin* editor, he shed considerable light on conditions along the Liard that spring, which were reported as follows:

> When on Brule portage a man named Hutton came to them starving. He and his partner, named Knute Nelson, a Dane from Chicago, had taken the cross country trail from Snyetown to Mud river post. About 40 miles from the post they had left their guns. Mr. Edwards, of the H.B. post there had given them food to go back for their rifles. They had gone back, but had run short of food. When near the crossing of Coal river a few miles from the post on their return, Nelson gave out and Hutton went on alone. In trying to raft across Coal creek he was carried down to the Liard and only succeeded in landing just above the Brule rapids. Two of the Oliver party went with him to the relief of Nelson and found him dead, but still warm. He was buried there.

Oliver's party reached Mud River Post June 1, 1899, but by then the prospectors who had wintered between Devil's Portage and Mud River had pulled up to Cranberry Rapids on the ice, built boats there and were far ahead of him.

> Some of these parties dragged their boats through the canyon around the Devil's portage, something that had never been done before. This was rendered possible by the water being four feet lower than usual. Wood of the Philadelphia party, wintering at Snyetown, had his feet badly frozen while exploring from Snyetown to Mud river post. He recovered, however. His home was in Wilmington, Delaware. A man named McCulloch, got his feet wet while travelling on the ice, and they were badly frozen. He was laid up all winter, but the several parties cared for him, and he was pushed on from camp to camp. In the spring Brooke and another of the party Oliver was with, took him on from Trout River, 70 miles to Mud river post. He was one of the first to get out, and recovered entirely. A man named Fleming was ill during the winter, and died after he reached the coast. Mr. Oliver heard that a man named Simonson had accidentally shot himself at Devil's portage. . . .

Simonson was a Swedish miner who at various times had panned the Saskatchewan River gravels at Edmonton and then set out for the Klondike. At the time of his death he was camped on the banks of the Liard with his friend Octave La Chapelle, who a few weeks earlier had found Martin Meneely's body. While Octave was examining a gun, it went off and killed Simonson. Following so soon on his discovery of Meneely's fate, this second tragedy unnerved Octave and as soon as possible he set out to return to Edmonton.

At Cranberry Rapids high water delayed Oliver and his associates for five weeks. There he saw the first cases of scurvy, but fortunately all of the men recovered. According to the *Bulletin*, he characterized "as absolutely false the stories of wholesale death and destruction on the Liard River, which had been so industriously circulated by the coast papers. Considering the number and kind of people who attempted the trip, the loss of life was surprisingly small. . . ."

Hearing that no one was having any luck on Frances Lake or farther north, Oliver decided to go home, and in the spring of 1899 he and his associates tracked their boat up the Dease River and then to the south end of Dease Lake. Then, packing blankets and supplies, Oliver walked the seventy odd miles to Telegraph Creek, took a canoe down the Stikine to nearby Glenora, and finally took passage to Wrangell and came home. He was a rugged individual, and in spite of being over sixty years old endured the hardships of the Liard region without serious ill effects. For the time being, Vaudin remained at Dease Lake.

About the same time that Oliver made his report to the *Bulletin*, W. A. Kerr, who had turned back from the Liard River area, told the editor that about four hundred men had been pressing along up that river and that of them forty had turned back. Mentioning the death of Captain Mason of the Philadelphia party and of Joe Butler of the Jones cattle party, he also told of a man named Davis who froze his feet and died at Mud River and said that he had seen a grave "at the Willis party's camp and another at the Chatworthy's [*sic*] camp." He said too that seven men in trying to cut a road past the rapids to Dease Post had become lost, badly frozen and nearly starved, but had finally worked their way out safely.

Like Oliver and Kerr, two other groups, one led by the Roses from Saskatchewan and the other including A. D. Osborne, also spent the winter of 1898-99 in the Cassiar. Unlike Oliver, however, these two parties finally went on to the Yukon. The Roses and their associates wintered along the Dease River without any unusual suffering, although all forty of their horses died. In the spring they pushed on to Dawson where, after an interval, young Ernest Rose joined the NWMP.

From the Mud River Post in February 1899, A. D. Osborne and the Jamiesons pushed along over the ice and reached Lower Post at the mouth of the Dease where the group broke up. By this time Osborne had also lost all his horses. In the spring, after visiting Frances Lake, the Jamiesons set out for Wrangell and home. Osborne, however, bought four horses and joined two men named Rowatt and Derrick who each had three horses. Leaving Lower Post about July 1 they travelled up the Frances River to the lake and reached Pelly Banks about the end of the month. As far as the lake they found little sign of Moodie's trail but from there on it was well blazed and fairly passable. Feed was good all the way. Murphy and Carroll, of Chicago, also made the trip with horses from the Mud River Post to Pelly Banks and on to Dawson. O'Neil, who had crossed the mountains from Fort Nelson with Murphy, went out by Wrangell. Three Montana men who had managed to keep their horses alive near McDame Creek took them to Pelly Banks and on to Fort Selkirk.

After descending the Pelly some distance with his horses, Osborne detected the onset of scurvy and decided to float down the river in a boat. Below the mouth of Ross River some rapids swamped it and he lost $175 in cash, his watch, and in fact almost everything except a sleeping bag. When his partners caught up to him, one of them took him farther down in a boat while the other took the horses across country to the mouth of Salmon River and eventually rejoined him at Fort Selkirk. As soon as he reached there and could get potatoes he recovered from scurvy. Then, having reached the Yukon, he decided to return to Edmonton.

The Liard-Cassiar region was hard not only on horses and Klondikers. It also saw the finish of the Jones, Lang and Geddis cattle. During the winter of 1898-99 near McDame Creek, storms and starvation killed all but six of the forty-six cattle Geddis had driven so far. H. Y. Jones, who had left Swift Current on April 9, 1898, and had sold some cattle at Fort St. John and at Fort Grahame, took the balance of about twenty-five through to the Mud River Post, where as the winter wore on he found a ready market for them. Unfortunately one of his men, Joseph Butler, was drowned in the Cranberry Rapids just below the Mud River Post about the time that the cattle drive was nearing a successful conclusion. Lang's cattle also reached the same vicinity and after withstanding all the hardships en route were also converted into meat for the miners.

It was fortunate for many Klondikers that these cattle reached the region and no wonder that once they arrived their doom was sealed. In this valley of the shadow that was the Liard watershed, with its frigid temperatures and its shortage of provisions, the Jones and Lang cattle helped to ward off starvation.

For, holed up in crude cabins at short intervals all along the Liard and Dease rivers from Hell's Gate to Dease Lake, men sometimes frost-bitten, sometimes emaciated with hunger and sometimes livid and wracked with scurvy, shivered out the dark dreary months. Some had to remain in their cabins all winter but others shacked up for a while and then started on again.

Charles Camsell, who had gone to Dease Lake in August 1898 and

221

worked in the Laketon and Telegraph Creek areas, had a wry story about this aspect of life in his *Son of the North*:

> The resident population of Laketon was small, not more than thirty people in all, but there were also a certain number of transients drifting in all through the winter, victims of the Klondike rush. One night, while we were having our supper, a knock came at our door. When the door was opened and the light fell upon the face of the man standing there in his rough winter clothing, I immediately recognized one of the two men we had met on Liard River in July and who had refused to give us a bite to eat. He came into the cabin and in due time was eating supper with us. He obviously did not recognize us and we did not enlighten him. We had evidently changed a good deal since he had seen us on Liard River.
>
> The conversation was gradually turned towards his trip up the Liard and he admitted having found nothing, that his map was no good and he was going home. He also referred to the fact that he and his partner had met three men while on their way up Liard River in July, that they looked half starved and in fact were "bent up like fish hooks." He said that he and his partner had often talked of that meeting and regretted that they had not given these fellows something to eat. Since that time he and his partner had experienced some of the hardships of the prospector's life. That experience had taught them understanding, and they had become much more sympathetic to those who were up against it.

Laketon, of course, was just one of the posts to which harassed Klondikers were turning for help. In the disaster area there were but a handful of responsible officials and trading-post managers. Telegraph Creek, the head of navigation on the Stikine during high water, was the official headquarters of James Porter, the gold commissioner or government agent for the Cassiar mining district. Reporting to him were two or three men, including Constable A. D. Drummond at Teslin Lake and Constable McLean at Glenora. This hamlet, about fifteen miles downstream from Telegraph Creek, was the head of navigation during low water periods, and in it lived the district managers for the Hudson's Bay Company and the Casca Trading and Transportation Company, Farquhar Matherson and William Marriott respectively. Matherson supervised four or five posts on Dease Lake and River and on the upper Liard. Marriott kept an eye on three or four Casca posts, including Mud River, Lower Post and Laketon, to which Scott Simpson had been moved.

Upon these few experienced men with their half-breed helpers and their small stocks of goods fell the burden of looking after a host of sick and starving Klondikers. Because all of these, from Porter, the senior government employee in the region, down to isolated post managers, were cut off from communication with their superiors in civilization, they had to solve the major problem that soon faced them on their own initiative.

As early as January 21, 1898, Constable Drummond at Teslin Lake wrote to Porter mentioning cases of illness or destitution, and reporting that with a helper he had made a five-day return trip and brought in a crippled and starving prospector. About the same time, Porter received a message from another starving man who was about eighty miles away along the trail to Teslin. At a cost of $93.50 to the government, he sent out to bring in the victim. On February 8, when Constable McLean at Glenora reported three cases of scurvy there, Porter arranged for "a sort of hospital at Glenora." Ten days later it had six patients, and before long eight more were placed in its care. Up to this point these patients were undoubtedly men who had entered the country from the coast or by way of the Ashcroft Trail – one of them seventy-four years old.

While Porter was busy helping these men, rumours began to reach him about victims of the Edmonton route, who were mainly much farther east. On March 13 he wrote to F. Matherson of the Hudson's Bay Company, asking his opinion of the seriousness of the problem of the Edmonton-based Klondikers, a problem which he suspected would become a major one. On March 15 Matherson replied, giving an alarming but undoubtedly good assessment of the situation. He said:

A large proportion of the people coming into the district over the so-called "Edmonton Route," both overland and via the McKenzie and Liard Rivers – are continuously turning up at our posts on the Dease and Liard Rivers, either short of supplies and money or completely destitute. I have just now returned from a journey down the Dease and Liard Rivers. While at our Lower Post, three men arrived there from the "Potato Patch," a place 30 miles above Fort Liard, coming on the overland trail in advance of a party of forty-five men. One third of this party, they informed me, had neither food nor money of their own, and depended entirely on their fellow travellers for means to enable them to continue their journey in this direction till they strike our Posts after which, I understand, they hoped to get along better. Besides these, it was believed by our post master Mr. Harry Edwards and by the prospectors wintering at the Lower Post, that there were twenty or thirty men down the river towards the Devils Portage and below the Devils Portage, who were also without provisions enough for the winter or for a journey to civilization. This last lot were supposed to have banded together for the purpose of having contributions from their more fortunate and better provided fellow travellers till they should reach the Hudson's Bay Posts where they counted upon getting further supplies by fair means or foul. . . .

Matherson went on to list a dozen or so cases where men, singly or in twos or threes, had reached the Hudson's Bay Company's posts at McDame Creek and on Dease Lake and had been given provisions for which the company knew it could never be reimbursed. Each of these posts had stocks of food sufficient for the normal trade of the area, but none of them was capable of feeding many extra men. Each of the traders was long experienced in the ways of the North and was entirely imbued with the northerners' code of feeding all needy passersby. The prospect of having to give out all of the company's food to miners who had no hope of paying was a difficult one to face. Each trader would gladly have shared all of his personal supply, but was naturally reluctant to face his remote superiors with the tale of having given away all of the company's goods. In Matherson's letter he also said:

> I have compiled the following table of the numbers of strangers travelling through or wintering in that country, being mostly an estimate I cannot vouch for its corrections, but it may be of some use to you.

Coming up the Liard at and below Devils Portage	100 men
On overland trail from Potato Patch	45
At Fort Halkett	16
At Lower Post & Brule Portage	58
Between Lower & Liard Post	10
Liard Post and vicinity	30
Francis Lake	45
McDame Creek & Horse Range	33
Black River Trail – wintering	19
French Creek	6
Dease River, above Post	15
Thibert Creek & Dease Lake	16
	393 men

> Most of those who have money or supplies intend going through towards the Pelly river, either this winter or in the ensuing summer, and those that have no means are making for civilization in this direction. In addition to the above it is reported that there are five or six hundred men scattered along the river [Liard] from the Devils Portage to Fort Simpson on the McKenzie River, but probably most of them will turn back. [Reference to five or six hundred men seems so greatly exaggerated that it can be disregarded.]

On March 16 Porter acknowledged Matherson's letter, recognizing that the Hudson's Bay Company's posts were rapidly being depleted of their food and wondering what could possibly be done. Too far away from Victoria to get any guidance before the emergency would be upon him, he, like every other official in the area, had to do everything he could to help the stranded wayfarers. He had no power to authorize the Hudson's Bay Company and the Casca Trading Company managers to dispense relief in the hope that their companies would be reimbursed by the provincial government, and yet between himself and these managers they had to provide for the Klondikers.

> There is one thing certain, and that is it will not do to try to keep food from these starving people as long as there is a pound of it in your stores, money or no money, therefore it is no use attempting to do so. The case is bad enough as it is without giving room for it to become more so.
>
> ... If you as managers here, for the Hudson's Bay Co. will do all you can to relieve those in distress and in absolute want on the Dease and Liard rivers, and keep a careful account of it, I will do my utmost in my official capacity to see that the Company gets paid for so doing. . . .
>
> I would strongly advise that each of your post masters be authorized to arrange for Indian hunters to kill game at each of the Posts for the benefit of the white strangers, as this would be a ready means of great saving of imported food.

On April 19, William Marriott of the Casca Company called on Porter and advised him that his company had a considerable store of supplies at its Laketon post and that this could be made available for a relief expedition. In contrast to the Hudson's Bay Company, the Casca Company was a relatively new organization in the field. Its line of communication came up the Stikine River from the coast, and at Glenora it kept a corps of pack mules which made regular trips to Laketon where the company maintained a considerable depot. Marriott suggested that if the provincial government would pay the bare cost of a relief expedition, he would be glad to organize it. Porter stated that although his powers did not go so far as to commit the government to paying for such an expedition, nevertheless, it seemed absolutely necessary to send it out.

On May 7 Porter received a petition from the Liard River signed by forty-two men asking for assistance. This is undoubtedly the one to which A. Scott Gillespie's diary referred, and it said:

Lower Post
Mountain Rapids, B.C.
April 3rd 99

To any representative of the Gov^t
of B.C. – to whom this petition
May come: –

We the undersigned beg to inform you that there are men on this river, Three at this post & several near here, who are disabled, entirely destitute & who unless government aid is sent immediately, must die. We have appealed to the H. B. Cos agent, but, he has refused to aid them in any way. We are ourselves unable to provide them with provisions or take them to civilization having all we can do to take care of our selves. We would urgently beg you to send at once such means of transportation as seems best & provide these men with the necessaries of life until such time as they can reach civilization. The men for whom we ask assistance are Fred. K. White, has scurvy, unable to walk – has no provisions. Alex McCulloch – feet badly frozen will not be able to walk for several months at least, has not more than 15 days grub. Nels Johnson has scurvy – been unable to walk for eleven weeks – has perhaps 30 days Grub, – Wm Barker has scurvy, has been pulled on a toboggan over a hundred miles and his comrades having no grub were unable to stay with him, so they left him here. he is very weak & will be unable to move for several months. He has not more than 30 dys Grub. W. H. Harris feet badly frozen cannot walk for months to come has perhaps 60 dys grub but has no means of travelling before it will be gone. In view of the great necessity now existing we beg you to take immediate action.

One of the men who signed it was A. Scott Gillespie. Commenting on this, Porter immediately wrote to the provincial secretary, saying:

On the receipt of this petition I at once came to the conclusion that it would not do to waist [sic] any more time, and again I looked at it in this way, that the Government might blame me were I not to act on my judgment and endeavour, if possible to save the lives of fellow men who were asking to be saved from starving to death. The following day I arranged with Mr. Marriott [Casca Trading Company] to send a special messenger with all haste to their agent at Laketon, with instructions to organize and equip a relief expedition and send them in a large boat down the river just as soon as it was possible to do so, and to bring all those who were found to be sick and destitute to Dease Lake. I trust that by the time this expedition returns to Dease Lake, the Government will forward full instructions to me as to the way they wish me to act in dealing with severe cases etc. etc. etc. It will likely be the first part of July before the expedition returns. . . .

By May 16, Porter having still received no word from Victoria once more wrote to the provincial secretary, stating that dozens of Klondikers had been arriving and that he had helped them all he could. Moreover, he had felt it necessary to ask the Casca Company to send out the relief expedition.

In this manner, without waiting to see who would ultimately pay for it, the men in the field sent the expedition on its way. On May 18, Scott Simpson of the Casca Company started it out from Laketon. Fred Camsell, who in 1897 had entered the area as a Klondiker, took charge of it and started out with two scows and a crew made up mostly of

Indians. The party reached Lower Post on May 23, and stayed there two weeks while it sent food to some of the outlying camps and brought in as many as possible of the worst sufferers to embark on the scows. On the way back to Laketon the water in the Dease River rose and for some time the scows had to wait for it to subside. As a result, the expedition ran out of food and had to rely on two good Indian hunters to kill moose.

After an absence of about two months, when the scows returned to Laketon they brought between fifty and sixty men, some of whom were so ill with scurvy that they had to be carried on and off at each camp. With a proper diet, however, many recovered very quickly. All of them were taken to the upper end of Dease Lake, whence they were transported to Telegraph Creek by pack train. In due course they reached the coast on the steamer *Strathcona*, and eventually went out to Vancouver or Victoria.

Reporting on the relief expedition on November 1, 1899, Superintendent I. T. Wood of the NWMP at Tagish, Upper Yukon, said: "According to the reports received from the Stikine district, the starvation on that trail far exceeded anything witnessed on the Yukon lakes. . . . Mr. Porter, the British Columbia agent, on the strength of the petition, forwarded a boat-load of provisions, notifying the British Columbia authorities of his action in the matter; he, I understand, received a reply by return mail to the effect that, as he had ordered and forwarded the provisions on his own responsibility he would have to bear the expense – the milk of human kindness had evidently been strained."

A letter book in the British Columbia Provincial Archives indicates that Premier C. A. Semlin wrote to Porter on April 29, saying: "The Provincial Government cannot accept the responsibility . . . as in its opinion the duty, if such exists, seems clearly to belong to the Dominion Government. . . . We will correspond with the Dominion authorities. . . ."

Then on June 12, after receiving another letter from Porter, the Premier replied that "the Government fully approve of your course and assume all responsibility for the same. . . . I do not anticipate any difficulty in adjusting accounts. . . ."

Futher studies might provide information as to whether or not the Dominion Government ever paid the bill, but this is enough for our purpose. Shortly after the expedition, however, the Casca Trading Company went out of business. Whether a deficit caused by the expedition was a contributing factor we do not know. In any event, the relief party saved many lives.

The men in the field had taken what steps they could and the comments they made help us to form a rough idea of conditions during that long, hard winter in the Cassiar. Gradually, as the earliest to get out of the area arrived in Vancouver and Victoria, word of the hardships they had endured began to reach the rest of Canada. Foremost in publicizing them was the *Victoria Daily Colonist*. The editor of that paper, biased as badly against the Edmonton route as the *Edmonton Bulletin* was biased in its favour, naturally felt that all Klondikers should have taken the sea route. He had little patience even with the route that left the CPR at Ashcroft and passed through Telegraph Creek on its way north to either Atlin or Teslin Lake, and no mercy on the Edmonton route. While other Canadian papers were moderate in their condemnation of the Edmonton route, the *Colonist* focused all its spleen on it.

By studying extracts from some of these papers, we can nevertheless get a more complete idea of the suffering in the Liard and Dease Lake areas during that winter. Exaggerated and unreliable as some of them were and the product of melodramatic reporters' emotional expansiveness, they do serve to paint a picture of the hardships a small fraction of the Klondikers suffered. Some reports were true and some were later shown to be entirely the result of the reporters' enthusiasm, but any one statement taken singly could well have been true. Moreover, regardless of the light they shed at the time, they are interesting because they reflect the redundancy and hyperbole of news items of that era.

One of the earliest to appear was a letter written to the *Winnipeg Free Press* from Sylvester's lower post on July 1, 1899, and signed by twenty-two righteously indignant Klondikers who had taken the overland route, saying in part: ". . . we think it our duty to send you this letter, as it may stop some from following our footsteps. We had to erect a hospital tent above the Cranberry Rapids and men have been hauled on toboggans for a hundred miles who were frozen and sick, some with the scurvy. This has been done on this route not by comrades but by strangers who hauled men they never saw before, and at the same time they had their own outfit to get up the river. Some men were moving up the river all winter. As provisions were getting very low for the sick, we had to make a demand on the Mud River post belonging to H.B.C. We did this by holding a miners' meeting."

In its September 19 issue the *Colonist* pulled out all the stops and set up an article under four headlines.

It listed fifteen men who had died, including Hoffman who had drowned on Great Slave Lake, Meneely, Joe Butler and others whose deaths were later verified, and these in general it recorded tersely. The reports of the others, the ones that were hard to confirm or were never

Died For Gold.

Lured From Edmonton Across Trackless Wild erness and Abandoned to Solitary Death in Most Appalling Form.

Survivors of the Spectral Trail Reach Civilization with Harrowing Tales of Named and Unknown Dead.

Men Cruelly Abandoned to Certain Doom Write With Touch-ing Simplicity of Visions of Home Seen by Last Flicker of Vital Spark.

confirmed, were packed with melodrama. For instance, the article quoted a Klondiker named Crawford who said: "I counted over 100 tragic deaths but can remember but a few of the names." Under the caption "Three Englishmen Unnamed" the reporter really let himself go, saying: "I found the bodies of three London Englishmen in one cabin; two were brothers; it was at night; there was a light in the tent, and I went in. A candle was just spluttering out. A man lay in the bunk, seemingly looking at me, so I said 'Hello,' but he still stared silently. I touched him and found that he was dead. I looked in two other bunks, and each contained a dead body — all dead of scurvy. The last entry in the diary lying close to the bunk, with some dried apples, read: 'Brother Jack passed away peacefully last night.' The three bodies were buried. Someone else took the names to write to friends."

Finally, quoting someone not credited by name, the article con-cluded: "I could give scores of other instances of deaths awful and swift, slow and starving. I can give details, but no names; I forget them. There has been an awful carnival of death on the Edmonton trail."

Each of these articles in the *Colonist* wrung an angry retort from the editor of the biased *Bulletin*. At times he was able to show that an article was totally untrue and at other times he had to admit its truth but found some way of softening its impact. Outraged by each article, he produced vitriolic ripostes that are gems of the journalistic style of his day. For their own sake, they are worth repeating.

One of his better efforts in June 1899, referring to an item in the *Colonist*, read:

CHEAP SENSATIONALISM

Readers of the daily press have been regaled for some time past with despatches from Victoria or Vancouver, retailing with all the thrilling fervor of a dime novel, the ghastly stories of wholesale murders, suicides and starvation which occurred on that "death trap," the Edmonton trail to the Yukon. Carried away by the fervor of the thing the industrious compiler of yellow journal despatches killed hundreds of people who took the trail and thousands who were never near it. Among the victims of this wholesale thirst for human life were six inoffensive prospectors from Halifax, N.S. Despatches from Victoria told how nine prospectors, from Halifax, starved, broken down, sick and lost were struggling with the last energy of despair after a few Indians who were trying to lead them out of the great lost land, out of the shadow of the "valley of death," (situated somewhere near Dease lake, though not marked on the map) out of the land of their starvation and suffering, out into the light again. Three of them got safely away from that dread land, in comparison to which Hades is a Paradise, the other six dropped behind and were lost on awful Hay mountain. "And when summer smiles again and the sun shines on Hay mountain and melts away the shroud of snow that wraps the bodies of the unfortunates in its cold embrace, what ghastly tragedies it will reveal; white glistening skeletons and grinning skulls which will be all that is left of those brave Halifax arganouts [*sic*] who sought for gold and found only death on the awful Edmonton route." The story was one calculated to move strong men to tears. The correspondent, however, over-reached himself. He was all right as long as he murdered people who never existed but when, emboldened by success, he thoughtlessly killed on Hay mountain six prospectors who actually did exist, he made the mistake of not arranging the matter before hand with them. As a result they innocently turned up, very much alive, as shown by a Halifax despatch of the 14th, which says: "The joyful intelligence was received today by Mr. Longford, a brother of one of the supposed unfortunates, that every one of the missing six had turned up safe and sound."

Comment is unnecessary.

On another occasion in August the *Colonist*, in referring to an interview with Jones who had driven his cattle to the Mud River Post, expanded his experiences into a doleful tale. The *Bulletin* demolished it by saying:

Of course having told his own story Mr. Jones is put through the usual course of questions as to hardships of the trail, with the usual result. Mr. Jones is made to say that 20 people were drowned in one storm on Great Slave Lake, and that several of their bodies have been found near Sylvester's Landing: the words "bodies have been found" forming a scare head in the article. In reference to this as a sample statement it may be remarked, 1st, that no such drowning ever took place, and 2nd From Great Slave Lake to Sylvester's Landing is some 700 miles, 400 of which is up the course of the Liard River, the great complaint against which is that it is so difficult for live men to get up, to say nothing of dead bodies. Mr. Jones is also made to say that all of Lang & Mansell's [sic] herd of cattle, except six head were lost at Dunvegan on Peace river. Mr. Jones may be a good deal of a liar, but the reporter must have depended on his own imagination for this one, as well as that about the alleged Slave lake drowning.

The extracts from the *Victoria Colonist,* some true, some fanciful, and all slanted in one direction, bring out the type of stark realities which the Edmonton-based Klondikers faced. The exact number of men who spent the winter in the Liard-Cassiar region can never be known; Matherson the local trader estimated that 393 did so, and that is undoubtedly a better guess than any that could be compiled now. Although on the one hand that figure included a number of men who had come in from British Columbia either by the Ashcroft trail or up the Stikine, on the other hand it probably did not include one or two score of Edmonton-based men who were on the lower Liard. It would seem safe, however, to assume that the whole Liard watershed that winter held a total of about 370 Edmonton-based Klondikers.

Twenty-six of them died during the winter. Out of the total saved by the relief expedition possibly some fifty had started from Edmonton, and after deducting them and the men who died, we are left with about 290 Edmonton-based Klondikers who managed to live out the winter in the Liard watershed by their own exertions. Of those, about forty returned to Edmonton by descending the Liard to Fort Simpson and another forty retraced their steps to Fort St. John or Peace River Crossing. Of the balance, about one hundred calmly went on to the Yukon in the spring, while possibly an additional 110 decided to chuck the venture and hurried out to civilization through Wrangell, bringing the total Edmonton-based Klondikers who headed for the coast to about 155, including those taken by the relief expedition.

Although the *Colonist* could conjure up some deaths which never happened, not even the *Bulletin* could whisk them all into its wastepaper basket. Scurvy took the greatest toll, seventeen. Starvation probably accounted for some, while sudden accidental death, mainly by drowning, brought a quick end to ten more Klondikers' hopes. Others froze their feet and suffered for weeks before their fellows got them out to civilization. A few required amputations.

For years newspaper reporters and others, eager for a titillating story, wrote of men murdered by their companions and of scores of men who disappeared and presumably met a solitary death. Most of these stories and rumours were without foundation. Undoubtedly an occasional prospector whose fate was never recorded did die, but there were very few of these. Moreover, a few men neither reached the Yukon nor returned to civilization, but, either to avoid the accusation of failure or because they had come to like the freedom that life in the far northwest provided, preferred to remain there to trap, trade or prospect. Many of these remained in the North for fifty years, and some of them could never be induced even to visit the outside. An example of this breed of men was Frank Watson, who, after making his way as far as the Liard River, decided to settle down at the lake near the Alaska Highway that we know as Watson Lake. He lived there long enough to witness the construction of that road.

It is tempting to use the phraseology of reporters and romantic writers and to call these hundred who reached the Yukon the pitiful remnant of the mighty host which left Edmonton. Though indeed they were only a fraction of those who started, they were far from being pitiful. They were the triumphant few who had pitted their strength and wits against all that the Edmonton route could dish out and had won. They were the hardy ones who had proved themselves. No one could have devised a severer test of a man's courage and endurance than the Edmonton Overland Route. Even those who won their way through it would have been far better advised if they had gone some other way.

For the Edmonton Overland Route, scarred with the wrecks of abandoned supplies and conveyances and strewn with the bleaching skeletons of thousands of horses, was a mistake and a terrible waste of human effort. Regardless of the fact that hundreds took it of their own volition; regardless of the facts that many frontiersmen from the Edmonton area took it successfully, that Edmonton merchants naturally advocated it and that the editor of the *Bulletin* advertised and defended it so valiantly; regardless of the fact that both the Northwest Territories and the Ottawa governments spent money on it, nevertheless, it was the least practical of nearly all the routes to the Yukon. To all it proved disappointing, to many it proved disastrous and to three dozen it proved deadly.

CHAPTER SIXTEEN

STATISTICS, SCURVY AND GREAT SLAVE LAKE MINING

The White Pass and Yukon Railway, heading from Skagway, Alaska, to Lake Bennett, Yukon, forty miles away, wrung the neck of Edmonton's All-Canadian routes to the Klondike. Organized in 1898, the company began construction work immediately and within a few months had built tote roads which circumvented the forbidding Chilkoot Pass. Preferring the White Pass five miles to the south, the new line doomed the former deadly bottleneck to unlamented and endless obscurity. By the fall of 1898 access to Lake Bennett and the Yukon River was child's play. With the demise of the ogre of the Chilkoot Pass came the death of all other routes including those out of Edmonton.

And it was just as well, too. For their fatal shortcomings were killing them anyway.

But, while they lasted and while the searchlight of publicity played on Edmonton – for those twelve months from mid summer 1897 to mid summer 1898 – Edmontonians participated in one of the truly stirring episodes in Canadian history.

For during that year some 1,500 prospectors set out along the Edmonton routes, and even though the laggards did not reach the Klondike till 1899, over seven hundred did reach that objective.

During 1897 nearly three hundred Klondikers had passed through Edmonton, but in a volume ever swelling through January, February and March 1898, and reaching a crest in April, the wave of milling Klondikers rolled on north. After that, through May, June and July, the flood subsided to a mere trickle and then it dried up, and Edmonton's streets returned to their normal loneliness.

The White Pass Railway had done its work and its most convincing helper was the backwash of Klondikers doubling back to Edmonton, overflowing with tales of frustration, disappointment and disillusionment. For during 1898 a large part of the traffic along Edmonton's routes to the Klondike, and particularly along the Overland Route, moved two ways. Eager adventurers northbound met hollow-eyed failures faltering back. The timid and the unfit and without doubt some of the more realistic were shaking the dust of the Edmonton route off their feet. They shook some of it into the smarting eyes of the editor of the *Edmonton Bulletin* but reserved most of it for newspapers such as the *Victoria Colonist*, which had always been hostile to Edmonton's routes. These papers often correctly but frequently unjustly spread the word far and wide. And traffic over the Edmonton routes ceased.

The first of the overlanders to leave had set out for Lac Ste Anne on August 24, 1897, and the first to give up and return reached Edmonton on October 10. The total of the drop-outs who became disgusted and went home is best shown by roughly rounding out the figures and studying the progress of the prospectors. During 1897 and 1898 about 775 overlanders left Edmonton heading for some point on the Peace River, and about 680 reached that stream. At Peace River Crossing about a hundred, fed up with hazing horses through muskegs though they were still set on going to the Klondike, took boats down the river and transferred to the Water Route. Of the remaining 580 who channeled their efforts to cover the next stages of their trip through two quite different routes which ended in Fort St. John on the one hand and Fort Nelson on the other, some 560 reached one or other of these places.

From the two widely separated points, these 560 started out on the next legs of their different routes, but before they converged on the Liard-Cassiar area, about one hundred had turned aside to mine in the Omineca or Finlay regions, while some seventy-five returned to Edmonton, leaving about 385 overlanders who reached the Liard-Cassiar region. To these should be added approximately 105 who had come up the Liard from the Water Route, bringing the total to enter that region to about 490, whom we may now consider as overlanders. Before the winter of 1898-99 set in, some sixty of these went on to Dawson, about fifty went out to civilization by way of Wrangell and ten turned back to Fort Simpson, leaving about 370 men who had started from Edmonton to face the winter in the Liard-Cassiar.

During the summer and fall of 1898 and the following winter twenty-six overlanders died in the Liard-Cassiar and another nine died before reaching there, giving us about 335 to account for. The next spring eighty men turned back towards Edmonton. Another 150 or so went out to the coast at Wrangell, while the remainder, about one

hundred, went on to Dawson, to bring the total overlanders who reached Dawson during 1898 and 1899 to about 160.

In total, then, of the 775 overlanders who left Edmonton, about 160
reached Dawson. Thirty-five died and the remaining 580 either stayed
to mine in the Omineca or other fields, or returned to civilization.

The Overland Route fell sadly short of success.

On the other hand, the wayfarers along the Water Route travelled
it to some purpose. Perhaps the best way to get some conception of
their numbers is to present our estimate in tabular form, adding the
warning that it is impossible to get accurate figures. The lack of records,
complicated by the erratic movements of small groups that switched
from the Overland to the Water Route, or vice versa, and other parties
that broke off from the mainstream of Klondikers to set out along a
number of minor routes, makes estimating extremely hazardous.

BY THE WATER ROUTE

Started from Edmonton 1897 and 1898 and reached		
Athabasca Landing		785
But 75 went upstream to Peace River Crossing	*75*	
Set out for Fort McMurray		710
Turned back before reaching there	*30*	
Reached Fort McMurray		680
Joined there by men from Prince Albert	*80*	
Total leaving Fort McMurray		760
Re-entering the water route from Peace River Crossing	*100*	
Reached Fort Smith		860
Returned to Edmonton or stayed on Great Slave Lake	*70*	
Reached Fort Simpson		790
Went up Liard (50 ultimately came back)	*105*	
Went downstream from Fort Simpson		685
Died	*35*	
Came back to Edmonton	*85*	
Reached Yukon by the Water Route		565

Our estimate of the total score of those who took one or other of the
routes is:

	OVERLAND	WATER	TOTAL
Total passing through Edmonton	775	785	1,560
Add those originating at Prince Albert		100	100
	775	885	1,660
Died	35	35	70
Turned back or remained in country	580	285	865
Reached Yukon	160	565	725
	775	885	1,660

By mid summer, 1898, the bloom had blown from the Edmonton routes, but for the next two or three months a few prospectors dribbled into the town and trickled out north. Disappointed Klondikers, however, continued to drain back into Edmonton for the next twelve months.

It will never be possible to arrive at the exact number of Edmonton-based Klondikers who died en route. In 1899 there were so many conflicting rumours, many of which turned out to be untrue or unconfirmed, that at the time estimates of the death toll varied widely. If we sift the various reports and include some which might be questioned, it appears that sixty-nine men and one baby died. Curiously enough, thirty-five of those who left by the Water Route succumbed and thirty-five who took the Overland Route. Of these, six died after reaching Dawson or else at other places in the Yukon where they decided to prospect. If we consider that these deaths, of which at least one was attributable to typhoid fever, were not the fault of the Edmonton route, we can still charge it with sixty-four deaths – a serious toll.

Of the sixty-four who died en route, three of the Water Route people and six of the overlanders died from causes such as hernia, heart attack, or being attacked by a bear, and it may be unfair to lay their deaths at the door of the Edmonton routes. For good measure, however, we have included them in the toll these routes took. There were rumours of men disappearing or being killed by their partners, and while most of these were the product of someone's imagination, it is nevertheless likely that a few men, maybe three or four, died who are not included in the totals above. Perhaps to take some account of these and thus to be on the safe side, we should increase our figure of sixty-four and say that seventy died as a result of taking the Edmonton routes.

Of the sixty-four of which we are certain, two died of starvation, four froze to death, six died of accidental causes of one sort or another, twenty were drowned and thirty-two died of scurvy.

Scurvy clearly took the greatest toll and was the most horrible way to die; drowning was sudden and was over in a matter of minutes, the victims of freezing suffered a day or so, but the victims of scurvy lingered in dreadful agony for at least two months.

Some idea of the course of this terrible malady can be found in the pathetic story of A. D. Stewart's illness on the Peel River. He had fallen and hurt his leg before Christmas, 1898, and was laid up for over two weeks before his diary for January 13 complains of his leg hurting and his difficulty in getting around.

Still unaware that he had scurvy, or at least not willing to admit it even to himself, Stewart, the man who six months earlier had expounded on the causes of scurvy, calls his affliction rheumatism. While his companions did all they could for him, he still had two months to suffer. The entries in his diary go on for another month, revealing what he went through and his remarkable bravery. They record the closing stages of scurvy from the standpoint of the victim – and a courageous one at that.

During that period his partner R. H. S. Cresswell also kept up his own diary, and its entries show us scurvy from the viewpoint of a dear friend who watched death come. From the two diaries we can get some idea of the nightmare of four men all suffering affliction of one sort or another during the sunless days of the winter while cooped up in a crude cabin sixteen feet by twelve feet and seven feet high. The unenviable situation can be clearly perceived in extracts in parallel columns from entries in the two diaries for the same days, skipping some of the more repetitious entries and at times the entries for several days.

STEWART	CRESSWELL
Jan. 14 – Leg less painful, but stiff at joint, and tendons back of knee very stiff.	Jan. 14 – Stewart and Skynner in cabin all day. Anxiously awaiting arrival of the sun.
Jan. 15 – Pain in leg excruciating. Passed awful night.	Jan. 15 – Skynner and Stewart in bed till five o'clock.
Jan. 16 – Did not get up today. In agony all day. Skynner made me a crutch and exchanges berths with me, but I find his too cold and move back to my own. Exhaustion terrible.	Jan. 16 – Stewart suffering great pain in his leg. Thinks it is acute rheumatism.
Jan. 17 – Bad night. Very weak and sick, almost fainted on rising . . . sun apparently trying to shine . . . Northern Lights of great magnificence.	Jan. 17 – Caught a hare in my trap. Roasted him for dinner. . . . Stewart suffering great pain.
Jan. 18 – Heated water for bath, but on trying to stand up to take one nearly fainted with pain. Back to bed again.	Jan. 18 – Skynner and Stewart in bed all day. Tallman and I as usual cutting wood.
Jan. 20 – Went outside this forenoon, and all but fainted. But for	

Cresswell who happened to pass, could not have got back. Exhaustion terrible. Weak as a baby. Tallman shows inside of right thigh completely discolored, red and black hue. He has had no bruise, and Skynner and I are much alarmed thereat.

Jan. 21 – Sleepless but not painful night. Beef tea three times a day seems to be strengthening me already. Great languor and weakness. Teeth seem to be loosening and gums sore. Can scurvy be setting in, too?

Jan. 23 – Passed a fair night. . . . Cresswell complains of weak back and pain in hips. Tallman's leg stiff, and Skynner feeling very poorly and full of rheumatic pains. Our damp cabin probably responsible. This is the worst month we have had, and we are all in poor spirits.

Jan. 24 – Passed a quiet day in bed. Weak but not in much pain. Last night got up and fainted in Tallman's arms. Exhaustion deplorable. Pain in legs agonizing. No words to describe the torture.

Jan. 27 – Had a splendid night's rest on my bed. Tallman's bed is leaky and let me down on boards, hurting my leg badly. Skynner feeling very poorly, and I think my case is worrying him.

Jan. 28 – Rested comfortably, but no sleep. Very cold and growing weaker again. Dull day and no sun. How I long for light instead of this everlasting darkness!

Jan. 21 – Stewart worse . . . perfectly helpless, almost fainted. Skynner also feeling poorly.

Jan. 23 – Stewart very weak and shivering with cold in cabin.

Jan. 24 – Stewart and Skynner both on sick list. My back and leg very sore. Stewart fainted at night and was asking for his daughter "Tot." Apparently he is thoroughly run down owing to his not eating meat.

Jan. 27 – Temperature 47 below. Coldest day of the season so far. Cut wood as usual. All the rest of the crowd feeling seedy.

Jan. 28 – Stewart and Skynner still laid up. Broke a new trail in the bush, at least a quarter of a mile from cabin for dry wood.

Jan. 29 – Pain is less excruciating. Can hear my partners discussing my case, but do not care to ask them what they think. They either fancy that I bear pain very badly, and am not so ill as I seem, or else that I am worse than I think I am.

Jan. 30 – Rested fairly well, thanks to Skynner, who sat up all night stoking the fire. Legs numb and painful all day. Tallman not feeling well and did not go out to work.

Jan. 31 – Pain in both legs very steady today, and causing me much suffering. Am longing for some fruit, or the sight of some flowers, or the children's faces. Thank God, January is over. If I can only last out till the first of May I may get down to Fort Mc-Pherson yet.

Feb. 1 – In great pain all night. Fearful pain in right shoulder. Very weak all day.

Feb. 2 – Partners decided last night to sit up in turns and keep fire going all night. Result agreeable to me. Passed a comfortable night, and feel better today, although still very weak. Kidneys badly out of order and causing me much distress. Found gums bleeding profusely and commencing to slough.

Feb. 3 – Am afraid that scurvy has now set in to complicate matters. If I only had the children's photographs!

Jan. 29 – Thawed ice off windows, making quite a difference in cabin.

Jan. 30 – Temperature 47 below. Skynner better. Stewart still ill. Skynner stayed up till 2.30 to keep fire going on account of Stewart feeling cold. Last of sugar for supper.

Jan. 31 – Temperature 47 below. All the crowd laid up, bar self. I cut wood, etc. Baked bread today. Stewart appears to be better. When his bed was made he seemed much stronger, and did not seem to be in much pain.

Feb. 1 – Stewart very despondent and perfectly helpless. . . . Complaining of pains in leg very bad, also appetite very poor.

Feb. 2 – Stewart suffering great agony, with frequent exclamations of "My God! My God!" He says pains have gone from legs to right shoulder, and that he cannot bear any more pain.

Feb. 3 – We have decided to keep fire going all night for Stewart. Skynner stayed up till 5 a.m., and then called me. Stewart says that he is better today; does not appear to be in much pain; only

stiff. In cleaning his teeth his gums
bled badly.

Feb. 4 – Had a good night's rest, but
fearfully weak all day. Find long
nights very wearisome. Acute pain
appears to have left me.

Feb. 4 – Stewart very weak. . . . .
Skynner up all night, Tallman re-
lieving him at 5 a.m. I had a very
bad night, owing to fire going all
night.

Feb. 5 – Agony in legs fearful, and
caused me to scream. Tallman
very indignant, and told me not
to make such a noise.

Feb. 5 – Stewart about the same. His
skin looks very yellow; his articu-
lation is bad; he is perfectly helpless.

Feb. 7 – Looked at my left leg this
evening and found it discolored
almost black from above the knee
to ankle. No more doubt now that
I have either scurvy or black leg
or something of that sort. . . . Am
longing for a dish of fruit and
some fresh flowers.

Feb. 7 – Temperature 47 below.
Stewart passed a bad night and
complains of teeth being loose.
He asks to have crusts cut off his
toast. Cannot hold his heavy pipe
in his mouth. We got him to sit
up for awhile in bed. His appetite is good. Skynner looks as
though he is worrying a great
deal.

Feb. 8 – Fearful shivering fit . . .
accompanied by coughing, which
racked me to pieces and caused
me great pain. . . . The long, dark
nights, the wakefulness and the
eternal thinking is maddening.
My vitality surprises me in the
face of such long-continued weakness and suffering.

Feb. 8 – Stewart about the same in
the morning. Appetite not so
good. His teeth are quite loose.
He will not eat things that are
good for him. It is very discouraging. He informed us at night that
he has an incipient attack of
scurvy. I have felt seedy all day
from not sleeping well.

Feb. 9 – Utterly exhausted all day.
Bad night's sleep. Left leg badly
discolored below the knee now.
No more acute pain, but very sore
all over, and back so weak that I
cannot turn in bed. Eating dry
evaporated potatoes. Tallman's
leg very much discolored but he
has no idea what he has.

Feb. 9 – Stewart passed a fair night.
Seemed to be in better spirits. We
get him up to make his bed, I
lifting him up. He commenced to
shake like a reed. He looked thoroughly exhausted. I have grave
doubts about his getting better.

Feb. 10 – Long nights utterly unbearable, and loneliness awful.

Feb. 10 – 53 below. Stewart seems
better today. Says he is very weak.

See the children continually. Indian woman nightmare. Longing for some fruit and flowers.

Feb. 12 – Quiet day in camp, Partners all out or asleep all day, and loneliness terrible. My exhaustion beyond telling. I feel that I am very near death or a crisis.

Feb. 13 – About 10 last night exhaustion following from movement drew me almost to death. Felt sure I was dying. Bade partners good-bye. I read 14th of John aloud, and prayers from Visitation of Sick. Breath labored and painful; pain in back and sides excruciating. Partners keep awake to see me die. Four times during night body and soul almost parted – a fearful night. No fear, but longing to be at rest. The Valley of the Shadow of Death. Towards morning fell asleep and awoke without pain, but as weak as a baby. Hope this is the crisis of my illness. Very weak all day, but in no pain. Skynner washed my head, face, hands and feet, which refreshed me. He has been most attentive to me.

Feb. 14 – Very weak all day, and very cold, but in no pain to speak of. Monotony of food very wearisome, and want of fresh meat distressing. Teeth all loose and gums very sore. In pitiable conditions. [This is the last entry in Stewart's diary.]

Appetite a little better. I did not feel the cold very much. Cut wood as usual. Felt pains in my leg at night.

Feb. 12 – Stewart got up this morning. After going back to bed he had a bad shivering fit, lasting for two or three hours. Complains of being sore and appears very weak.

Feb. 13 – Stewart appears stronger today and brighter. Ate a hearty supper. After the above note was written Stewart had a relapse and completely gave up. He shook hands with us all, and finally asked me to read a chapter in the bible and a prayer. As I had gone to bed, Skynner did it for me. He says he was passing through the "Valley of the Shadow of Death" no less than four times.

Feb. 14 – Stewart appears to be a little better, although a little weaker than usual. He tells me he prayed to God about his children – what would become of them if he was called away? And he said the answer came back that they would be cared for.

From here on we give extracts from Cresswell's diary.

Feb. 15 – Skynner's head bad again. Stewart . . . complains very much of cold. Appears to be getting peevish. Says he could easily pull his teeth out.

Feb. 19 – Stewart better. We rigged up his bed today so that he can sit up straight. He sat up for three-quarters of an hour.

Feb. 21 – Stewart about the same. He informed us tonight that he had decided to go back home as soon as the river opened, and that his Yukon trip is at an end.

Feb. 23 – Stewart about the same; complains of cold and teeth being very loose. It is hard work to make him eat anything. We got Stewart up to-night to make his bed. We wrapped him up in a blanket, near the stove. I was holding him up, when suddenly he gave out and fell right into my arms, his legs barely escaping the stove. Skynner and I carried him back to bed, and he quickly rallied. He put up a game fight tonight, which is very encouraging.

Feb. 26 – Temperature 51 below. Stewart very quiet all day. He had a slight vomit; seems to be very weak, and will not eat anything that we advise.

March 1 – Stewart very much brighter. Was up today and did first-rate, but had a bad shivering fit afterwards.

March 6 – Stewart got up today as helpless as a two-year-old kid. I once thought he was going to die in my arms.

March 7 – Stewart getting better. We now get him to take a little exercise in bed by moving his arms and legs.

March 8 – Stewart about the same. Put fresh underclothes on him.

March 10 – Stewart . . . lies in a half stupor, and does not speak unless spoken to.

March 11 – Stewart's appetite very poor. . . . No pain in body. This has been a hard week, as Tallman is now off work, and it is with hard work that Skynner and I can keep him doing his two miles on the track. It is very trying on us, and difficult to keep one's patience. We are hoping for warmer weather, as it will help our invalids.

March 12 – Went around island twice with Skynner. Walked 8½ miles. After Skynner and I came in from our walk we gave Stewart a good straight talking to, which put new life into him. He had not eaten all day and kept asking for cold water, which we did not want him to have; so, getting angry, he said "Here, boys, this thing has got to stop," and immediately he sat up, I sitting beside him. He sat up for half an hour and finished strong, and has promised us that he will do all we ask him. So we are going to try once more and see what we can do with him, and we consider that this is his last chance. He had no dizziness after sitting up. Took beef tea and toast and stewed apples for tea.

March 13 – This has been a sad day for us, for we have to record the death of A. D. Stewart, which took place at 12.30 p.m. We all got up feeling bright, and hoping our invalid was on the mend, as he had promised us he would sit up for three-quarters of an hour in his chair.

242

So at 11.30 a.m. Skynner and I started to arrange things. We put a blanket round his chair, and put a mackinaw coat on him. He wished us to leave him alone, but to be sure of his not falling I sat beside him. After his sitting up on the bed I assisted him into the chair, and he seemed fairly strong; but soon afterwards he went into a faint. I held his head while Skynner gave him a little brandy and water. We put him back to bed, and shortly afterwards I put my hand on his forehead, which was cold. I called Tallman, telling him I was afraid that Stewart had passed away. We felt for pulsation of the heart, but could detect none, and it was with sad hearts we had to confess that our old friend and partner had been called away. At night we wrapped him in blankets and placed him in the tent intending to bury him when the warmer weather arrived. Skynner raised the flag at half mast. Stewart died in no pain; in fact, he had none for two or three weeks.

Alphonso Waterer, a man dragooned against his will by the miners' committee and told off to help two scurvy sufferers at Destruction City, presents a picture even more grim. Speaking of his experiences in the death shack, he said:

As the time passed away I noticed a great change in our two charges; poor Springer was going fast down the hill and the other was beginning to rally. Springer was not only suffering from the scurvy but also with some very bad form of blood poisoning and I can assure you that in handling these men and washing their clothes we were running the risk of losing our own lives by inoculating the cuts and scratches on our hands as everything which came from their bodies was of the foulest description and as black as ink. On the night of Feb. 14th Springer became very feeble and towards morning he beckoned me to his bunk side; his voice was gone and he could scarcely whisper. With arms extended and his glassy eyes fixed upon me I approached near to him when he placed his arms around my neck and embraced me. . . .

[After Springer died] the other man who had been mending gradually day by day when he knew Springer was dead ordered us to give up some effects which he claimed and which were in a small box at the head of Springer's bed, but I explained to him that we had not the power to search any part of Springer's outfit until the arrival of the committee, at which he began to use very bad language and called us all kinds of wicked names. We knew that he had a six shooter hidden away somewhere in the blankets and that he would use it if he thought fit, as his temper was not a very sweet one, so we watched him and when he saw that we meant what we had said he made a break for it, whereupon my partner seized him by the hands and took it away from under the blankets; a Colt's 44 loaded in all chambers, and it is needless to say that he never recovered it again. . . .

All through the night the wind howled with the fiercest fury, bending the spruce trees in all shapes; and I am left alone with a corpse and a sick and crazy man, a position envied by nobody, but an addition to my stock of mental anguish.

. . . All that I could do was to watch him and after a while he became totally exhausted and looked like dying and when I got close to him I saw that his gums were jet black and protruding from his mouth, and this was where the black blood was coming from. I tried to assure him of this fact but he remained in a semi-conscious state for a long time and his condition was most deplorable and critical. I bathed him all over with warm water changed all his clothes, and he eventually returned to consciousness but could remember nothing which had happened, and clamoured aloud for the burial of his dead partner, a service which I was totally unable to render single handed.

Although of all the forms of suffering on the Edmonton routes, scurvy was by far the most hideous, no human suffering could compare with what the horses endured. At least four thousand of them, far too sensible to have made a mad trip like this of their own volition, did so in the service of the Klondikers who cared little for their welfare and in many cases had very vague ideas about their requirements. To use an expression which World War II brought into our language, they were expendable.

The overlanders started out with varying numbers of horses, depending upon the mode of travelling they planned to adopt: using either double sleighs or toboggans for the first part of their trip and then switching over to pack saddles, or restricting themselves to pack horses right from the start. If at the outset they packed all their supplies on horses, each man needed from eight to ten of them. Then, theoretically, as they ate into their supplies they could gradually dispense with some of their animals, presumably by selling them to traders or Indians as they went along or by merely abandoning them. When they reached Fort Nelson, for example, they expected to need only half the horses with which they had started. They left Edmonton thinking that one of their problems would be how to dispose of their surplus horses without too much financial loss.

The grim realities of the overland trail quickly settled that problem and in most cases the Klondikers soon found themselves short of horses. Frisking along, shaking their heads and snorting, four thousand horses set out north from Edmonton. A couple of months later, with hollow ribs and drooping heads about two thousand limped into Peace River Crossing. The rest had died of starvation or ill treatment in the Swan Hills. Well over one thousand more left their bones to bleach in the muskegs and pine forests between Peace River Crossing and the

Cassiar. The winter of 1898-99 finished off most of the thousand or so that did reach the Cassiar. As far as is known, no Edmonton horses reached the Klondike.

Perhaps it should be noted that no women reached the Yukon by the Overland Route. As shown by the list in Appendix IV, twenty women in all set out, nine overland and eleven by water. All of the nine eventually returned to Edmonton safely while five of those who took the Water Route did so. The other six who went down the Mackenzie eventually strode into the Yukon.

Like the Overlanders of 1862, nearly all the Klondikers of 1897 who pressed on, following the vision of gold before them over mountain and muskeg and through canyon and cataract for nearly a year, found on their arrival at Dawson that the rich diggings of their dreams dissolved into ice-lined gravel gulches. Most of them met disappointment. On their arrival at Dawson they found other hundreds ahead of them, all expressing the same opinion as that in a letter sent to the *Edmonton Bulletin*: "From what I have seen and heard this country is not anything near what it was boomed up to be. There are a few good creeks but that is all." And the few good creeks were swarming with miners. Long before those who left Edmonton got through to the Klondike every inch of ground on the creeks there had been staked. Many Klondikers stayed only a week and caught the first means of transportation back home.

There were exceptions, but very few. Some worked in Dawson for wages or as employees of other men who had arrived earlier and struck it rich. W. J. Graham, who came in by way of the Liard, started a brick yard. H. Woodward, who had accompanied him, secured a modest bench claim for which he refused three thousand dollars. Segers, the steamboat captain, wasted little time in idle panning. When he reached the broad Yukon, he paid his passage up to Dawson and then within a few days hired on as captain of a boat plying that river. Writing back to his daughter in Edmonton, he said he was making more in a day than he had made in a month with the Hudson's Bay Company.

F. M. Robertson, who had come in by way of Fort McPherson, was in on the rush to Dominion Creek and had enough stamina to secure a claim which paid moderately well. Speaking of his experiences in that rush, he vowed that if he ever met a similar opportunity nothing would tempt him to go through what he endured. He said that he was one of five or six thousand men all waiting for the deadline that would start the rush to the creek. At the signal, they all set off running and a regular stampede ensued. Three men died as they ran pelting along the trail and many men dropped out completely exhausted. Robertson reached the creek and, as soon as he had cut and put up his stakes, fell down exhausted. For three hours he just lay there, suffering such incredible cramps that he could not reach down to take the boots off his bleeding feet.

Perhaps the most fortunate, or long-headed, of the Edmonton-based Klondikers was R. H. Milvain. Soon after reaching Dawson he teamed up with a mining engineer and the pair of them staked good claims. They worked these so successfully that, after some years, they sold their interest to the Guggenheims, who thereupon employed Milvain as manager. For the next fifteen years or so he spent most of his time in the Yukon, but left it to enlist during the 1914 war. He was severely wounded in France and eventually retired to his old home in England.

Less lucky was Milvain's former partner Jack Garnett, who was some time getting over his scurvy but eventually joined another party which went up the Gravel River and across to the Stewart and down to Dawson. According to Milvain's memoirs, "He had been 2 years on the way. He caught typhoid fever after arriving in Dawson and died in a few days. A better man to make a trip with would be hard to find. He was never out of temper, understood all about camping and was always anxious to do rather more than his share of work. He took the rough with the smooth without a grumble."

W. J. Morse, who had come in by the Peel River, soon gave up the idea of mining and eventually showed up at Shingle Point, Alaska, where he procured an outfit from some whalers and for some time was a successful trader.

F. C. Kendricks, J. T. Montgomery and possibly others of the combined canoe and sleigh party reached Dawson overland on June 6, 1899. As he went along Kendricks had been acquiring fur and, when he arrived at Dawson and assessed the prospects there, he traded the fur for enough gold dust to pay his way back to Ontario and to have a small nest egg left over.

Ernest Corp did not wait till he got to Dawson to turn his hand to profitable employment. Hearing that hay was selling there at two hundred dollars a ton, he and his partners cut and cured five tons on the banks of the McQuesten River. Then they cut timber and, to avoid putting all their eggs in one basket, made two rafts which in due course they beached at Dawson. There they "sold the hay for 10c a pound, and the log rafts for $200, giving the four of us $1,200 for about three weeks' pleasant work."

There also they encountered a phenomenon about which many Klondikers were to comment. "We had been in Dawson about three days when each of us had a bad cold. Here we had been on the trail for over a year, often in soaking wet clothes, but felt none the worse for it, and now, living in comfort, bad colds caught us all."

After trying a creek or two and taking an occasional job, Ernest Corp, like so many other Edmonton-based Klondikers, went out to civilization.

It took Eben McAdam a week or two to face up to the inevitable, for him to write in his diary: "Our party is now dissolved, and Andrew and myself are living alone. Henry secured a job as ships carpenter on the steamer 'Cudahy,' and left a week ago. Constant is wandering around on his own hook. Charlie leaves today for home via Whitehorse and Scagway. McGinnis is remaining here, but what his intentions are we do not know. Understand, however, from outside sources, that he is going home via St. Michael's and San Francisco. The end is not an unpleasant one, and we are parting good friends. Charlie drew up a short release, dissolving the company. So the end has come."

As far as the mining scene went, R. H. S. Cresswell, who had nursed former mayor Stewart during his last illness, met similar disappointment. He came to like the Klondike, however, and before long owned a tobacco and liquor store there and continued this activity for some years. Apparently he never returned to Hamilton but lived out a long life in British Columbia's coastal cities.

Many of the Klondikers who set out from Edmonton stopped to prospect along the Finlay, in the Omineca and at other spots that appealed to them and were quite content to forget about going to the Yukon. Ferriss and his partner Bob McDermid, who had gone through so many vexations in the Swan Hills, were a pair of these. In the fall of 1898 they had stopped along the Ingenika River and the following spring were reported as being well pleased with what they had found. Several others had reasonable luck in the Omineca area and came out to Edmonton the next spring for further supplies to take back to their claims.

During at least the next year or so many who had stopped to work the bars upstream from Fort St. John continued to make a living. All of them mined when they could and augmented their income by trapping. Several others tried their luck by panning their way up the Wapiti and Smoky rivers – tried and were disappointed. As a result, and because they liked the area and the life, they turned almost exclusively to trapping. Prior to the Klondike Rush very few white trappers had entered what we know as the Peace River country but after 1898 several stayed, made a living and found the type of life which suited them. While this was true of the Peace River country, it also held good for all the area as far northwest as the Liard River, but the concentration of trappers became less as they went north.

It has been said that the Peace River country got its earliest farmers from the Klondikers, but the statement does not bear examination. It is true that by the time the Peace River country was homesteaded several of these ex-Klondikers were scattered there trapping and formed a framework of old-timers on whom some of the homesteaders could lean, but they had little inclination to farm. One official report of 1900 stated that only one Klondiker, a man by the name of McLeod, was settling down to farm and he was operating a cattle ranch at Spirit River.

One of the Klondikers who did not remain in the Grande Prairie area very long was Captain O'Brien of the Helpman party. After a slow trek through the Swan Hills, when the last of them reached Lesser Slave Lake in June 1898, the group split up. Major Helpman, Captain Hall, Dr. Hoops, Dr. Hollwright and Messrs. Jeffreys and Bannister decided to float down the Peace River. Lord Avonmore, Colonel Le Quesne and Captain O'Brien, taking Sam Cunningham, the guide from St. Albert, went up the Smoky and Wapiti rivers to prospect. Their summer's work was disappointing and in September all but O'Brien returned to Edmonton and eventually to Ireland. Late in November O'Brien too returned, fed up with prospecting, and, since he had legal training, set up a practice which he carried on for several years in Wetaskiwin.

The bulk of the Helpman party, which went down the Peace River in the spring of 1898, pricked up their ears when they got to Great Slave Lake. They were among the first prospectors to start sniffing along the shores of that inland sea. After working all summer and wintering at Fort Resolution, Dr. Hoops and Dr. Hollwright came back to Edmonton in May 1899 with excellent samples of galena from a point said to be forty-five miles west of Resolution – the vicinity of our Pine Point mine. At least some of the members of this party, which Edmontonians had derided, put their fingers on a major ore body.

Several other Klondikers spent the summer of 1898 at Great Slave Lake, and, in the fall, some men from Chicago, Messrs. Dautrey, Rogers, Staudigall and Collin, startled the *Chicago Times* with their samples of galena. Only lack of markets and the extreme isolation of the region kept Great Slave Lake from bursting out as a rich mining area.

Ed Nagle, a well respected and successful trader with posts at various places, who was supervising the one at Fort Resolution during the winter of 1898-99, watched the staking activity with great interest. Ed, an Irishman, had had a fascinating career. As a young man he had served against the Fenians and went on to become a buffalo hunter out of Winnipeg. He also served as a scout in the Northwest Rebellion of 1885. Eventually he had gone into trading in the North and operated his own steamer.

Always in touch with the local Indians, who are said to have used the nearby galena deposits to melt into bullets, Ed acted on their information and staked a number of claims. Writing from Fort Resolution on October 3, 1898, he related the distaste with which he regarded some Klondikers who watched an Indian bring a piece of quartz rich in mineral into the post. They ridiculed the native and told him that it was valueless, but made certain to find out where he found it. They then sneaked off to stake the area he had found.

It was Ed Nagle who sent out the news of the stampede to the east end of the lake. The rumour that triggered this rush was probably a report of the work being done by the Yukon Valley Prospecting and Mining Company. Like the Helpman party, this company's men also divided forces and while J. M. Swigert and others went on to the Klondike, several men under W. J. McLean and a man named Willis stayed to study the Pre-Cambrian rocks of the vast lake. They searched the north shore, and possibly the islands, and finally concentrated their efforts on a claim said to be about two hundred miles east of Fort Resolution. News of this work came to Fort Resolution in the middle of January, 1899, when the temperature was forty-five below, and immediately all the men there, mainly defeated Klondikers who were waiting to go back to Edmonton, set out for a point 150 miles away to the northeast on the frigid and inhospitable shores of the lake. There many staked claims and came back, wondering, perhaps, what had possessed them to go at all.

All this discovery and staking around the long lake was forty years ahead of its time. So too was our indefatigable friend R. M. Springer, who had been a member of the Warmolts party and who, in the spring of 1898, returned from Fort Simpson. A year later he created some excitement in Chicago when he tried to organize a colony of miners and agriculturalists to settle on Great Slave Lake. Among his other schemes was one involving transportation. He came to Edmonton in March 1899 representing a Chicago company which was trying to sell the idea of a so-called ice-locomotive which would draw a train of cabooses. The back wheels were to be eight feet in diameter so that in going through deep snow the body would be clear of the drifts. If he could arouse enough interest in Edmonton and raise some financing there, he proposed to start manufacturing his conveyances in the town. He advised the town council that he would welcome a five-thousand-dollar bonus, a free site and some tax exemption, but the scheme fell through.

If the plans made by the Helpman party, the Yukon Valley Prospecting and Mining Company and Springer for developing the Great Slave Lake area came to nothing, and Springer's new method of transportation fell on its face, so did most of the other plans involving transportation. Other entrepreneurs failed too, notably the Alaska Mining and Trading Company, which had spent so much money on steamers for the Water Route. Even though the rush over the Edmonton routes had fallen off so completely, A. C. Waters of that company in Chicago wrote to Edmonton in March 1899 saying that he expected to start his boats running late in April. He too was disappointed, however, for in July three of the company's steamers, one at Athabasca Landing, the *Alpha* at Fort McMurray and the *Chesrown* at Fort Smith were seized by the sheriff and the lot were sold for $520.

The Alaska Mining and Trading Company had been bankrupted because the rush through Edmonton had died. The White Pass and Yukon Railway had killed it. Now there was no need for improved transportation north out of Edmonton. Northern traffic had reverted to what it had been before the rush and the Hudson's Bay Company's steamers and a few private traders' scows could handle it.

Similarly, the once glowing fires of all the promising schemes for roads and railways to the Yukon had burned themselves out. Moodie's road by way of Fort Grahame was forgotten, W. P. Taylor's trail to Fort Nelson became a memory. The railway that Pugsley had advocated and the one that Dibble had surveyed by way of Fort St. John and the Omineca were put on the shelf with their reports. Even the Indians avoided using the haunted Chalmers Trail over the Swan Hills, although it was clearly marked by a litter of discarded impedimenta, stark white skeletons of horses and the grave of a Klondiker's daughter.

Back at the starting point, at the end of steel, whence these horses and this little girl had set out, Edmontonians found that the fever of the Klondike Rush had fizzled out as suddenly as it had flared up. By August 1898, some seven miles of the White Pass and Yukon's track had been laid and a good tote road that ran ahead of it eliminated the climb over the summit of the pass which had been the bane of the Klondikers. Now, over this road, goods could be freighted from Skagway to Lake Bennett for ten cents a pound. Although it was to be some weeks before the editor of the *Bulletin* was to refer to it as the "now historic rush," the stampede through Edmonton was over.

While it had lasted, Edmonton had seen stirring times and the long-delayed beginning of prosperity. For the Klondikers had done well by Edmonton. In all, some 1,500 had set out from there and, if each had spent four hundred dollars to outfit himself, over half a million dollars of new money, much of it in gold pieces, had tinkled into Edmontonians' tills.

But aside from the money, which was really not much even for those days, the Edmonton area received publicity such as mere advertising could not have brought. The Klondike Rush put it on the map. Moreover, with their own eyes hundreds of newcomers had seen how arable Edmonton's far northern soil was. Even Klondikers returning disappointed remembered Edmonton and spread its fame. Many fell back upon the town or took a nearby homestead.

Actually, Edmonton's hour had come. Even as the last Klondiker was starting off north, the economic clock, newly wound by the realization of the wealth of rich lands around the little town, struck, and Edmonton began to race ahead. During the next three years as thousands of settlers came in to farm the adjoining lands, its population doubled to 2,626. Three years later it had nearly trebled even that figure. The Klondikers had nudged it awake, but settlers set it on its feet. For they had come to stay to work the riches of its lands and to live in the immediate area; the Klondikers, though colourful and courageous, had been mere transients hurrying north into the vast forests of its hinterland.

Though they had hurried through, they had filled a stirring year of Edmonton's life – a year which Edmontonians of the day thought they could never forget. But, when the traffic over the Chalmers Trail dropped to zero and Athabasca Landing fell back to its former loneliness, when Livingstone and Greer closed their hotel at Fort Assiniboine and no one bothered to remove the trees that fell over the "Klondike" Trail, Edmontonians turned their attention to catering to farmers and did forget. When within five years Edmonton's population doubled and redoubled, four newcomers walked the streets to every single old-timer and these newcomers were too busy opening up new subdivisions and dealing in farm land to pay attention to old-timers' mumbling tales of the Klondikers.

The newcomers could remember only the foolish things of the Klondike Rush, the froth and the follies which floated to the top of the tales. They remembered the failure of the Chicago Steam Sleigh, Texas Smith's barrels, and the Helpman party's helplessness. And new fictions grew out of old fibs until no tale was too impossible to believe – not even the story that one party of Klondikers required four horses to pack its cartons of toilet tissue.

Foolhardy the Edmonton-based Klondikers may have been, but not fools. On the basis of very scanty information about routes available at the time, they chose unwisely, but having chosen they pressed on. In today's easier atmosphere of security and overtime, of propane-heated construction camps, where electricity operates the nightly movies, in these days of internal-combustion transportation by land, water and air, in these days of computers which assess the rate of return on a year's labour and investment to determine whether a man would profit more by work or by welfare, perhaps it is hard to assess the simple persistence of the Klondikers.

Few indeed found the rich diggings of their dreams. And yet perhaps in the secret folds of their brains they never expected to. The search was enough; the excitement, the sheer thrill of far and forbidding places and the long trip were reward enough. Unlike today, when in general all but a handful of men talk of pay and guaranteed wages and dream of overtime and a northern living allowance, these men knew little of security and cared less. Each felt he could live and make his way under any circumstances, and what did it matter if by going to the Klondike he used up two of his years? Would he not be as well off in the end as if he had stayed home? And indeed, if in a cascade or on thin ice he met with accident and never came back, might he not, if he remained in the Edmonton area, be equally likely to be killed by a falling tree, a flooded river, or even a runaway horse?

The trip to the Yukon was its own reward. Like their fathers or grandfathers who, one or two generations earlier, had rushed to California or the Cariboo, the Klondikers had taken part in a history-making trek. For a year or two they had lived. For a year or two they had fought their way through the dangers and difficulties of the North, pitting their strength and their courage against them and enjoying the risks and the solitude. One or many pokes full of gold would have been desirable but would still have been mere frosting on their cake. They knew what many have forgotten – that satisfaction comes more often from trying than from succeeding. Though some of them were illiterate and perhaps had never heard of Tennyson, they would have agreed with the motto he ascribed to Ulysses, "To strive, to seek, to find and not to yield."

Mainly they had proved that they were men – men to whom in later years younger men would point and, with awe in their voices, say: "*He* went to the Klondike."

They saw the trek to the Yukon as an adventure and a gamble which might not pay off. If it did not, they'd start again. But by pressing on, not looking too closely at the cost in labour or hardship, neither analysing nor advertising their courage, they took their places in the great trek. That many turned back is perhaps a tribute to their common sense; that 725 pushed on to the diggings is a tribute to their versatility and virility.

They were of the bone and sinew that built Canada.

All during the long years when Edmonton was growing into a great city, over the years when the All-Canadian Routes to the Klondike came to be regarded as foolish, the great swaying forests along the 1,500-mile trail returned to their primeval soughing silence. In them the fur-company traders resumed the isolated tenor of their ways. On the island at Grand Rapids new foliage hid the clutter left by Klondikers and around it the roaring waters, oblivious as ever of man and his interests, continued their wild tumbling rush downstream. By rapid or rill, along the Liard, Athabasca, Peel and the Porcupine, men cast up by the Klondike Rush, scattered here and there like glacial boulders, settled in to enjoy the good life of trapping, panning or trading. Keen of vision, slow of speech, and dreamy of expression, they had found their own bonanzas.

Then after the passage of decades there came a day in 1941 when far out in the world of "civilization" bombs rained on Pearl Harbor and a military road had to be rushed to Alaska. Once more the maps came out, once more Edmonton became the jumping-off place, and once more (and for the last time) the pack horses were called out and sent into the valleys beyond Fort St. John. Once more courageous, versatile and mighty men set out for the Yukon, this time with bulldozers and trucks.

By that time farmers had filled the Peace River country and, heedless of W. P. Taylor's memory, were ploughing up the trail he had laid out. By that time access to Fort St. John, a hamlet in a farming community, was to be had in dry weather by a desperately long day's drive from Edmonton. By that time the old posts the overlanders knew, Fort St. John, Fort Nelson and Watson Lake (Lower Post), had air strips. Out of each of these, pack horses carrying surveyors sought a way for a highway and within weeks, aided by all the endurance and might of internal-combustion engines – giant bulldozers, snorting Le Tourneaus and roaring lowboys – a tote road came into being. By August 5, 1942, over a road which in essence followed the Overland Route, the first truck from Fort St. John rolled into Whitehorse, 1,030 miles away. The Edmontonians of 1897 had been vindicated.

In a rough way the Alaska Highway followed Taylor's return route from Fort St. John to Fort Nelson. From there, still treading in Taylor's steps for a few more miles, the highway turned west, but like the Klondikers A. D. Osborne, the Jamieson brothers and Geddis and his cattle, it continued farther west until by turning north and descending the Trout River it crossed the Liard at the Hot Springs above the Grand Canyon. Thence it continued up the river past Fort Halkett, the Whirlpool Canyon, the old Mud River Post, the Mountain Portage, Cranberry Rapids, Lower Post and the Liard Canyon. Then, swinging to the west of the overlanders' route, it followed the shores of Teslin Lake, headed for Marsh Lake and then followed the Yukon River into Whitehorse.

From sod-roofed shacks here and there, a few of the original overlanders wandered out to see the miracle of these snorting machines, grunting and pushing and roaring as through coulee or cut they shoved up this grade. If, here and there in this onetime Valley of the Shadow, unobserving, these caterpillars crunched the mouldering logs of shacks which over forty years earlier had heard the last anguished cries of scurvy-stricken overlanders, or covered their bones with twenty feet of fill, who was to know or care? For as the overlanders had played their parts, this highway was to play its new part as a speedway to the Yukon.

The Overland Route, however, was not alone in hearing the clamour of the snorting machines. Oil had to be piped to Whitehorse to support the effort along the Alaska Highway and from near Fort Norman to Whitehorse bulldozers pushed the Canol Pipeline through – pushed it across the summit where Ernest Corp had fallen through the ice and later helped to bury Victor McFarland; where, like Trojans, Miss Jones and Rosie, the German girl, had tugged their loaded sleds.

Each group in its time, the men who built the Alaska Highway, the men who strung the Canol Pipeline and the men who trekked to the Klondike through Edmonton – rugged, courageous and single-purposed men – fought their ways through the forbidding terrain of Canada's North. To all three ventures they brought all their toughness and all their talents – the men of the modern age with their bulldozers, trucks and technology, the Klondikers with their pack horses, rafts and snowshoes. And all in their own time enlivened the frontier pages of Canada's colourful story.

APPENDIX I

Distances to Dawson City by the Overland and the Water Routes
according to McDougall and Secord's *Guide to the Gold Fields*

OVERLAND ROUTE

Section of Route	*Mileage*
Edmonton to Pembina River	60
Pembina River to Fort Assiniboine	30
Fort Assiniboine to Lesser Slave Lake	120
Lesser Slave Lake to Grouard	30
Grouard to Peace River Crossing	80
Peace River Crossing to Dunvegan	48
Dunvegan to Pine River Crossing	83
Pine River Crossing to Nelson River Forks	120
Nelson River to foot of canyon Liard River	125
Portage around canyon	35
Head of canyon to Brulé Portage	40
Brulé Portage to Dease River	75
Dease River to Frances Lake	100
Frances Lake to Pelly River	50
Pelly River to Dawson City (downstream)	450
TOTAL	1,446

WATER ROUTE

	Mileage
Edmonton to Athabasca Landing (good wagon road)	90
(Freight from 75¢ to $1.00/100 lbs.)	
Landing to Grand Rapids (downstream & clear sailing)	167

Grand Rapids to McMurray	87
McMurray to Smith's Landing	289
Smith's Portage — 16 miles of bad rapids	16
Next 1,287 miles navigable all the way	
Smith's Landing to Resolution	194
Resolution to Providence	168
Providence to Fort Simpson	161
Fort Simpson to Wrigley	136
Wrigley to Fort Norman	184
Fort Norman to Good Hope	174
Good Hope to Peel River	252
Up Peel River to McPherson	18
Up Poplar River to Chain of Lakes	44
Across portage 400 yards	
Downstream to Bell River	5
Downstream to Porcupine	50
Down Porcupine River to Yukon	250
Up Yukon River to Dawson	300
TOTAL	2,585

APPENDIX II

Supplies for one man for one year according to
McDougall and Secord's *Guide to the Gold Fields*

GROCERY LIST

400 lbs. Flour	$10.00		8 lbs. Compressed		
150 lbs. Bacon	16.50		Vegetables	3.25
100 lbs. Navy Beans	4.50		1 lb. Pepper	.25
40 lbs. Rolled Oats	1.40		½ lb. Mustard	.25
20 lbs. Corn Meal	.75		¼ lb. Evaporated Vinegar	.75
10 lbs. Rice	.75		75 lbs. Evaporated Fruits	10.00
25 lbs. G. Sugar	1.63		20 lbs. Candles	3.20
10 lbs. Tea	4.00		6 Tins 4 oz. Extract Beef	3.00
20 lbs. Coffee	8.00		4 Pkg. Yeast Cakes	.40
2 doz. Condensed Milk	4.50		1 Pkg. Tin Matches	.75
10 lbs. Baking Powder	5.00		½ lb. Ground Ginger	.20
2 lbs. Baking Soda	.20		6 lbs. Laundry Soap	.37
20 lbs. Salt	.40		6 Cakes Borax or Tar Soap	.50
20 lbs. Evaporated			2 Bottles Jamaica Ginger	.50
Potatoes	5.00		25 lbs. Hard Tack	2.00
5 lbs. Evaporated			1 lb. Citric Acid	.90
Onions	2.50			$91.45

HARDWARE LIST

1	Camp Cook Stove	$7.00	1 7 × 7 Heavy Duck Tent	4.50
1	Fry Pan	.25	1 Jack Plane	.90
1	Coffee Pot	.75	1 Inch Framing Chisel	.25
2	Granite Cups	.30	1 Whip Saw, 6 feet	7.50
1	Bake Pan	.75	1 Hand Saw	1.00
1	Set Nested Kettles	2.40	2 Files	.25
1	Galvanized Water Bucket	.40	1 Draw Knife	.75
			15 lbs. Assorted Nails	.75
2	Granite Plates	.30	1 Drifting Pick and Handle	1.25
1	Knife, Fork and Spoons	.25		
1	Butcher Knife	.25	1 Long Handle Shovel	1.00
1	Axe and Handle	1.00	1 Gold Pan	.75
1	Small Hand Axe	.60	200 ft. ⅜ inch Rope	1.20
1	Whet Stone	.10	5 lbs. Oakum	.60
1	Hammer	.50	10 lbs. Pitch	1.00
1	Brace and Bits	1.25	2 Caulking Irons	.60
1	pair Gold Scales	2.00	1 pair Goggles	.15
1	38-55 Winchester Carbine	16.00	1 Compass	1.00
			1 Quartz Glass	.60
100	Cartridges	3.25	1 lb. Quick Silver	.90
				$62.30

This Hardware List includes nearly all that would be
required if the party consisted of five or more.

CLOTHING OUTFIT

2	Suits Heavy Knit Underwear	$8.00	1 Mackinaw, Coat, Pants, Shirt	11.50
6	Pair Wool Sox	1.75	1 Pair Heavy Buck Mitts, Lined	1.75
1	Pair Heavy Moccasins	3.00		
2	Pair German Stockings	1.00	1 Pair Unlined Leather Gloves	.75
2	Heavy Flannel Overshirts	3.50	1 Heavy Duck Coat, Pants and Vest	11.50
1	Heavy Woolen Sweater	1.50		

1 Pair Overalls	1.25	6 Towels		1.50
2 Pair 12 lb. Blankets	14.00	1 Pocket Match Box		.15
1 Waterproof Blanket	2.75	Buttons, Needles and		
1 doz. Bandana		Thread		.25
Handkerchiefs	1.25	Comb, Mirror, Tooth		
1 Stiff Brim Cowboy Hat	1.50	Brush etc.		.50
1 Pair Hip Rubber Boots	5.00	Mosquito Netting		.50
1 Pair Prospector's High		1 Dunnage Bag		1.00
Land Boots	4.50	1 Sleeping Bag		12.50
				$90.90

Medicine Chest	$ 4.00	Packs, Saddles, complete	6.00
Horses	25.00	Flat Sleighs	8.00

Flour put up in 50 pound double sacks. Everything is sacked that can be, and no packages more than 50 lbs. All goods put up and packed in the very best manner. No charge for packing except extra sacks, which are 10¢ each. In these lists nothing but necessaries are included. There are many other things that are usually taken, but are not absolutely necessary. Lumber suitable for boat building is from $15 to $20 per 1,000 feet here.

MCDOUGALL & SECORD

APPENDIX III

Edmonton Bulletin tabulation of boats June 23, 1898,
by the Water Route

The following is a list, as complete as it is possible to secure, of the gold
seekers who have left Athabasca Landing this spring to go north by the
Athabasca-Mackenzie route:

Name of Parties	No. of Men	Name of boat	Where from	Destination	Weight of Supplies
Heider	3	No name	Chicago	Peel	3 tons
McKay	3	No name	Ontario	Peel	3 tons
New Brunswick	2	No name	N.B.	Peel	3 tons
Flarin	3	Bella	S. Dakota	Peel	4½ tons
Stannard	2	No name	U.S.	Peel	4½ tons
Clark	6	Nellie	Toronto	Peel	6 tons
Newark	4	Horse Shoe	Newark, N.J.	Liard	4½ tons
Fish	4	Soo Mich.	U.S.	Peel	4½ tons
Diamond 5	5	Diamond 5	Chicago	Peel	5½ tons
Woonsocket	10	Woonsocket	Woonsocket, R. I.	Peel	8 tons
F. Wilson	7	York	Hamilton	Peel	8 tons
Link	5	Chester	Chicago	Peel	6 tons
Sturgeon	4	Chicago	Chicago	Peel	6 tons
Buck & Co.	5	Montana	Great Falls	Liard	5 tons
Green Bros.	3	Bessema	Chicago	Peel	3½ tons
Mitchell	5	No name	Toronto	Peel	6½ tons

Phillips	6	Northern Bell	Hamilton	Peel	7 tons
Findlay	9	River Horse	U.S.	Unknown	12 tons
Cooper	4	No name	U.S.A.	Peel	4 tons
Bush Bros.	6	Chicago	Chicago	Peel	5 tons
Los Angeles	7	No name	Los Angeles	Peel	6 tons
Mills	5	Jessie	Minneapolis	Peel	5½ tons
Jos. Wilson	6	No name	Ontario	Peel	7½ tons
Tramay	7	No name	P.Q.	Peel	4½ tons
Bell & Reid	4	Joker	Edmonton	Peel	4 tons
Gillman	4	Iowa	Iowa	Peel	4 tons
St. Anna	5	St. Anna	U.S.	Peel	6 tons
Healy	6	No name	England	Peel	6 tons
Davenport	3	Clara	Patterson, N.J.	Peel	3 tons
McKay, 2 boats	7	No name	Willson, Mont.	Peel	8 tons
Anderson, 3 boats	9	Shamrock, Thistle & Rose	Montreal	Peel	10 tons
Idaho	4	Idaho	Idaho	Peel	5 tons
Palon	6	No name	Montreal	Peel	7 tons
Windsor	3	No name	Windsor	Peel	3½ tons
Adams	3	Israel	St. Hyacinthe	Liard	4 tons
Martin Mathews	5	M.S.	Chicago	Peel	6 tons
Purdy & Nixon	2	Try Again	All over	Unknown	3 tons
Party without leader	5	Excelsior	All over	Peel	6 tons
Windsor, No. 2	5	Annie	Windsor	Liard	6 tons
Loutic	34	(4 scows)	McMurray	McMurray	36 tons
H. B. Co.	65	(16 scows)	Edmonton	McMurray	175 tons
"I Will"	5	—	Chicago	Liard	5 tons
Hamilton	8	—	Hamilton	Peel	8 tons
Lyster	7	Dr. Lyster	Detroit	Liard	9 tons
Callander	5	No name	Winnipeg	Liard	2 tons
Chicago	4	Undine	Chicago	Liard	4 tons
Chicago	2	Undine No. 2	Chicago	Liard	3 tons
Russell	3	Biddy	Edmonton	Peel	3 tons
Johnson	3	Priscilla	Soo, Mich.	Liard	3 tons
Pain	3	Say When	Qu' Appelle	Liard	3 tons
Keighlish	4	No name	U.S.A.	Peel	3½ tons

Dillman	5	No name	Chicago	Peel	4 tons
Manning	3	No name	U.S.A.	Peel	3 tons
Capt. Howell	6	No name	Winnipeg	Peel	3 tons
Montreal M & T Co.	6	May	Montreal	Peel	7 tons
A. D. Stewart	7	Get There	Hamilton	Peel	6 tons
Halifax City	9	Halifax City	Halifax	Liard	7 tons
Garden City	6	Garden City	Chicago	Peel	8 tons
Behn	4	Scout	Chicago	Peel	5 tons
Minne-ha-ha	7	Minne-ha-ha	Minneapolis	Peel	7 tons
Three Friends	3	Emma	Minneapolis	Peel	3 tons
Clatworthy	5	Quo Vadis	England	Peel	4 tons
Parson Bros.	3	No name	England	Peel	3 tons
Ed. Nagle	16	(5 scows)	Edmonton	Ft. Resolution	60 tons
Minstrel Boys	2	Minstrel Boys	England	Peel	2 tons
Waldy	3	Squaw	Unknown	Won't say	3 tons
Mary Ella	3	Mary Ella	Homestead, Pa.	Peel	3 tons
Blakley	4	No name	Won't say	Peel	3 tons
St. Albert 2 boats	6	St. Albert			
		St. Anthony	St. Albert	Liard	5½ tons
Clara Bella	2	No name	Niagara	Liard	2 tons
Sparrow	15	Sparrow	Minneapolis	Peel	7 tons
Enterprise	8	Enterprise	Detroit	Peel	10 tons
12 Boats	40	Names, destination and particulars unknown.			

APPENDIX IV

Women who set out from Edmonton

	From	Left Edmonton Overland	By Water	Got as far as	Returned to Edmonton
Mrs. Allen	?	Spring, '98		Ft. Grahame	?
Mrs. A. Booth	Halifax		Mar. 1/98		?
Mrs. S. Brown	Detroit		Spring, '98	Yukon	
Mrs. A. C. Craig	Chicago		Sept. 1/97	Yukon	
Mrs. G. E. Garner	Fresno	Aug. 24/97		Beyond Ft. Grahame	Sept. 5/98
Mrs. C. B. Heizer	Cincinnati	Feb. 19/98		?	?
Mrs. A. Hoffmann	Sandon, B.C.		May 15/98	Yukon	
Mrs. Horsfall	Winnipeg		Aug. 15/97	Yukon	
Miss Jones	England		Spring, '98	Yukon	
Mrs. L. L. Lampman	Williston, N.D.		Spring, '98	Up Liard	Sept., '99
Mrs. G. W. Larrabee	Buffalo	Feb., '98		Beyond Ft. Assiniboine	?
Mrs. Le Francois	Woonsocket		April, '98	Destruction City	Summer, '99
Mrs. Nansen	?	Spring, '98		Ft. Grahame	Summer, '99
Mrs. H. S. Neisler	Buffalo	Feb., '98		?	
Rosie	Sandon, B.C.		May 15/98	Yukon	
Miss Semple	Cincinnati	Feb. 19/98			Feb. 25/98
Mrs. O. Sommer	Chicago		Feb., '98	Grand Rapids	June 29/98
Mrs. A. P. Toneilli	Chicago	Feb., '98		?	?
Mrs. C. Westhead	Buffalo Lake		Spring, '98	Ft. Norman	Fall, '99
Mrs. H. M. Woods	Cincinnati	Feb. 19/98			Feb. 25/98

INDEX

271